Ted Bundy and The Unsolved Murder Epidemic

Matt DeLisi

Ted Bundy and The Unsolved Murder Epidemic

The Dark Figure of Crime

Matt DeLisi
College of Liberal Arts & Sciences
Iowa State University
Ames, IA, USA

ISBN 978-3-031-21417-2   ISBN 978-3-031-21418-9   (eBook)
https://doi.org/10.1007/978-3-031-21418-9

Cover credit: eStudioCalamar

This Palgrave Macmillan imprint is published by the registered company Springer Nature Switzerland AG
The registered company address is: Gewerbestrasse 11, 6330 Cham, Switzerland

Acknowledgements

I owe a debt of gratitude to many people for this book. I thank Ann Rule, Elizabeth Kendall, Al Carlisle, Stephen Michaud, Hugh Aynesworth, Polly Nelson, John Henry Browne, William Birnes, and Robert Keppel. Without their scholarly, forensic, or literary work drawn from their personal experiences with Bundy, we would have had no exposure to his behavioral history, personality functioning, and psychopathology from which to develop criminological insights. His dark figure of crime would have remained so.

Several friends and colleagues enhance my understanding of homicide and other pathological criminal offending. These include Eric Beauregard, Michael Welner, Oliver Chan, Alan Drury, Mike Elbert, Julien Chopin, Enzo Yaksic, Jon Caudill, Chad Trulson, Park Dietz, Ann Burgess, Reid Meloy, and Michael Vaughn.

Josie Taylor at Palgrave Macmillan is a wonderful champion of this project and I appreciate her enthusiasm and support. The entire team at Palgrave has been great to work with once again.

Of all of my publishing endeavors, this project created the most buzz among family and friends. Thanks to Melissa, Jamison, Landon, Finley, Winston, Barkley, Lincoln, Ziggy, and Ferris DeLisi for your love, support, and encouragement, and a special mention also goes to Christian Gallt for keeping tabs on the book's progress. I also thank my old friends John Coltrane, Lee Morgan, Hank Mobley, Donald Byrd, Roy Hargrove, Herbie Hancock, and Miles Davis for providing an uplifting counterbalance to the somber content herein.

Contents

About the Author

Matt DeLisi is Distinguished Professor, College of Liberal Arts and Sciences Dean's Professor, Coordinator of Criminal Justice, and Faculty Affiliate of the Center for the Study of Violence at Iowa State University. A renowned scholar, Professor DeLisi is one of the most influential and prolific criminologists in the world with over 470 scholarly publications including over 30 books on an array of topics in the social, behavioral, and forensic sciences. He has provided expert services and consultation on capital murder and homicide cases in multiple federal and state jurisdictions. In 2013, Professor DeLisi testified to the United States Senate Judiciary Committee and consulted on criminal justice policy to a variety of federal stakeholders including the United States Attorney General, National Institute of Justice, Federal Bureau of Investigation, and others. For eight years, Dr. DeLisi served as a research specialist with United States Probation and Pretrial Services and engaged with scores of practitioners in the federal judiciary and correctional spheres.

1

Introduction

Fear is pain arising from the anticipation of evil.[1]
   Aristotle

Ted Bundy is the most infamous, recognizable, and influential criminal in American history. For those who remember his exploits from the 1970s, Bundy was a source of fear, revulsion, and intellectual fascination as he perpetrated scores of sexual homicides, kidnappings, property crimes, and jail escapes spanning the Pacific Northwest to Florida. An inveterate psychopath, Bundy beguiled law enforcement personnel and media commentators alike and managed to cultivate public interest in his crimes and psychopathology until his execution in January 1989, an event that was itself a public spectacle.

Horrified by the criminal exploits of a seemingly normal person, at least by his appearance, the American public wanted to understand Bundy's motivation and offense history, and the case galvanized the bourgeoning true crime genre in the United States. More than three decades later, interest in Bundy has not abated evidenced by the abundance of films, documentaries, and true crime books about him. Several feature films on Bundy exist including *The Deliberate Stranger, The Stranger*

© The Author(s), under exclusive license to Springer Nature   1
Switzerland AG 2023
M. DeLisi, *Ted Bundy and The Unsolved Murder Epidemic,*
https://doi.org/10.1007/978-3-031-21418-9_1

Beside Me, *The Riverman*, and *Extremely Wicked, Shockingly Evil and Vile* with actors Mark Harmon, Billy Campbell, Cary Elwes, and Zac Efron in the role of Bundy, respectively.

Bundy is also frequently discussed on true crime television programs, such as *Criminal Minds* and some of the forensic features of his modus operandi and offense conduct appear in classic American films, such as *The Silence of the Lambs*. His criminal career and personality pathology coincided with and contributed to criminology and criminal justice programs emerging as academic growth areas within higher education. Surely there is nothing new about Ted Bundy. Is there?

Despite the bevy of works on his life and crimes, uncertainties, contradictions, and controversies remain. Foremost, it is unknown how many homicides Bundy perpetrated. The uncertainty about his murder total stems in part because when describing his murders, Bundy deceived, manipulated, and outright lied to interviewers, all cardinal features of the interpersonal dimension of psychopathy. At minimum, the victim count is approximately thirty adult and adolescent females, but other estimates, including occasionally from Bundy himself, place the victim count at greater than one-hundred victims.

That is at least one-hundred sexual homicides.

Similar questions surround whether Bundy only murdered adolescent and young adult women or did he also kill males, whether he killed prior to adulthood especially during late childhood or early adolescence, and whether he killed in a larger geographic area beyond primarily the Pacific Northwest and Rocky Mountain areas of the United States.

In this regard, Ted Bundy is merely symptomatic of much broader societal problems. Debates about his murder total implicitly recognize that most crime is never known to law enforcement. The incidence of all crime, including murder and serial murder, is far greater than official crime statistics indicate. Criminal records are *estimates* of an individual's actual involvement in crime and are at best a sampling of the true amount of offending and violence that occurred. The disparity between an offender's arrest count and other data sources, such as victim reports, correctional records, and an offender's self-report of their criminal activity reflects a criminological concept known as the dark figure of crime. Thus, debating an individual offender's total victim count is not merely true crime conjecture, but reflects a critical statistical and substantive issue in criminology.

The dark figure of crime is intimately connected to another criminological axiom: the asymmetry in offending. With crime, Mother Nature is no egalitarian. Across cultures, approximately five percent of the population engages in habitual, chronic, lifelong antisocial behavior. This group, commonly known as career criminals, accounts for more than half of the total incidence of crime in any society. More problematic is the career criminal group perpetrates an even larger share of the most severe forms of crime spanning predatory offenses, such as murder, kidnapping, and rape. The apex of this form of crime, sexual homicide, is the most pathological and rare, and accounts for only one percent of all homicide offenses. It is also disproportionately the purview of the most pathological offenders.

Although they usually spend the majority of their life in confinement and under correctional supervision, sexual homicide offenders also exhibit considerable expertise in their offense behavior that allows them to kill for a lengthy period of time before their ultimate capture. The most sadistic and psychopathic of them have keen forensic awareness where murders are committed in such a clandestine way that the victim's body is never found, where victims who are not known to be missing are targeted and thus the murder is never discovered, and where their modus operandi is fluid and versatile. These offenders also travel constantly, and the combination of switching jurisdictions as they variously bludgeon, strangle, and stab their victims in order to change jurisdictions to variously bury, destroy, or desecrate the bodies results in a lengthy offending period.

The confluence of these criminological and forensic issues has resulted in an epidemic of unsolved murders in the United States, one that is estimated at between 250,000 and 350,000 open, unresolved, or cold cases. Between 1960 and the early twenty-first century, unsolved murders increased by nearly eighty percent, an appalling miscarriage of justice, but one that generally stays off the public radar until the discovery of a new serial sexual homicide offender, such as Samuel Little, the emergence of a new pathological offender who is linked to multiple unsolved homicides, such as Todd Kohlhepp, or the passing of a long-incarcerated serial sexual homicide offender, such as Rodney Alcala. All of these offenders are profiled herein.

Unsolved murders have paradoxically increased despite greater resource allocations to law enforcement, pervasive increases in surveillance capacity and quality, the proliferation of computers to monitor transactions and thus an individual's movements, and a general tightening of the informal social controls within society. The laissez-faire social norms of the 1960s and 1970s are wholly foreign to today, but we face the contemporary challenge that just five out of ten murders are cleared by arrest. Most of this decline in solvability relates to a subculture of distrust, animosity, and uncooperativeness that exists at both the neighborhood and individual levels. The unsolved murders epidemic in the United States has morphed from a technological resource problem to a social problem primarily rooted in antagonism and social conflict.

This book uncovers the dark figure of crime by revisiting the life and crimes of Ted Bundy and seeks to reconcile the contradictions and controversies about his life that underscore the unsolved murder problem. Although he is commonly portrayed as a brilliant, successful man, empirical evidence about his life suggests this was a façade that distracted observers from his considerable dysfunction and underachievement, which are expected given someone with his behavioral disorders and psychopathology. The conventional orthodoxy is that Bundy was an affable, debonair winner whose life suddenly transformed in January 1974, when he was approaching thirty years of age, as he initiated a murder spree that would span a mere few years until its culmination with his capture in February 1978. Given the pace, confidence, and acumen with which Bundy killed during this period, and the forensic and criminological features of those crimes, it is highly unlikely that he had not murdered previously.

Consistent with the science of the dark figure of crime and the life history of the most severe offenders, my thesis is that Ted Bundy's criminal career is far lengthier, versatile, and extensive than the official 1974–1978 period, and his murder count is likely closer to one-hundred or more than thirty. Confidence in this relates to Bundy's offending history, his behavioral tendencies, and his psychopathology, which is extensively documented and rich in criminological detail and forensic significance. An offender who was as profusely psychopathic, homicidal, and beset by multiple paraphilic disorders as Bundy could not have kept these forces at bay for nearly three decades.

Importantly, there is suggestive and at times compelling circumstantial evidence across his life that Bundy, in fact, did not keep these forces at bay. Like most serious offenders, there are numerous behavioral warning signs, or prodromes, of his ultimate behavioral maladjustment and sexual violence. The notion that Bundy abstained from homicide offending until it emerged *de novo* in 1974 is simply not consistent with criminological and forensic science.

Fortunately, Bundy and others who knew him quite well provided substantive, incisive, often brilliant insights about his behavioral functioning and the likely contours of his offending career and homicidal activity. Some of these books include explicit conservations with Bundy about his own dark figure of homicide offending, and how his actual victim count far surpasses any law enforcement evidence of his crimes. He also divulged the specific behaviors that he and other sexual murderers engage in to ensure that victims are never located, let alone identified. In many respects, Bundy served as an expert witness on the unsolved murder problem in the United States.

These books are the primary data sources upon which I develop my thesis and involve authors who knew Bundy as a coworker, patient, interviewee, legal client, suspect, or intimate partner. These include Ann Rule's true crime classic *The Stranger Beside Me* about her friendship and experiences working with Bundy, and how her opinion of him worsened as more details of his crimes emerged throughout the middle to late 1970s. Dr. Al Carlisle's *The 1976 Psychological Assessment of Ted Bundy* is a forensic assessment of Bundy after his commitment to prison in Utah for an aggravated kidnapping conviction that contains numerous clinical observations about his psychopathology, antisocial development, and likely hidden homicide offending. Like me, Dr. Carlisle strongly suspected that Bundy murdered far earlier and more extensively than is chronicled in his official record.

Investigative journalists Stephen Michaud and Hugh Aynesworth's *The Only Living Witness: The True Story of Serial Sex Killer Ted Bundy* and *Ted Bundy: Conversations with a Killer: The Death Row Interviews* offer among the most comprehensive insights from Bundy during the course of approximately 150 hours of interviews during his confinement on Florida's death row. By providing Bundy the opportunity to speak in third person as if he was a consultant on his own murders, Michaud and Aynesworth extracted voluminous details about Bundy's life of crime, some of which are effectively admissions about how long he murdered, and the various ways that he, or "an offender like him," was able to get away with so many murders for so many years.

Polly Nelson's *Defending the Devil: My Story as Ted Bundy's Last Lawyer* and John Henry Browne's *The Devil's Defender: My Odyssey Through American Criminal Justice from Ted Bundy to the Kandahar Massacre* offer unique perspectives from defense counsels who represented Bundy, and thus had the unique vantage of hearing startling admissions from him about his homicide career and other features of his offense history. As his legal confidants, Browne and Nelson personally heard some of the most shocking and revelatory statements about the full extent of Bundy's homicide career, which indicate the degree to which a single offender can exacerbate the unsolved murder problem.

Elizabeth Kendall's *The Phantom Prince: My Life with Ted Bundy* is a memoir of her intimate relationship and domestic partnership with Bundy between 1969 and 1974 that contains numerous fascinating and forensically meaningful anecdotes about Bundy's behaviors and personality functioning. Kendall had daily access to Bundy for several years, and her lived experiences are littered with incidents which indicate that he likely murdered more often and significantly earlier than when he burst on the American culture in the mid-1970s. Her memoir also documents the various gaps in his life where Bundy's location and behaviors are unaccounted for as he engaged in extensive travel to perpetrate his murders.

Written with William Birnes, Robert Keppel's *The Riverman: Ted Bundy and I Hunt for the Green River Killer* is an account of the unlikely collaboration between Keppel, the homicide investigator who worked the Bundy murders in Washington State and Bundy, who offered his forensic insights into the offense conduct of Gary Ridgway, the infamous Green River Killer, another case on which Keppel worked. The book covers two distinct phases of their relationship, the consulting period in 1984 where Bundy, awaiting his execution on death row in Florida, provided penetrating insights into the modus operandi and behavioral features of the Green River Killer that were clearly, albeit indirectly, a reflection of Bundy's own crimes. The second phase, in 1989 just prior to his execution, involve seminal admissions from Bundy about some of his crimes that make clear the murder count is exponentially higher than records indicate, and that many victims would never be found due to his use of burial or dismemberment. Collectively these primary sources contain a treasure trove of data and direct quotations from Bundy that reinforce my thesis.

Owing to his grandiosity, the loquacious Bundy also left many breadcrumbs, and at times, offered startlingly informative clues about the true incidence of his crimes and the full depths of his behavioral history and criminal depravity. Drawing on these personal memoirs and investigating treatises, my theoretical approach also incorporates criminological science to offer a connective thread toward understanding Bundy's offending career and casting light on the controversies that surround it. Serving as an exceptional case study, my reappraisal of Bundy's offense history is a microcosm of the unsolved murder epidemic he helped to set into motion.

Chapter 2 "The Dark Figure of Crime" offers several data sources which indicate that the incidence of crime, including murder and serial murder, is far greater than official records indicate meaning that an offender's criminal record is at best a sampling of their true criminal activity. Drawing on biographical data from Samuel Little and Rodney Alcala, serial sexual homicide offenders who themselves likely killed one-hundred victims and were contemporaries of Ted Bundy, and a bevy of studies of sexual offenders, conservative estimates are that the total of unsolved murders in the United States ranges from 250,000 to 330,000 and there are also approximately several hundred thousand unanalyzed sexual assaults kits, a disproportionate amount of which implicate serial offenders.

Complicating matters further, the most pathological, forensically aware offenders target victims whose disappearance is undetected and who are not known to be missing, a population known as the "missing missing." These factors coupled with linkage blindness, a tendency for law enforcement organizations to overlook or misidentify the serial offenders responsible for crimes across jurisdictions, facilitated the decades-long offending careers of the worst offenders who accumulated scores of murders, most of which remain unsolved.

Chapter 3 "Asymmetry" investigates the empirical regularity that approximately five percent of the population is pathological in their offending career relative to nominal offenders and non-criminals. This small group accounts for more than half of the incidence of crime in the population, and an even larger share of the most violent felonies including murder and rape. Drawing on landmark birth cohort studies that documented the existence of the most active offenders, it is clear that the most exceptional offenders are primarily responsible for the dark figure of crime. Given that just one percent of all homicides are sexual homicides, this means that the worst offenders, such as serial sexual murderers, bear tremendous responsibility for unsolved murders in part due to the perniciousness of their personality disorders and sexual deviance. Based on the dismal results shown by recidivism research, there is little evidence that pathological offenders reform their conduct, and instead continue their predatory acts immediately upon release from prison custody.

Chapter 4 "Clinical" examines the broad concept of clinical disorder in the behavioral sciences that is essential for not only understanding Bundy's psychopathology, but also for recognizing that given the extremity of these conditions, it is virtually impossible that severe conduct problems, including homicides, were nonexistent prior to the official 1974–1978 murder career. The personality disorder of psychopathy, which Bundy and sexual homicide offenders like him clearly instantiated, is used to highlight the concept of clinical disorder as well as provide a foundation upon which to understand his emotional and behavioral dysfunction. There is ample convergent validity between psychopathy and the most pathological forms of criminal offending. In many respects, the specific clinical features of psychopathy facilitate an instrumental, relentless, and remorseless mode of offending that produces far more victims than law enforcement authorities are aware of, and that are ever reported missing.

Chapter 5 "The Entity" explores his comorbid psychopathology, or the other clinical conditions that affected his conduct and can be used to understand it. Here, Bundy's discussions with investigative and media interviewers are especially helpful in digesting his motives, his physiological and psychological drives, and his struggle to contain these drives. Much of Bundy's psychopathology involved sexually deviant behaviors, or paraphilic disorders, that explained the versatility with which he would sexually abuse an array of victims. Moreover, his intellectual functioning facilitated a forensic awareness that allowed Bundy to perpetrate sexual assaults and sexual homicides without leaving much in the way of physical evidence, an asset that resulted in most of his crimes remaining unsolved.

With this criminological, forensic, and psychiatric profile in mind, Chapter 6 "Timeline" revisits Bundy's criminal career and specifically his homicide career to show that based on extant evidence, was significantly more involved than the putative 1974–1978 period. Evidence of support that Bundy killed many more victims and for a much longer period of time originates from multiple sources including his defense counsel, with whom he occasionally divulged frank details about his life, his former girlfriend with whom he divulged that his murder career was far more expansive than law enforcement knew, and with media investigators who interviewed Bundy at length. Some of these admissions stem from Bundy's final confessions where he begrudgingly confessed to murder in part to manipulative correctional authorities and forestall his inevitable execution.

Chapter 7 "The Open Road" explores additional psychological, sociological, and societal factors that facilitated Bundy's extraordinary criminal career that likely helped him to avoid detection until his official homicide career starting in 1974. A cunning and forensically aware offender like Bundy was able to exploit the social mores of middle to late twentieth-century America where hitchhiking was commonplace, and thus he was able to easily access and procure victims, and where the omnipresent surveillance and technological footprint of today was nonexistent. I also rely on the bourgeoning criminological concept of criminal energetics to explore physiological explanations for Bundy's prodigious criminal behavior, which at its peak potentially involved more than one abduction, rape, and murder per day.

Chapter 8 "Unsolved" utilizes the relatively recent case of multiple homicide offender Todd Kohlhepp to illustrate how the most pathological offenders perpetrate scores of crimes many of which remain unsolved for many years unless serendipitous events and unlikely confessions bring the case to resolution. Currently, the unsolved murder problem in the United States is estimated at between 250,000 and 330,000 cases many of which are the responsibility of the worst offenders whose forensic acumen has ensured that a significant proportion of these murders will never be solved. In an ironic twist of fate, Ted Bundy volunteered to work with Robert Keppel, the homicide detective who had investigated his crimes, as a consultant on the Green River Killer another prolific sexual murderer who was adept at avoiding the police for most of his offending career. In this consultant role, Bundy provided granular insights into the mindset and offense conduct of the worst offenders in part because he relied on his own murderous experiences.

Chapter 9 "No Body, No Crime" examines the challenges and dynamics that arise when interviewing psychopaths and the surprising incidents of honest disclosure that can occur. At times, the interviewer can use clever ploys, such as allowing the subject to speak in third person about their crimes to dissociate them from their conduct, something that Michaud and Aynesworth did during their death row conversations with Bundy. This approach provided numerous insights into Bundy's offense behavior and its full extent that was previously unknown, which is consistent with the criminological concept of the dark figure of crime.

Chapter 10 "What Would Have to Be True?" covers three themes, behavioral stability, offending frequency, and moral depravity that dominate the lives of the most violent and serious criminals. Bundy's official 1974–1978 criminal career is critically examined for the time that elapsed between murders and the driving distances that were involved, data which provide contextual information to acknowledge the likelihood that his murders began far earlier in life. A syllogism of sorts is also presented to offer all of the pieces of evidence that would have to be disproven to effectively challenge my thesis that Bundy murdered across life and killed at least 100 victims. Finally, I suggest an appropriate lasting legacy of Ted Bundy one that matches his reprehensible character and his inhumane conduct.

Chapter 11 "Resolution" acknowledges that whether it was Samuel Little setting his spiderweb to catch disadvantaged and disempowered women in the ghettos, Rodney Alcala luring women to remote locations for the photoshoot that he convinced them would launch their modeling career, or Ted Bundy trolling the nation's college and universities for young women or obliging hitchhikers on the nation's vast highways, the United States was once a loosely connected, frontier society where changing behavioral mores unwound the bonds that previously regulated behavior. It was a perfect milieu for obsessively motivated, psychopathic, sexually deranged career criminals whose wanderlust drove them across the nation many times over to the most remote and clandestine settings imaginable. Fortunately, a paradigm shift in criminal justice procedure and forensic science technology has occurred that dedicates more resources to investigating unsolved murders and processing untested sexual assault kits than ever before in American history. Several National Institute of Justice initiatives and recent federal legislation is leading the way to provide some resolution toward reducing the unsolved murder epidemic in the United States.

Notes

1. J. Alexander (2013).

Reference

Alexander, J. (2013). *Best Aristotle quotes*. Crombie Jardine Publishing.

2

The Dark Figure of Crime

The conditions of the crime scene were indicative not only of extensive pre-event planning but also post-event planning and superb execution, leading to the conclusion that the offender previously had been successful at committing murder. This killer was more experienced at cold-blooded murder than any of us were at watching people like him.[1]

Robert Keppel

"I got away with numerous murders, of women, in my life over the span of 50 years."[2] That was Samuel Little's plain spoken, straightforward admission to Texas Ranger James Holland during an interview on the television news program *60 Minutes* in September 2020. Little, who died three months after the program aired, confessed to the staggering total of ninety-three murders spanning nineteen states across several decades of relentless criminal activity. The preponderance of his murders was in Florida and California, specifically in Miami and Los Angeles, the latter of which Little divulged that he murdered approximately twenty women. His incredible murder career was part and parcel of a commensurately extensive and versatile criminal history that spanned more than a half century with convictions for rape, armed robbery, aggravated assault on

© The Author(s), under exclusive license to Springer Nature Switzerland AG 2023
M. DeLisi, *Ted Bundy and The Unsolved Murder Epidemic*,
https://doi.org/10.1007/978-3-031-21418-9_2

police, burglary, theft, drunk driving, drug possession, and numerous other law violations.

A lifelong drifter who would murder women and then often immediately relocate to another city or out of state, Little accumulated documented criminal justice system contacts in Alabama, Arizona, Arkansas, California, Florida, Georgia, Illinois, Kentucky, Louisiana, Maryland, Massachusetts, Mississippi, Missouri, Nebraska, Nevada, New Jersey, Ohio, Oregon, Pennsylvania, South Carolina, Tennessee, and Texas. To put this into perspective, the geographic spread of Little's criminal history is nearly twice as extensive as the average lifetime travel history throughout the United States of the typical American citizen. The average American has visited twelve states.[3] According to the Federal Bureau of Investigation, with fifty of these murders confirmed at the time of his death, Samuel Little's official and confessed totals render him the most prodigious serial murderer in the history of the United States.[4]

Until the very end of his life when Little began confessing his crimes to a criminal justice system investigator with whom he developed a trusting professional relationship, the overwhelming majority of Samuel Little's whereabouts, movements, and homicidal activity during his eighty years of life was undetected and unknown. Only he and his victims knew about their final encounter.

On July 24, 2021, Rodney Alcala died in prison custody in California where he awaited his execution stemming from his capital convictions dating to 1980. Infamous for his appearance on *The Dating Game* television show in 1978 and also likely among the most prolific sexual homicide offenders in American history, Alcala was convicted of multiple homicides in multiple states and is suspected of dozens to potentially hundreds of murders and other violent felonies across several decades of remorseless criminal activity.

Ironically, Alcala was victorious in his *The Dating Game* appearance and was selected to date the young female contestant, Cheryl Bradshaw. However, she declined the opportunity when she became unnerved and viscerally affected after briefly meeting with Alcala. She had an unspecified but intense feeling that something was profoundly wrong with Alcala. Little did Cheryl Bradshaw know at the time, but her forensic instincts likely saved her life.

A photographer who would use the pretense of a photo shoot to procure victims, Alcala possessed a large cache of hundreds of photographs of children, adolescents, and adults, both female and male, some of whom are presented in a sexually explicit manner. The majority of the people in his photograph collection have never been found. It is widely believed these photographs are personal mementos of the children, adolescents, and adults that he had sexually assaulted and murdered throughout his criminal career.

One of those photographs appeared to match a cold case in Wyoming involving a woman named Christine Thornton, a homicide victim whose remains were found in a remote area of the state in 1982. In September 2016, investigators from the Sweetwater County Sheriff's Office in Wyoming, Detective Joe Tomich and Detective Jeff Sheaman and local prosecutor Daniel Errasmouspe flew to California to interview Alcala about their unsolved case. At the time, the infirm Alcala had been moved from the death row population at San Quentin to the California State Prison at Corcoran. He was physically unwell and generally lethargic in his movements. True to his psychopathic and sadistic nature, Alcala was less than cooperative with detectives and mostly responded to their inquiries about outstanding homicides with passive aggressive displays of petulance, denial, and defiance.

His passivity changed when the investigators showed Alcala photographs of the Wyoming terrain that included the crime scene. As if he had teleported to the moment where he likely murdered the young woman, Alcala perked up and admitted that he knew the area well.

He knew the area very well.

Alcala's response to a photograph of Christine Thornton was even more striking. For approximately five minutes, Alcala held the photograph of the woman and with his index finger methodically traced the outline of her body. He did this over and over again. He said nothing.

Seemingly in a trance, Alcala transitioned from tracing the body of the woman to tapping the image of her body with his finger. His tapping of the photograph increased in intensity, and became significantly louder. To the investigators, it was as if Alcala was simulating, or reenacting, a stabbing, and there was a noticeable increase in his arousal during this tracing and tapping event. In his creepy and ominous manner, not unlike what Cheryl Bradshaw experienced during her *The Dating Game* contact, Alcala was alive with the memories of what happened between him and her. To the investigators, he appeared to be mentally reliving killing Christine Thornton.

After this unsettling event, Alcala simply looked at them, effectively intimating that his silent stare was the extent of the confession he would provide them.[5] After his death, and absence of definitive evidence that could link Alcala to the cold case, the murder charge in this case was dismissed.[6] It remains unsolved.

In September 2015, I delivered one of the keynote addresses to a sexual offender symposium sponsored by United States Probation and Pretrial Services in Des Moines, Iowa. The other keynote speaker was a criminal profiler within the Federal Bureau of Investigation's National Center for the Analysis of Violent Crime, specifically the Behavioral Analysis Unit 3 that handles crimes against children, and the event had an audience of more than one-hundred attendees most of whom were federal criminal justice practitioners, state correctional officials, and judicial officers from multiple jurisdictions.

The two addresses examined a broad range of topics pertaining to sexual offenders. A recurrent theme across both presentations centered on the difficulty estimating how many sexual victimizations occur since the bulk of sex crimes are never discovered let alone reported to the police. Most sexual victimization occurs in the shadows. Victimization data tell one story, official data, such as arrest and conviction information often tell another. And offender self-reports, where offenders divulge what they do when no one is around to stop them, provide still another estimate.

To reinforce this point, I asked audience members to raise their hand if at any point in their life they ever engaged in behavior for which they could have been arrested. Approximately everyone raised their hand. That bears repeating. In a large lecture hall at a conference hotel filled with criminal justice practitioners, the lifetime prevalence of self-reported crime perpetration is approximately one-hundred percent. I also asked audience members to raise their hand if they had ever been arrested for any of these violations.

No one did.

Fortunately, in a normative sample like criminal justice professionals, the overwhelming majority of those undiscovered criminal events were alcohol violations during youth specifically drinking alcohol before age twenty-one (or age eighteen for the older participants who experienced an earlier age of consent to use alcohol), use of fake identification to purchase alcohol, and related conduct. In the grand scheme of things, their hidden criminal behavior was rather trivial and frankly never needed to be discovered by the justice system.

The same could not be said about the federal sexual offenders from our research. These offenders, whose sexual crimes spanned sexual abuse, rape, lewd and lascivious acts with a child, and a variety of statutes relating to child pornography, also self-reported far more criminal offenses than their criminal records indicated, but the seriousness of their crimes was much more troubling. During polygraphed treatment sessions, nearly seventy percent of the federal sexual offenders admitted they had sexually abused a victim prior to their current supervision. On average, the offenders had victimized nearly four victims.

During treatment sessions, the offenders divulged wide variance in the number of people they had abused, ranging from zero to twenty-four victims. The majority of these victims of rape, sodomy, or oral copulation were children and adolescents, and nearly thirty percent of the sexual offenders had no official criminal history prior to their current federal supervision, and many of which were convicted of possession of child pornography.[7]

In comparing the magnitude of sexual violence as indicated by self-reports versus official records, several data points conveyed the scope of how much victimization and other human suffering is hidden and goes unresolved. The two most prolific sexual abusers in the study had twenty-four and twenty-two victims, respectively, but had never been arrested for a sexual offense. Three offenders reported twenty-one victims each had only five arrest charges for sexual crimes. An offender who reported nineteen victims had only two sexual arrest charges. An offender with sixteen self-reported victims had just one arrest, and an offender with thirteen victims had zero arrests for sexual crimes.

A replication study reinforced the striking evidence for the dark figure of sexual crime. nearly seventy-four percent reported a prior contact victim. Fifty-seven offenders without prior arrest record for sexual crimes nevertheless have sexually assaulted a victim at some point during their life. The most prolific of these offenders reported twenty-five victims. Overall, the most prolific sexual abuser in the study reported forty victims, but had only eight arrest charges for sexually based offenses.[8]

My findings are consistent with broader trends in the criminological literature. Meta-analysis, which is a quantitative review of research studies to produce estimates of a global overall effect, found that among online sexual offenders, one in eight have sexually abused a prior victim, which is a prevalence of twelve percent. However, in studies where self-reported data are available, more than one in two sexual offenders, or a prevalence of fifty-five percent, have sexually abused a victim during their life.[9] More problematic is these victimization data only indicate the number of people who have been victimized, they do not indicate the total number of sexual crime incidents or events, which can occur on a daily basis over a period of years and yet never generate police response.

The difference in magnitude between the number of victimizations that occur relative to known victims is enormous. A landmark study that documented this empirical reality examined 561 community members who engaged in paraphilic, or sexually deviant, behaviors and found these individuals collectively perpetrated 291,737 paraphilic sexual acts, an average of over 520 incidents of sexual deviancy. The arithmetic mean for extra-familial pedophilic acts against male children was nearly 282, substantially higher than the mean against female children which was 23.2. The means for pedophilic acts within the family, or incest, were much lower and here female family members, usually daughters, incurred more abuse. The evidence for a range of behaviors spanning rape, exhibitionism, voyeurism, frottage, sexual sadism, and many others was substantially higher than would ever be known by criminal justice system data.[10] Overwhelmingly, the sexual violence was invisible to justice system investigators.

As they repeatedly offend and get away with it, sexual offenders continually adapt from their experiences and learn how to best manipulative environments to isolate victims for abuse. Criminological studies of first-time convicted sexual offenders have shown that on average, offenders sexually victimized others for nearly eight years before their first arrest. Much of that victimization never sees the light of day in court. The offender in their data who was best able to avoid detection perpetrated sexual assaults for over forty-one years before his first police contact. In terms of the sex crime events that occurred, the mean was nearly 217 events with a range of one to 5,524 sexual crimes.[11]

These estimates are from male sexual offenders upon their first official conviction for sexual violence, not from serial sexual homicide offenders for whom estimates of sexual violence are much higher. Methodological issues aside, these are appallingly high totals of sexual violence and raise questions that are even more staggering when considering the most prolific sexual homicide offenders, such as Little and Alcala, who perpetrated violent crime at high levels across several decades of the middle to late twentieth century.

If Samuel Little willingly confessed to strangling ninety-three women, how many others did he kill that he was not willing to discuss? Which of these "personal" murder victims did he keep to himself? How many other women did he sexually abuse, but not murder? As he drifted across most of the contiguous United States and preyed on those living in the shadows of life, how many rapes and murders were there? How many of the children, adolescents, and adults in Alcala's fetishistic trove were sexually abused? How many times did that abuse occur? How many were ultimately murdered? Why were so many never seen alive again?

These diverse anecdotes, insights, and research findings from serial murderers, law enforcement investigators and prosecutors, and researchers illustrate a concept in the behavioral sciences known as the dark figure of crime. Since the advent of crime statistics in the early nineteenth century, several commentators noted that different data sources can reveal a divergent empirical portrait of the incidence of crime. In an American context, a seminal account of the dark figure of crime was published in an arcane social science journal in 1967 when criminologists Albert Biderman and Albert Reiss observed:

> The history of criminal statistics bears testimony to a search for a measure of "criminality" present among a population, a search that led increasingly to a concern about the "dark figure" of crime—that is, about occurrences

that by some criteria are called crime yet are not registered in the statistics of whatever agency was the source of the data being used.[12]

The dark figure of crime highlights the methodological disparities that emerge when comparing official records of crime, such as a person's record of arrests and convictions, colloquially known as a "RAP sheet," to victimization reports, such as the National Crime Victimization Survey, to the individual's own self-report of their offense history.

Although various crime measures offer both strengths and limitations regarding their validity and reliability, the most compelling issue that emerges when comparing crime data is that more often than not, criminal offenders get away with crime. That is true for underage alcohol drinking among normative populations with no criminal history, that is true of those who perpetrate sexual violence, who aggress for years with only their victims aware of the event, and that is true of Samuel Little, Rodney Alcala, and, as will be examined in great detail, Ted Bundy.

The scientific evidence supporting the dark figure of crime is formidable. For example, a study using data from the National Crime Victimization Survey, a nationally representative survey of American households, found that only twenty-five percent of rapes are reported to the police. A similar proportion, just twenty-five percent of other sexual assaults are also reported to the police. Of course, this means that three of four sexual assault victimizations in the United States are not reported to law enforcement. It is not cleared by arrest. It is not solved. It does not produce legal closure. Perhaps most importantly, it does not stop the offender from perpetrating these criminal acts again. Moreover, the National Crime Victimization Survey does not measure victimization among persons younger than twelve years, thus, the dark figure of crime is effectively built into the survey.

An advantage of the National Crime Victimization Survey is it allows participants to indicate the reasons why their victimization was not reported to the police. In the case of rape victimization, the most common reasons are the victim considers it a private matter and took care of it informally, is afraid of reprisal by the offender or others, or the event was reported to another official. Other reasons include the perception that it was a minor incident and the victim did not necessarily construe it as a crime, they did not want the offender to get into trouble, perhaps because they were acquaintances or intimates, and various negative viewpoints about police. These include the perception that the police would not consider their victimization to be important, the belief that the police would be inefficient and ineffective at solving the crime, or that the police would be biased and cause the victim additional distress.[13] For these and other reasons relating to case attrition and the challenges inherent in the prosecution of sexual violence, it is estimated that only about one percent of sexual violence ultimately results in conviction.[14]

Contrasting victimization and arrest data on rape and sexual assault casts light on the dark figure of crime, but another data source showing a large magnitude of sexual violence that goes undiscovered is unsubmitted sexual assault kits, formerly known as rape kits. After a sexual assault, the surviving victim can participate in an invasive physical examination in which biological specimens are collected from various parts of the body to be submitted to a crime laboratory where the DNA is compared to profiles in national databases, such as the Combined DNA Index System, or CODIS. CODIS is installed in over 200 local, state, and federal laboratories and by April 2021, more than 20 million DNA profiles have been uploaded to it.[15]

Unfortunately, the promise of the CODIS database cannot be reached when many cases where viable biological data are collected during sexual assault examinations are not tested for comparisons to samples in CODIS. Consequently, the forensic connection cannot be made when forensic evidence sits dormant. Currently, approximately 300,000–400,000 unsubmitted sexual assault kits languish in police evidence storage and have not undergone analysis.[16]

Testing unsubmitted sexual assault kits regrettably does not always mean that a case will achieve legal resolution. Generally, the reasons for this relate to the victim's confidence in the case. In seventy-three percent of cases in one study, the victim did not wish to participate in the investigative process due to poor cooperation with the detective, a desire not to prosecute the case, or lack of follow-up with the detective during the original investigation. Nearly one in ten cases could not be advanced because the statute of limitations had expired, which is not an issue in murder cases.[17] In other jurisdictions, fewer than one percent of cases of previously unsubmitted sexual assault kits that produced a CODIS hit resulted in new criminal charges, overwhelmingly because the statute of limitations has expired on the case, the victim could not be located, or the victim declined to participate for a variety of reasons.[18]

Fortunately, some jurisdictions have prioritized the testing of previously untested sexual assault kits, and their findings once again substantiate the dark figure of crime in addition to revealing the disproportionate role of the most active offenders. In Cuyahoga County, Ohio, a geographic area that Samuel Little once trolled and perpetrated murder, testing of sexual assault kits indicated that twenty-seven percent of cases were connected to serial sexual offenders. Moreover, among stranger sexual assaults, thirty-five percent did not produce a DNA match indicating that the perpetrator had managed to avoid arrest or at minimum managed to avoid arrest for an offense where DNA could be collected.

DNA testing of previously unsubmitted sexual assault kits not only shows the salience of serial sexual predators, but also indicates other forensic features that are consistent with the behavioral histories of highly prolific offenders like Little, Alcala, and Bundy. Sexual assaults by serial offenders are more likely to occur in a vehicle, to occur outdoors often in remote areas, and to involve a stranger, such as one that was recently contacted in the course of prostitution, offered a quick photo shoot, or picked up while hitchhiking along the nation's highways. In the Cuyahoga County, Ohio data, nearly two of three serial sexual assaulters targeted strangers.[19]

It is not surprising that serial predators impose such criminal harm, but importantly, their criminal activity is not limited to sexual assault, but instead encompasses a broad range of crimes. In the aforementioned data, nearly one in ten offenders identified by testing sexual assault kits has previously been arrested for murder. Homicide offending was more common among high-volume generalist offenders, and among sexual specialists whose arrest activity primarily included rape and kidnapping.[20] This means that as untested sexual assault kits remain inert in storage in police custody, the highly recidivistic offenders, a proportion of whom murder, remain in the community, continue to offend, and inexorably expand the dark figure of crime. There is a strong interconnection between repeated sexual violence and murder.

It is one thing to recognize the dark figure of crime when comparing the ratio of one's own underage drinking behavior to one's nonexistent arrest activity or recognizing that most sexual violence goes undetected, it is another to see the magnitude of the dark figure for homicide offending. According to the Office of Justice Programs within the United States Department of Justice, there are 250,000 unsolved murders in the United States, and approximately 6,000 additional unsolved murders are added to that total each year.[21] That equates to five-hundred new unsolved murders each month. A variety of factors relating to criminal justice system limitations, surveillance capacity, lack of evidence, poor witness corroboration, refusal of witnesses to cooperate with law enforcement, and other factors contribute to unsolved murders.

Other estimates suggest an even larger dark figure of murder. According to Project Cold Case, which presents data from the Murder Accountability Project, there were 967,856 murders in the United States between 1965 and 2020 and 636,855 of these were cleared by arrest. This means that slightly less than sixty-six percent of murders were solved across these decades with 331,001 murders remaining unsolved.[22] The quantity of unsolved murders in the United States is roughly comparable to the quantity of collected, but untested sexual assault kits.

In the event of unsolved murders, it is at least *known* that an individual is a homicide victim, and in most cases, the victim's body has been found and identified. In many unsolved murder cases, there are viable suspects, but for a variety of evidentiary reasons, there is not enough probable cause to make an arrest. However, the expanse of the dark figure of crime is even more concerning when a murder is undiscovered, unreported, and, more troublingly, it is not even known that the murder victim has been murdered. In many of these cases, it is not known that the murder victim is missing.

Tens of thousands of people have been murdered in the United States where no one is fully aware that a crime occurred. Criminologist Kenna Quinet referred to this phenomenon as the "missing missing." According to Quinet,

The most successful serial killers know to select the unmissed as victims if they intend to kill for an extended period of time. How many people are missing but have never been reported as missing? One way to get at this number may be to do an analysis of serial murder cases to determine how many of the victims were missing persons never reported as missing, or were reported as missing with the case having been prematurely or incorrectly closed or purged.[23]

Drawing on various data sources that provide quantitative estimates of the missing missing, Quinet calculated that the number of people murdered by serial murderers is likely tenfold higher than previously known. Since they target the missing missing, the most prolific serial offenders perpetrate a disproportionate share of unsolved murders.

Additional data sources document the assorted risks that befall missing persons. A fascinating study reviewed more than 32,000 law enforcement reports of missing persons that had been canceled, that is, the person was no longer missing, and in some cases the report was canceled because the missing person was found deceased. Overall the proportion of missing persons who were found dead showed sharp sex and age differentials. Among missing males, the risk of being found dead was 1 in 119, for females, the risk was 1 in 299. For both males and females, the risk of missing persons being found dead increased as a function of age.

Very different results were found for the proportion of those found dead where the cause was homicide. Among males, the overall proportion of those found dead who were homicide victims was one in 114; for females, the ratio was one in fifteen. Moreover, the age effect reversed. Younger males and younger females were more likely than older males or older females to be homicide victims. Among females ages 14–18 years, the proportion of those found dead who were victims of homicide was one in four. Among females ages 19–24, the ratio was also one in four. Among females between the ages of 25–29, the proportion of those found dead who were victims of homicide was one in three.[24] These risks of homicide victimization among missing persons are astronomically high.

Historically, about one in four murders are stranger cases where the offender and victim are unknown to the other, and these crimes are especially prevalent in the offense conduct of serial murderers.[25] Serial murderers generally prey on populations whose lifestyle or immersion in criminal activity increases the likelihood they will be unmissed. Persons engaged in prostitution, drug selling, drug use, and other criminal activity are more likely to be transient and to live "off the grid," meaning their whereabouts are significantly more untraceable and uncertain relative to an individual with conventional, stable, identifiable, nondeviant lifestyles.

Persons living high-risk lifestyle are frequently in and out of vehicles, stay at temporary motels, go away with clients for brief periods of time, or are incapacitated on substances during periods of binge drug usage, and are thus generally unreachable. As a result, murders are more likely to become unknown events in the dark figure of crime when they involve potential victims who go unmissed. Indeed, the killers themselves know this. In describing the scenarios of his own murders, Samuel Little offered this cruel observation, "They was broke and homeless and they walked right into my spider web."[26]

During his consulting role in the Green River Killer case, Ted Bundy suggested, "you're dealing with a class of victims who are hard to trace and are hard to investigate."[27] He observed the victim would recurrently disappear, but then reemerge. Because of their uncertain location and movements, others were unlikely to ever report them as missing. It was simply believed the victim was away and would appear later. Bundy likely offered this advice with considerable confidence because his victims were never considered missing as they were abducted in plain sight or from the open road as they traveled the nation's highway system.

Far more audacious is the targeting of victims who are neither transient nor unmissed, but whose disappearance will similarly never be discovered. Rodney Alcala and certainly Ted Bundy filled this niche. They targeted people during the course of normal social activity, such as children at play, adolescents and young women socializing or walking to class, or those who were traveling or hitchhiking. These victims were murdered and their bodies would never be discovered for a variety of reasons, namely the body was incinerated by fire, devoured by animals, degraded by weather and water, or buried. It was as if they disappeared, and for all practical purposes, they did.

The National Missing and Unidentified Persons System, also known as NamUs, is able to furnish some data on these disappearances. Among active NamUs unidentified persons cases, the majority of bodies are unrecognizable in several ways. Only about one in four active cases involves a body with a recognizable face. The remaining three out of four cases are facially unrecognizable in part as a consequence of the violence inflicted at the time of death, and, in some cases, as a consequence of the overkill violence inflicted after death. Nearly thirty-seven percent of cases involve bodies with partial skeletal remains, nearly sixteen percent have near or complete skeletal remains, and about six percent of cases involve bodies with partial skeletal remains with some soft tissue. Slightly more than thirty percent of bodies are completely decomposed, nearly four percent are charred or burned, nearly four percent are in a state of mummification, and nearly one percent are degraded by insect activity and infestation.[28] Damaging a face and body beyond recognition is a sure sign of the forensic awareness that serial sexual homicide offenders' practice. It is also an indication of the Hell these offenders inflict upon their victims.

A historical allusion places the dark figure of murder into context. In March 1975, the Seattle and King County Washington law enforcement departments established the Ted Missing and Murdered Women Task Force to investigate cases of missing women and unsolved murders in the Pacific Northwest, most of which were presumed to have been murdered by Ted Bundy. Roger Dunn, an investigator within the task force, uncovered *ninety-four* unsolved murders of young women between January 1969 and May 1975 that had forensic features that were consistent with Bundy's offense behavior.[29] At various points of his life during his relationship with Elizabeth Kendall, Bundy acknowledged that his homicide offending initiated at least as early as 1969, suggesting that his total victim count potentially approach one-hundred murder victims merely within Washington State.

Ironically, the typical operations of the criminal justice system at times propagate the dark figure of crime including for homicide cases. Criminal justice systems are decentralized and geographically bound to cities and municipalities in terms of law enforcement organizations, and counties in terms of sheriff's offices and prosecutors. In the case of police departments, each has a discrete jurisdiction where the organization is charged with responding to the criminal activity that occurs within.

In many cases, a law enforcement organization would have no awareness of an offense occurring in another jurisdiction especially if the other jurisdiction is hundreds of miles away, or worse, in another state. These organizational features are particularly problematic if an individual offender perpetrates criminal acts across multiple jurisdictions. The disconnect between criminal justice systems was more acute during the middle to late twentieth century when criminal records and fingerprint cards existed in paper format and had to be mailed for confirmation and sharing. Nearly nothing was computerized and automated. Criminologist Steven Egger referred to the disconnect between investigative agencies on cases that likely involved the same perpetrator as "linkage blindness."[30]

Linkage blindness has multiple sources. Primarily, linkage blindness has an innocuous cause. Agencies simply are not aware of analogous cases that exist in other jurisdictions because they lack exposure to those other cases. On the other hand, petty professional conduct among justice professionals is another reason for linkage blindness. Reluctance to cooperate with other agencies because of concerns about the maintenance of jurisdictional or professional turf, professional jealousy, and perceptions that coordination with another agency could reduce their own likelihood of making an arrest are some examples. Criminal justice agencies that refuse to cooperate with one another and fail to share information unwittingly help the most prolific offenders.

Serial murderers create logical dilemmas that also contribute to linkage blindness. For instance, theoretically it seems highly unlikely that the same offender would be responsible for dozens to hundreds of murders across numerous jurisdictions, just as it seems improbable that the same offender would commit murder in five, ten, twenty, or more states. Thus, the extraordinary frequency, chronicity, and geographic spread of an individual serial murderer's homicide offending is at times almost so extreme that it is implausible to believe. As a result, linkage blindness is another contingency that a forensically aware, highly calculating serial murderer can exploit to not only facilitate continued offending, but also to help reduce the likelihood of being caught.

Another important reason for the dark figure of crime including unsolved murders is that the criminal justice system processes criminal defendants for the particular and specific offenses for which there was probable cause to arrest and charge them. They are not prosecuted for the general likelihood of being a multiple murderer, even if a defendant has confessed to multiple murders. Criminal prosecution is narrow and specific, not broad and general. Moreover, the legal process is not always successful and does not always result in a conviction.

From a crime control perspective, several things can go wrong during the judicial process, and this is evident at various points during Samuel Little's offending career. For example, Little was the prime suspect in the murder of Melinda LaPree whose body was found in Gautier, Mississippi in October 1982 and who had been seen with Little in Pascagoula, Mississippi approximately one month earlier. During the course of that investigation, two additional women who were working as prostitutes reported that Little had seriously assaulted them as well. In November 1982, Little was arrested in Pascagoula for theft and authorities noticed his resemblance to the wanted person in the LaPree murder. Little was formally charged with the LaPree murder and two counts of aggravated assault against the two women; however, the grand jury failed to indict Little on these charges.

However, legal maneuvering regarding Little was not finished. Although the Mississippi grand jury failed to indict Little, he was soon thereafter extradited to Florida where he was the prime suspect in the September 1982 murder of Patricia Ann Mount in Forest Grove, Florida. In January 1984; however, he was acquitted of murder in the Mount case. The itinerant Little would also be charged for another attempted murder in October 1984 in San Diego, California, but the jury in that case was unable to reach a verdict in the attempted murder charge and instead convicted Little of false imprisonment and assault.[31] Convictions for less serious crimes mean shorter sentences, shorter periods of confinement, and sooner release into society to begin the process anew.

A final data source about the dark figure of crime is both speculative and potentially persuasive, and involves the trophies, totems, or mementos that many prolific, violent offenders hold dear. Ted Bundy had two separate trophy collections from his likely victims. In 1973, his girlfriend Elizbeth Kendall found a bag filled with women's underwear in Bundy's room. None of the garments belonged to Kendall. Bundy had no good explanation for whose underwear it was and where the garments came from, and it is believed these were the underwear of many of his victims prior to this time.[32] The underwear denotes a greater significance because Bundy's usual method of sexual assault involved the woman taking off her own clothing culminating in the removal of her underwear. To Bundy, it was a final act of evil foreplay before the rape and strangulation.

He had other collections. In 1975, after his arrest in Utah for the attempted kidnapping of Carol DaRonch, Bundy returned to his residence and destroyed his personal cache of photographs that law enforcement had not discovered during their search of his apartment. How many of those photographs correspond to the dark figure of unsolved murders is unknown. It is known with considerable confidence that the number is greater than zero.

The baleful Rodney Alcala and his large collection of photographs are haunting images of people who have never been found, and the diversity of the photographs, which can be viewed via news organizations,[33] suggests the variable methods he would use when zeroing in on his victims. Many of the photographs show persons in various stages of undress, some in sexually provocative poses, and some of which are effectively pornographic. Other photographs reveal individuals who are not aware they are being watched, let alone being photographed. These photographs reveal Alcala in social settings, some of which are indoors and others outdoors, mixing with a broad range of people, but leering at a particular person of interest. His telephoto lens finds its prey.

And still other photographs involve other individuals, usually young women but also adolescents and even children, who appear alone, outdoors, and in remote locations. No one else is around, in order to provide the requisite privacy for an intimate photo shoot with a mysterious and dashing young man. At least that was the pretense. Only Alcala knew what happened thereafter.

No wonder he responded to the Wyoming investigators and their photographic display with such perverse vigor as he basked in the memories of his undiscovered sexual violence.

Notes

1. Keppel and Birnes (2005, p. 17).
2. https://www.cbsnews.com/news/serial-killer-samuel-little-60-minutes-2020-09-06/, Accessed September 8, 2021.
3. https://livability.com/topics/education-careers-opportunity/how-many-states-has-the-average-american-visited/, Accessed August 25, 2022.
4. https://www.fbi.gov/news/pressrel/press-releases/fbi-confirms-samuel-little-is-most-prolific-serial-killer-in-us-history, Accessed September 8, 2021.
5. https://www.cbsnews.com/news/serial-killer-rodney-alcala-the-killing-game/, Accessed September 7, 2021.
6. https://www.wyomingnews.com/rawlinstimes/news/charge-against-dating-game-killer-dismissed/article_fd74fdbe-ff8c-571a-8239-b676e7a5c418.html, Accessed September 7, 2021.
7. DeLisi et al. (2016).
8. Drury et al. (2020).
9. Seto et al. (2011).
10. Abel et al. (1987).
11. Mathesius and Lussier (2014).
12. Biderman and Reiss (1967, p. 1).
13. Bachman (1998).
14. Brouillette-Alarie and Lussier (2018).
15. https://www.fbi.gov/news/pressrel/press-releases/the-fbis-combined-dna-index-system-codis-hits-major-milestone, Accessed September 20, 2021.
16. Strom et al. (2021).
17. Fallik and Wells (2015).
18. Wells et al. (2019).
19. Lovell et al. (2018) and Lovell et al. (2017).
20. Lovell et al. (2020).
21. U.S. Department of Justice. (2020). The crisis of cold cases. Retrieved July 15, 2021 from https://www.ojp.gov/files/archives/blogs/2019/crisis-cold-cases
22. https://www.murderdata.org/p/blog-page.html
23. Quinet (2007, p. 327).
24. Newiss (2006).
25. Riedel (1998).
26. https://www.cbsnews.com/news/serial-killer-samuel-little-60-minutes-2020-09-06/, Accessed September 8, 2021.

27. Keppel and Birnes (2005, p. 195).
28. Weiss et al. (1998).
29. Keppel and Birnes (2005, p. 51).
30. Egger (2002).
31. Associated Press. (2018). Timeline retraces the whereabouts of a career criminal, alleged serial killer. https://www.foxnews.com/us/timeline-ret races-the-whereabouts-of-a-career-criminal-alleged-serial-killer.
32. Keppel and Birnes (2005, p. 85).
33. https://www.cbsnews.com/pictures/serial-killers-secret-photos-24-9-10/30/, Accessed September 15, 2021.

References

Abel, G. G., Becker, J. V., Mittelman, M., Cunningham-Rathner, J., Rouleau, J. L., & Murphy, W. D. (1987). Self-reported sex crimes of nonincarcerated paraphiliacs. *Journal of Interpersonal Violence, 2*(1), 3–25.

Bachman, R. (1998). The factors related to rape reporting behavior and arrest: New evidence from the National Crime Victimization Survey. *Criminal Justice and Behavior, 25*(1), 8–29.

Biderman, A. D., & Reiss, A. J., Jr. (1967). On exploring the "dark figure" of crime. *The Annals of the American Academy of Political and Social Science, 374*(1), 1–15.

Brouillette-Alarie, S., & Lussier, P. (2018). The risk assessment of offenders with a history of sexual crime: Past, present and new perspectives. In P. Lussier & E. Beauregard (Eds.), *Sexual offending: A criminological perspective* (pp. 349–375). Routledge.

DeLisi, M., Caropreso, D. E., Drury, A. J., Elbert, M. J., Evans, J. L., Heinrichs, T., & Tahja, K. M. (2016). The dark figure of sexual offending: New evidence from federal sex offenders. *Journal of Criminal Psychology, 6*(1), 3–16.

Drury, A. J., Elbert, M. J., & DeLisi, M. (2020). The dark figure of sexual offending: A replication and extension. *Behavioral Sciences & the Law, 38*(6), 559–570.

Egger, S. A. (2002). *The killers among us: An examination of serial murder and its investigation* (2nd ed.). Prentice Hall.

Fallik, S., & Wells, W. (2015). Testing previously unsubmitted sexual assault kits: What are the investigative results? *Criminal Justice Policy Review, 26*(6), 598–619.

Keppel, R. D., with Birnes, W. J. (2005). *The riverman: Ted Bundy and I hunt for the Green River killer.* Pocket Books.

Lovell, R., Huang, W., Overman, L., Flannery, D., & Klingenstein, J. (2020). Offending histories and typologies of suspected sexual offenders identified via untested sexual assault. *Criminal Justice and Behavior, 47*(4), 470–486.

Lovell, R., Luminais, M., Flannery, D. J., Bell, R., & Kyker, B. (2018). Describing the process and quantifying the outcomes of the Cuyahoga County sexual assault kit initiative. *Journal of Criminal Justice, 57*, 106–115.

Lovell, R., Luminais, M., Flannery, D. J., Overman, L., Huang, D., Walker, T., & Clark, D. R. (2017). Offending patterns for serial sex offenders identified via the DNA testing of previously unsubmitted sexual assault kits. *Journal of Criminal Justice, 52*, 68–78.

Mathesius, J., & Lussier, P. (2014). The successful onset of sex offending: Determining the correlates of actual and official onset of sex offending. *Journal of Criminal Justice, 42*(2), 134–144.

Newiss, G. (2006). Understanding the risk of going missing: Estimating the risk of fatal outcomes in cancelled cases. *Policing: An International Journal of Police Strategies & Management, 29*(2), 246–260.

Quinet, K. (2007). The missing missing: Toward a quantification of serial murder victimization in the United States. *Homicide Studies, 11*(4), 319–339.

Riedel, M. (1998). Counting stranger homicides: A case study of statistical prestidigitation. *Homicide Studies, 2*(2), 206–219.

Seto, M. C., Hanson, R. K., & Babchishin, K. M. (2011). Contact sexual offending by men with online sexual offenses. *Sexual Abuse, 23*(1), 124–145.

Strom, K., Scott, T., Feeney, H., Young, A., Couzens, L., & Berzofsky, M. (2021). How much justice is denied? An estimate of unsubmitted sexual assault kits in the United States. *Journal of Criminal Justice, 73*, 101746.

Weiss, D., Schwarting, D., Heurich, C., & Waltke, H. (1998). Lot but not forgotten: Findings the nation's missing. *National Institute of Justice (NIJ) Journal, 27*(9), 58–69.

Wells, W., Fansher, A. K., & Campbell, B. A. (2019). The results of CODIS-hit investigations in a sample of cases with unsubmitted sexual assault kits. *Crime & Delinquency, 65*(1), 122–148.

3

Asymmetry

I'm the only Ph.D. in serial murder.[1]
Ted Bundy

The notion that most criminal activity is hidden, undiscovered, and ultimately not reported to law enforcement personnel is only one axiom in the criminology canon. A related and equally important idea is that criminal activity within the offender population is as variable in its volume and expression as any other human behavioral endeavor. On any behavioral outcome or psychological characteristic, most people are average. Statistically much smaller exceptions appear to be very low or very high on any outcome or characteristic whether it is intelligence, wealth, or personality features. In terms of crime, some never engage in criminal behavior, most dabble in trivial forms of delinquent activity especially during late adolescence and early adulthood as the underage drinking poll at the sexual offender symposium revealed, and still others appear to engage in antisocial and violent conduct beginning very early in life and consistently thereafter. The same typifies crime seriousness. The most serious forms of crime, such as homicide and certainly sexual homicide very rarely if ever occur among the least antisocial individuals in the

© The Author(s), under exclusive license to Springer Nature   **33**
Switzerland AG 2023
M. DeLisi, *Ted Bundy and The Unsolved Murder Epidemic*,
https://doi.org/10.1007/978-3-031-21418-9_3

population and instead are primarily the purvey of the most violently pathological, chronic offenders.

That criminal behavior occurs along a distribution ranging from very low to very high is consistent with a concept in the behavioral sciences known as population heterogeneity. In practice, the concept is population heterogeneity is evident to any practitioner who has ever worked with criminal offenders, and the implicit recognition that most offenders are average, a small group appears to be low-risk and are easy to manage or supervise, and another small group appears to engage in crime to a significantly greater degree than other criminal offenders. The policing adage that removing twenty or so very active offenders from the streets can reduce a city's crime rate by half is indicative of the importance of population heterogeneity.[2] The braggadocious chapter opening quotation from Bundy also reveals that the worst offenders themselves have a general sense about the exceptionality of their antisocial capacity relative to other people.

The concept of population heterogeneity and empirical documentation confirming the existence of a small group of very active offenders might not have achieved scientific importance if not for the efforts of a team of criminologists at the University of Pennsylvania conducting research in the middle to late decades of the twentieth century. These scholars, including Thorsten Sellin, Marvin Wolfgang, and Robert Figlio, were keenly aware of both the dark figure of crime and the diversity of behaviors among the offender population, and conceptualized a large-scale study to further the knowledge base on these topics. Their general idea was to follow an entire birth cohort of boys born in Philadelphia and track their behavior until adulthood to assess the prevalence and incidence of crime.

The conceptualization of the project took many years and required coordination with multiple juvenile justice and criminal justice agencies. As early as 1960, Sellin and his colleagues arranged a deal with the Juvenile Aid Division of the Philadelphia Police Department to save the delinquency case files for research purposes instead of the agency destroying them as is customary. After years of planning, coordination, and data collection, their efforts produced a birth cohort of 9,945 males born in Philadelphia in 1945 who lived in the city at least from ages ten to eighteen. They produced several influential findings.[3]

Similar to the criminal justice professionals from the sexual offender symposium, most of the boys in the birth cohort had clean records. Specifically, sixty-five percent of the males in the birth cohort were never contacted by police suggesting that at least as measured by official arrest data during adolescence, the majority of the population is basically law-abiding. Perhaps more accurately, most of the population engages in relatively trivial offenses that never rise to the level of requiring police attention. Among the thirty-five percent of youth who did have police contacts, it was usually a one-off or limited occurrence involving a small number of police contacts. These contacts usually did not involve serious felonies. Most delinquents were infrequent, benign, and generally inconsequential.

The same was not true of 627 boys, slightly more than six percent of the entire birth cohort. These youth had five or more police contacts and were deemed chronic offenders. Relative to their occasionally antisocial peers, chronic offenders recurrently generated juvenile justice system interventions due to their frequent and serious antisocial conduct.

This small core of chronic offenders imposed a heavy burden of violence and victimization. They accounted for more than half of all delinquent offenses in the entire birth cohort, and their disproportionate contribution was even more glaring for crimes such as murder, where chronic offenders accounted for seventy-one percent, rape, where chronic offenders accounted for seventy-three percent, robbery, where chronic offenders accounted for eighty-two percent, and aggravated assault, where chronic offenders accounted for sixty-nine percent.

Research findings about the small group of chronic offenders was a compelling indication of how diverse criminal careers are, and also illuminated the calamitous toll they impose in terms of serious criminal violence. Heartened by their research findings, the criminologists at the University of Pennsylvania replicated and extended their study by examining a much larger birth cohort of over 27,000 males and females born in Philadelphia in 1958.

Although the study population had changed, the overall message of the criminal havoc imposed by a small core group of offenders was unchanged. In the latter birth cohort, seven percent of the youth were chronic offenders, and they accounted for more than sixty percent of all delinquent acts and between sixty percent and seventy-five percent of the most serious forms of crime spanning murder, rape, robbery, and aggravated assault.[4] In these studies, nearly all of the homicide offenders perpetrated a single murder.

Replication of the asymmetry in criminal offending and the burden imposed by approximately five to ten percent of the population is certainly not limited to Philadelphia, and has been consistently reported using data from diverse nations in Europe, Asia, Australia, South America, and hundreds of research sites in North America. The replication that a small group of pathological offenders impose a heavy societal toll challenges the idea that cultural features, ethnic composition, or social stratification factors mostly explain criminal offending, and instead reveal the importance of individual-level factors relating to personality pathology and broader psychopathology. This small group of the most chronic and serious offenders, who are overwhelmingly male, goes by several names including the severe five percent, life-course-persistent offenders, habitual offenders, chronic offenders, and, most commonly, career criminals.[5]

In addition to their pathological criminal behavior relative to other offenders and the large swath of the population that does not engage in serious crime, career criminals exhibit a variety of behavioral features that are crucial to understanding their developmental history and the likely course of their antisocial behavior. One of the most important is the precocious or early onset of their conduct problems and symptoms of their psychopathology. When criminal propensity is extreme, it has little recourse but to reveal itself, and that emergence comes early. Relative to normal delinquent development that occurs during middle to late adolescence as individuals traverse the difficult terrain in transitioning from child to adult status, career offenders begin exhibiting delinquent behavior much earlier in life.

The past is prologue.

Among this group, it is common to have arrest activity prior to age ten and interviews with family members, neighbors, and peers indicate that other aberrant behaviors also started early in life even before the child entered kindergarten. During a wholesome period of life when their prosocial peers are doting on their parents and teachers, making friendships, and playing with toys, career criminals bully other children, steal, engage in violence toward animals, lie pervasively, and cause problems in virtually every social context.

Usually, their broadband conduct problems produce repeated police contacts, court appearance, and in some cases, correctional interventions as seen among the chronic delinquents in the Philadelphia birth cohort studies. It is typical, as was the case in Samuel Little's offending career, for career criminals to experience multiple out of home placements to group homes, juvenile detention centers, training schools, or reformatories. In other circumstances and consistent with the dark figure of crime, there is less evidence of official justice system intervention; however, self-reports of other behavioral history clearly indicative maladaptive development and ominous signs of perverse sexual interests, homicidal thoughts, and personality disturbances. These were seen consistently in the backgrounds of Little, Alcala, and Bundy.

Due to the virulent nature of their personality functioning and their high criminal propensity, career criminals are generally versatile in their offense conduct, that is, there is evidence of all sorts of criminal activity spanning diverse forms of violence, property offenses, drug violations, public-order crimes, and other law violations. Depending on opportunity structures and situational contingencies, they will commit virtually any form of crime. Although their offense history is general in a global sense, there are also specific forms of crime that an offender will perpetrate over and over.

Even criminal behavior reflects matters of taste, preference, and idiosyncrasy.

This is particularly true for rarer crimes that most offenders lack arrest activity for, namely murder, rape, and kidnapping. Once an offender has engaged in these forms of crime, they are exponentially more likely than offenders who have not previously committed these crimes to perpetrate them again. There is continuity in extreme crime.

Several criminological research examples show the likelihood of homicide continuity. A variety of studies examined small groups of convicted murderers who served time in prison for their murder conviction, were ultimately paroled and released from custody, and subsequently murdered again. Although the majority of convicted murderers do not murder again, a significant number of them do. Across studies, the murder rate of former murderers ranged between 3,200 per 100,000 residents to nearly 3,900 per 100,000. Those estimates likely do not seem very high until they are compared to the national homicide rate, which in the United States in 2020 was 6.2 per 100,000. The murder rate among those who have already murdered is several hundred times greater than the current murder rate in the United States.[6]

Another study of a cohort of institutionalized delinquents examined the evidence for continuity in offending by specific types of crime and the greatest evidence was seen for homicide offending. Offenders who had previously committed a homicide offense had 1,467% increased odds of subsequently committing a homicide offense and 797% increased odds of subsequently committing any violent offense. These models controlled for a variety of factors that are important correlates of criminal behavior including sex, race, age, and five other forms of criminal activity.[7] For some offenders, murder begets murder.

The exponentially higher risk for murder among those who have killed previously is striking with the observation that most of the criminological studies are limited to offenders who have killed only twice. Most studies do not contain serial murderers or serial sexual homicide offenders. But if killing once before confers nearly 1,500% higher odds of killing again, what are the odds among those who have murdered dozens of times? What are the odds among those who have murdered hundreds?

The asymmetry in offending research makes clear that a minority of offenders begin their life of crime early, offend at a higher rate than other offenders, commit crime in a more voluminous fashion, and are exponentially more likely to perpetrate extreme violence. Consequently, these offenders experience multiple justice system interventions; however, unlike nominal offenders, judicial and correctional efforts to rehabilitate their conduct have no salutary effect. The most pathological offenders are effectively impervious to correctional methods designed to reform their conduct. The University of Pennsylvania criminologists observed this fact in their seminal birth cohort research.

Thus, we must conclude that the juvenile justice system, at its best, has no effect on the subsequent behavior of adolescent boys and, at its worst, has a deleterious effect on future behavior. For it is clear that, if a selection process is operating which routes hard core delinquents into the courts and correctional institutions, no benefit is derived from this encounter, for the subsequent offense rates and seriousness scores show no reduction in volume and intensity.[8]

True to this conclusion, prison incapacitation and death were the only interventions that slowed the offending careers of Little, Alcala, and Bundy. Unless confined, they will offend.

Despite the severity of the career criminal group, the promising finding is that the justice system can make significant crime reductions if it effectively neutralizes those who are the worst of the worst offenders. Imprisoning the five percent can cut crime in half and produces even larger reductions of the most violent felonies. For these reasons, pathological offenders often animate crime control legislation. In the federal criminal justice system, for instance, legislative attempts to curtail the repeated criminal activity of the most severe offenders includes initiatives, such as the Armed Career Criminal Act. The Armed Career Criminal Act was established as part of the Comprehensive Crime Control Act of 1984 and provides a 15-year mandatory minimum sentence for its violation among offenders who have three or more previous convictions for a violent felony, serious drug offense, or both.[9]

Offenders charged under this legislation have extensive criminal histories with more than ninety percent in the highest three federal criminal history categories and nearly half in the highest category, Criminal History Category VI. Nearly eighty-four percent have prior convictions for violent offenses, including murder, rape, robbery, or assault. Nearly seven percent had previously been convicted of a homicide offense. Some of these offenders have truly stunning offending histories with seven violent convictions on average and a range of violent convictions spanning three to forty-five.

Against the backdrop of continual criminal activity, the United States Sentencing Commission has performed analyses of offenders sentenced under the Armed Career Criminal Act in 2019 and found evidence of three general pathways. Nearly fifty-five percent of offenders exhibited a mixed pathway that involved a combination of violent and drug trafficking offenses. Slightly more than twenty-nine percent of offenders followed a violent pathway comprised of serious violent crimes, but no prior convictions for drug trafficking offenses and just over sixteen percent followed a drug trafficking pathway with three or more convictions for drug trafficking offenses without prior convictions for crimes of violence.

The mix of offenses within these pathways showed important differences. Among those in the violent pathway, sixty-five percent had robbery or armed robbery convictions, sixty-four percent had assault convictions, eleven percent had homicide convictions, three percent had prior rape convictions, and thirty-three percent had convictions for other violent offenses. This pathway had extensive public order, burglary, larceny, weapons violations, fraud, drunk driving, and other property violations. The mixed pathway had the most versatile blend of offenses spanning violent, property, drug, and public-order crimes, but did not have as extensive involvement in the most serious crimes spanning murder, rape, and armed robbery.

In the drug trafficking pathways, there were no violent convictions, but extensive conviction history for drug trafficking, drug possession, public-order crimes, larceny, fraud, weapons violations, and drunk driving. Generally, their criminal activity centered on drug use and sales and attendant property offenses to obtain money for drugs.[10] These nationally representative data on the most chronic offenders are noteworthy in that murder and rape convictions are relatively rare with prevalence estimates of eleven percent and three percent, respectively. This puts into perspective how pathological sexual homicide offenders are who commit dozens of rapes and murders.

Despite its potential to incapacitate the most active offenders, the Armed Career Criminal Act is not frequently used and currently constitutes less than one percent of all federal cases. Defendants convicted under the Act constitute just over two percent of all federal prisoners. Moreover, as expected by their recalcitrant offending conduct, nearly sixty percent of armed career criminals recidivate within eight years of release from federal confinement, and the median time to rearrest is a mere sixteen months. The most common new offenses are assault, public-order crimes, drug trafficking, larceny, and burglary. Nearly four percent commit a new murder, nearly five percent commit a new rape, nearly six percent commit a new armed or strongarm robbery, and nearly five percent commit a new other violent offense, which could include kidnapping.

Recidivism varied by offender pathway with those in the violent pathway showing the most noncompliant profiles. Among Armed Career Criminals released between 2009 and 2011, for example, nearly sixty-three percent of those in the violent pathway recidivated and the median time to first offense was fifteen months whereas fifty-five percent of those in the mixed pathway recidivated with a median time to first offense at twenty months. Both pathways had a median of three new arrests *after* their conviction and confinement for being Armed Career Criminals, and the majority of offenders in both pathways had assault for their new offense.[11]

As a consequence of their extensive criminal history and their disproportionate involvement in the most serious crimes, pathological offenders are recurrently in and out of prison, as seen in Samuel Little's correctional history, are sentenced to death and remain in custody for decades as a culmination of their correctional history, as seen in Rodney Alcala and to a lesser extent Ted Bundy, or are sentenced to prison but experience intermittency because of escapes from custody or recurrent detainers from other jurisdiction who want to prosecute the defendant for unresolved criminal activity, as seen in Ted Bundy's correctional odyssey. Generally, prisoners have exhausted numerous opportunities with community-based sanctions, such as probation, deferred sentences, or suspended prison sentences, and they tend not to fare well after release from custody. Recidivism data whether using federal or state prisoners are pessimistic and show the reduced likelihood that an offender will disengage from their criminal activities.

The United States Sentencing Commission examined recidivism among all federal releasees in 2005, which included 25,431 former prisoners. In the federal system, there are six criminal history categories ranging from low to high that are comprised of underlying criminal history points, which range between zero and thirteen or more. The offender's prior convictions are assigned one, two, or three depending on whether the offense resulted in an imprisonment term, whether the offense was committed while the offender was an active criminal justice system client, and whether the crime involved violence. Traffic, petty, and misdemeanor offenses do not figure into criminal history points. Had Little, Alcala, and Bundy been in the federal system, these procedures offer perspective about how abnormally prolific and severe serial sexual homicide offenders' criminal careers are.

The association between criminal history points and failing after release from federal prison progresses in a generally linear fashion. About thirty percent of those with zero criminal history points recidivate in the eight years after release from federal custody. That figure is seventy-four percent for those with eight criminal history points and approaches eighty-six percent for those with thirteen or more criminal history points. A similar pattern occurs for criminal history categories. Re-arrest rates are thirty-four percent for category I, fifty-four percent for category II, sixty-three percent for category III, seventy-five percent for category IV, seventy-eight percent for category V, and eighty percent for category VI. Other than firearm offenders, who are also usually engaged in violence, those convicted of violent crimes including murder and rape had the highest rearrest rates for recidivism, and, at fourteen months, were the fastest to re-offend.[12] There is a certainty of continued offending that is most acute among those who perpetrate the rarest, most severe crimes.

The United States Sentencing Commission conducted a study of 10,888 federal drug traffickers who were sentenced between 1991 and 2005 and released from the Bureau of Prisons in 2005. The drug traffickers accounted for nearly forty-three percent of all federal prisoners released that year, and the sample was followed for eight years post-release. Across the follow-up period, fifty percent of federal drug traffickers were arrested for a new crime or for a violation of their supervised release conditions. Among those who recidivated, the median time until the first arrest was twenty-five months. Criminal history was strongly associated with rearrest: the more chronic, the greater the recidivism. Those in the lowest criminal history designation had a recidivism prevalence of thirty-five percent whereas those in the highest criminal history designation had a recidivism prevalence of seventy-seven percent.

Among those rearrested, nearly thirty-one percent were reconvicted and over twenty-three percent, or nearly one in four, were sent back to federal prison.[13]

Similarly, distressing recidivism data are also seen in prison systems across the United States excluding the federal Bureau of Prisons. A study of nearly 100,000 prisoners released from prisons in thirty-four states in 2012 and followed until 2017 found that sixty-two percent are rearrested within three years and seventy-one percent are rearrested within five years. Nearly twenty-eight percent of all releasees had been convicted of the most serious crimes including murder, rape, kidnapping, armed robbery, and aggravated assaults. The notion that prisons are disproportionately populated by pathological offenders is seen in data revealing that seventy-four percent of prisoners have five or more arrests and more than forty-three percent have ten or more arrests. They average more than five convictions. A strong gradient is seen in the recidivism data where prisoners with the lengthiest criminal records recidivate sooner and a greater proportion of them fail over the study period. Among the prisoners with ten or more career arrests, fully eighty percent recidivate within five years after release.[14]

There is also continuity in offending within specific offenses. As expected based on its legal seriousness, homicide offenders served the most time in prison with a median sentence of 150 months. Unfortunately, their lengthy prison terms do little to reduce their recidivistic tendencies. Those who had been convicted of a homicide offense were the most likely to subsequently be arrested for a new homicide offense and more than forty-one percent of released murderers recidivated with a new violent offense.[15]

Study after study produces research findings that arrive at the same inescapable conclusion: the worst offenders do not refrain from crime even after a prison term and effectively never desist from criminal behavior. Instead, any notion of behavioral change means they can modify their behavior as they learn from various experiences, and exploit opportunity structures to mix their offense conduct across violent, property, drug, and other offenses. Once there is evidence of a rare and extreme crime; however, the likelihood of perpetrating that crime again is orders of magnitude greater than an offender who refrains from the rarest of crimes.

True to their sociological training, the University of Pennsylvania criminologists had a relatively limited set of explanatory variables including age, race, and social class with which to understand variations in delinquent offending. However, the real explanatory power is found when one delves within demographic statuses and studies the fundamental psychological and psychiatric tendencies within. That is where the population heterogeneity is found. For the worst offenders, the frequent, diverse, and early emerging criminal activity does not occur in a vacuum, but instead can be understood as largely the outgrowth of underlying individual-level characteristics that are driving the pathological criminal behavior.

Those individual-level factors relate to personality disturbances and sexual deviancy. Among multiple homicide offenders especially those who perpetrate sexual homicide, evidence for antisocial personality disorder, psychopathy, and paraphilic disorders, such as sexual sadism and pedophilia is plentiful. There is strong overlap, or convergent validity, between career criminals and specific forms of psychopathology, such as psychopathy. Compared to other serious offenders, the most chronic and violent delinquents are more psychopathic, more narcissistic, more unemotional, more fearless, more impulsive, more callous, and display greater cruelty.[16]

These forms of psychopathology motivate, potentiate, and enable criminal activity, but do so in a compulsive and perseverative way. It is as if the worst offenders have a calling to perpetrate sexual violence as well as the forensic savviness to obscure their criminal acts. Shortly before his death, Samuel Little horrified investigators when describing the compulsive motivation driving his need for fatal strangulations, "She was fighting for her life, and I'm fighting for my pleasure."[17]

The most pathological career criminals who perpetrate serial murder are seemingly propelled by the dark psychological forces within them. For example, although Rodney Alcala raped and murdered adult females as well, he once cited his sadistic and murderous pedophilic interests as reasons *not* to sentence him to death. During the penalty phase of his second capital trial in California, Alcala admitted in court that he kidnapped, raped, and nearly murdered a child in 1972 and served time in prison for the offense. After his release on parole, Alcala admitted possessing child pornography that resulted in a parole revocation and additional time in confinement. He also divulged his responsibility for numerous rapes and violent assaults of other child victims, but suggested that he was "absolutely harmless" since he would not have access to children in prison, and, as a consequence, should receive life imprisonment as opposed to death.[18]

Alcala's deadly psychopathology is consistent with other offenders who sexually abuse and murder children. Forensic researchers found that homicidal child molesters have a more severe behavioral profile than non-homicidal ones. In their study, homicidal child molesters more commonly victimized strangers, were more psychopathic, were more likely to have antisocial personality disorder, were more likely to be sexually sadistic, and to display multiple personality disorders and other paraphilias. More than eighty-two percent of the homicidal group were sexually sadistic and about fifty-three percent were both pedophilic and sexually sadistic. The respective prevalence of those constructs for the non-homicidal group was zero percent for both. The homicidal group also demonstrated higher levels of deviant arousal to pedophilic and adult assault stimuli. In terms of criminal careers, the homicidal group had nearly three times more arrest charges than the non-homicidal child molesters. The homicidal child molesters also were significantly more likely to have a history of other violent arrests and convictions.[19] The worst offenders—sexual homicide offenders—exhibit a variety of features that facilitate their violent conduct.

Nearly a half century after the publication of *Delinquency in a Birth Cohort*, criminology owes a debt of gratitude to Wolfgang and his University of Pennsylvania colleagues for their bedrock empirical work on the small group of the worst offenders. But even their impressive birth cohort design was limited by the age of their study population, and, although there were some murderers, limitations in their extremity of conduct. And they were able to offer no insights into what goes on underneath the hood of the worst offenders, what they called etiological factors. One of those clinical features of the worst offenders, specifically Ted Bundy, is examined next.

Notes

1. Keppel and Birnes (2005, p. 297).
2. In statistics, the Pareto principle is the same general idea, namely that the majority of behavioral outcomes stem from a minority of participants.
3. Wolfgang et al. (1972).
4. Tracy et al. (1990).
5. DeLisi (2005), DeLisi and Piquero (2011), Moffitt (1993), and Martinez et al. (2017).
6. Welner et al. (2021).
7. DeLisi et al. (2019).
8. Wolfgang et al. (1972, p. 252).
9. 18 U.S.C. § 924(e) The Armed Career Criminal Act.
10. U.S. Sentencing Commission (2021).
11. U.S. Sentencing Commission (2021).
12. U.S. Sentencing Commission (2017).
13. U.S. Sentencing Commission (2017).
14. Durose and Antenangeli (2021).
15. Durose and Antenangeli (2021).
16. Vaughn and DeLisi (2008).
17. https://www.cbsnews.com/news/serial-killer-samuel-little-60-minutes-2020-09-06/, Accessed September 8, 2021.
18. *Alcala v. California* (2007).
19. Firestone et al. (1998).

References

Alcala, Rodney James v. The Superior Court of Orange County and the People of the State of California, G036911, S. Ct. C42861, 2007.

DeLisi, M. (2005). *Career criminals in society*. Sage.

DeLisi, M., Bunga, R., Heirigs, M. H., Erickson, J. H., & Hochstetler, A. (2019). The past is prologue: Criminal specialization continuity in the delinquent career. *Youth Violence and Juvenile Justice, 17*(4), 335–353.

DeLisi, M., & Piquero, A. R. (2011). New frontiers in criminal careers research, 2000–2011: A state-of-the-art review. *Journal of Criminal Justice, 39*(4), 289–301.

Durose, M. R., & Antenangeli, L. (2021). *Recidivism of prisoners released in 34 states in 2012: A 5-year follow-up period (2012–2017).* U.S. Department of Justice, Office of Justice Programs, Bureau of Justice Statistics.

Firestone, P., Bradford, J. M., Greenberg, D. M., Larose, M. R., & Curry, S. (1998). Homicidal and nonhomicidal child molesters: Psychological, phallometric, and criminal features. *Sexual Abuse: A Journal of Research and Treatment, 10*(4), 305–323.

Keppel, R. D., with Birnes, W. J. (2005). *The riverman: Ted Bundy and I hunt for the Green River killer.* Pocket Books.

Martinez, N. N., Lee, Y., Eck, J. E., & SooHyun, O. (2017). Ravenous wolves revisited: A systematic review of offending concentration. *Crime Science, 6*(1), 1–16.

Moffitt, T. E. (1993). Adolescence-limited and life-course-persistent antisocial behavior: A developmental taxonomy. *Psychological Review, 100*(4), 674–701.

Tracy, P. E., Wolfgang, M. E., & Figlio, R. M. (1990). *Delinquency careers in two birth cohorts.* Plenum Press.

United States Sentencing Commission. (2017). *The past predicts the future: Criminal history and recidivism of federal offenders.* Government Printing Office.

United States Sentencing Commission. (2021). *Federal Armed career criminals: Prevalence, patterns, and pathways.* Government Printing Office.

Vaughn, M. G., & DeLisi, M. (2008). Were Wolfgang's chronic offenders psychopaths? On the convergent validity between psychopathy and career criminality. *Journal of Criminal Justice, 36*(1), 33–42.

Welner, M., DeLisi, M., Baglivio, M. T., Guilmette, T. J., & Knous-Westfall, H. M. (2021). Incorrigibility and the juvenile homicide offender: An ecologically valid integrative review. *Youth Violence and Juvenile Justice.* https://doi.org/10.1177/15412040211030980

Wolfgang, M. E., Figlio, R. M., & Sellin, T. (1972). *Delinquency in a birth cohort.* University of Chicago Press.

Wolfgang, M. E., Figlio, R. M., & Sellin, T. (1987). *Delinquency in a birth cohort.* University of Chicago Press.

4

Clinical

There are so many people. This person will never be missed. It shouldn't be a problem.[1]

Ted Bundy

A clinical disorder is a coherent condition that has a set or constellation of traits, features, or symptoms, has a specified developmental course with an onset, continuity, and remittance, if any, and is applied or diagnosed when an individual's presentation and behaviors appear to "match" the disorder. The cardinal feature of any clinical disorder is behavioral impairment. In prior eras of psychiatry through the fourth edition of the *Diagnostic and Statistical Manual of Mental Disorders,* or *DSM-IV*, clinical disorders existed in categorical terms: a person either met diagnostic criteria for the disorder, or did not. Those who displayed symptoms of the disorder but not enough to warrant a diagnosis were referred to as subclinical. In 2013 with the fifth edition of the *Diagnostic and Statistical Manual of Mental Disorders,* known as DSM-5, there was an intentional shifting of perspective away from discrete diagnostic conditions to a spectrum perspective where individuals were located on a distribution that reflected their place on a range of symptoms.[2]

© The Author(s), under exclusive license to Springer Nature Switzerland AG 2023
M. DeLisi, *Ted Bundy and The Unsolved Murder Epidemic,*
https://doi.org/10.1007/978-3-031-21418-9_4

Understanding an individual's place in a distribution of symptoms is helpful for understanding their behavioral impairment. Among persons with zero symptoms of mental disorder, there is usually a correspondingly low behavioral impairment and thus adequate behavioral functioning. For instance, imagine an individual who is self-interested, assertive, and generally indifferent to others in terms of how his conduct affects them. While this person has admittedly unpleasant descriptive features, consider that he is also married, has children, is employed, supports himself and his family financially and emotionally, and participates in several community organizations. Irrespective of how aversive his personality might be, it has no detrimental effect on his behavioral functioning across life domains. The person does not have a clinical disorder.

Consider a different individual who has the identical features, but the self-interest and indifference to others are more pronounced, and the assertiveness is stronger and more often manifests as overt aggressiveness. This person has been married, but his personality features caused considerable discord and the marriage ended in divorce. The person has also lost several jobs as a result of his dysfunction in getting along with others. Frequently employed, he just as frequently is fired or quits. Due to his occupational instability, he has serious financial problems and often has to stay with friends or family to avoid homelessness. This person meets the criteria for a clinical disorder.

For those who are frequently arrested and placed into correctional custody, the Samuel Littles and Rodney Alcalas of the world, the notion of clinical disorder is straightforward and uncontroversial. Their behavioral dysfunction is clear to see. However, such an assessment is more challenging for an equally violent and antisocial individual who manages to avoid police contact for the majority of his offending career. In these scenarios, the evidence of clinical impairment is not so easy to diagnose when the person appears to maintain work, school, and relationship demands.

Despite the popular notion that Ted Bundy gave the appearance of normal psychological and psychiatric functioning, he was in fact no stranger to clinical disorder, and exhibited multiple conditions that not only were clinically significant, but also truly pathological in their expression. This is critical for understanding his life history and his crimes.

The extreme volume of his sexual homicides and other offenses did not unfold from a normal, normatively functioning person. In this regard, Little, Alcala, and Bundy were forensically the same basic type of person. As Bundy himself observed when describing his murders, "We're not talking about normal sexual gratification. We're not talking about *normal* anything!"[3] The extremity of the violence was commensurate with the extremity of the psychopathology that Bundy struggled with across life. This chapter explores just one component of his psychopathological profile: psychopathy.

Psychopathy is a clinical construct often considered a personality disorder that has a coherent set of interpersonal, affective or emotional, lifestyle, and antisocial features. Persons with psychopathy are grandiose, conning, and manipulative in their interactions with others, and use various means of coercion, persuasion, and charm to meet their needs. They are impulsive, irresponsible, and display a preference for hedonic, risky, and stimulating experiences. They gravitate toward substance use and sexual gratification.

They have severe impairments in emotional functioning, often appearing as cold, indifferent, and unfeeling, usually exhibit little to no remorse or guilt for their conduct, and refuse to accept responsibility for their actions. These emotional deficits are the cardinal feature of the disorder. The videos of Samuel Little calmly and casually describing his various murders to the Texas Ranger investigator and the cruel and unfeeling manner in which Rodney Alcala interacted with the Wyoming investigators are examples of these emotional deficits.

In the behavioral domain, psychopaths fail in a spectacular fashion and their life is usually characterized by poor self-regulation, early conduct problems, juvenile delinquency, versatile criminal acts, such as violent, sexual, property, and public-order offenses, and noncompliance with the justice system. Among the other forms of personality disorder, psychopathy is most consistent with antisocial personality disorder, which is characterized by pervasive disregard for and violation of the rights of others.[4] However, psychopathy is a rarer, more pernicious condition. Whereas most offenders who have antisocial personality disorders are not clinically psychopathic, the overwhelming majority of clinical psychopaths also meet diagnostic criteria for antisocial personality disorder. The basic definitions of psychopathy and antisocial personality disorder likely immediately remind readers of the worst offenders' demeanor and criminal behavior.

They are recipes for crime.

Like most psychological conditions, psychopathy is a multifactorial construct, which means that its etiology or cause is attributable to a sublime mix of genetic and environmental factors. The genetic causal features of a condition are known as its heritability, which sounds similar to the colloquial concept of a condition being inherited. A general rule of thumb is that the more acute, pronounced, or vivid the condition, the higher its heritability estimate, meaning that the bulk of its origin is attributable to genetic factors. Thus, highly heritable pathological conditions are not only evident during childhood, they are present at birth. Research on children as young as two years, for instance, indicates clear evidence of callous and unemotional traits that are congruent with the affective deficits seen among adults with psychopathic personality.[5] This fact is disconcerting to some but nevertheless is true.

Twins are a natural research tool because they allow researchers to statistically estimate the effects of nature (e.g., genetic relatedness) and nurture (e.g., environmental effects). The use of twin data among elementary school children allows for precise estimates of how much variance in psychopathy is owed to genetic factors and how much variance is owed to environmental factors. Studies of children as young as seven years found that among twins with psychopathic features and extreme antisocial conduct, genetic factors account for eighty-one percent of the variance. Among twins without psychopathy but with similarly extreme antisocial conduct, genetic factors account for just thirty percent of the variance.

A related study with children as young as nine years reported heritability estimates of seventy-five percent for the most psychopathic and behaviorally impaired youth. And while environmental inputs are essential to the development of psychopathy especially those involving abuse, neglect, and drug exposure, genetic factors are most responsible for the disorder.[6] Moreover, when both antisocial conduct and psychopathic features are extreme in their expression, the genetic load is highest.

A quick foray into the behavioral genetics of psychopathy is useful because of the features of Bundy's life that often receive causal significance for his personality functioning and homicidal acts. Overwhelmingly, these causal features are *environmental* including his confusing parentage (whom Bundy thought was his sister was actually his mother and whom Bundy thought were his parents were actually his grandparents), his family instability and move across the country, his potential exposure to adverse childhood experiences, his exposure to and consumption of violent, sadistic pornography, and his tumultuous early adult dating relationships.

Whatever the significance of these events in Bundy's antisocial development, it is crucial to note these events operated on an individual who was already a nascent psychopath. In this way, the signal developmental events in Bundy's childhood were moderators of a child who was already trying to manage bizarre and compulsive behavioral instincts, such as arranging an array of knives around the body of a female relative while she slept. Bundy did this at age three years. His aunt Audie described that Bundy stood in a daze and stared at his sleeping aunt with the knives around her, to which she awoke with considerable concern.[7]

This event is incredibly revealing and forensically meaningful. At age three years, normally developing children engage in the most basic goal-directed activities, such as walking up and down stairs, showing increased motor competence and versatility, recognizing basic emotions, such as happiness, sadness, and anger, speaking with greater clarity and sophistication (e.g., moving from single words to simple sentences), and related developmental milestones. A typical child of this age is simplistic in their behavior.

Contrast these milestones to Bundy's conduct. Already by age three years, Bundy noticed his young female relatives and had a nebulous physical interest in them. His interest had a violent valence involving the display of knives. Unlike normally developing children whose only knowledge of knives would be in a mimicry context, such as watching one's parents using a knife to prepare food in the kitchen, Bundy had the goal directness to know that knives could be used for violent means, and in his precocious way, fused that sense of violence to physical attraction to young females. He did not arrange the knives around an inanimate object or a sleeping dog. Instead, he went to his female relative's room while she slept and arranged the knives around her.

The affective display Audie describes is also clinically important. Once the knives are arranged, Bundy appeared in a trance as if transfixed by what the knives encircling a woman meant to him. It appeared he was in a dream world. When his relative awoke and showed concern at his conduct, there is no evidence that their concern upset Bundy in any way. Even as a 3-year-old boy, he did not appear to be phased by their concern, fear, or distress. It was an early warning sign of the remorselessness to come.

Even in children who exhibit pronounced psychopathic features, there are other variables that can alter its expression. For instance, numerous studies indicate that environmental advantages can buffer the effects of psychopathy, and Bundy's intelligence was a likely moderator of his psychopathy. Unlike most criminal offenders who are intellectually below average and poorly educated,[8] Bundy had above average intelligence and used that cognitive capacity to moderate or constrain, at times, his psychopathic motivations that centered on the fusing of aggression and sexual gratification. It is likely that his intelligence, specifically his verbal intelligence, allowed Bundy to charm potential victims and largely avoid police detection for most of his criminal career unlike less successful psychopaths who are recurrently in jail, prison, and community supervision across life, offenders such as Little and Alcala.

With his verbal acuity, Bundy was able to manage his emotions generally well during childhood, but there were also warning signs suggesting that his apparent behavioral control masked troubling undercurrents in his conduct. His fledgling psychopathy was not always so well moderated, and there are recurrent incidents in Bundy's life in which he was aggressive and had poor behavioral control. In his youth, these incidents involved fights with other boys and cruelty toward animals.

An interesting harbinger in Bundy's childhood involved a fight where he struck another boy named John Moon over the head with a large stick. The attack was from behind, the same modus operandi he would employ time and again during his homicide career. His personal attack style was already established. Reflecting on that event, Bundy's childhood friend Terry Storwick described the affective malevolence that appeared to overtake Bundy's eyes when in the throes of violence. He suggested that Bundy's blue eyes would transition to black whenever he got mad or was about to have a physical confrontation. Even a critical comment from a friend could generate this reaction.[9]

* * *

Dr. Hervey Cleckley is a seminal scholar in the modern study of psychopathy and his book *The Mask of Sanity*, published in 1941, is his signal work. Cleckley's work identified many of the key characteristics of psychopathic personality as we understand them currently. Ironically, Cleckley worked as an expert witness for the prosecution in Bundy's capital cases in Florida and testified that Bundy was clinically psychopathic. Since Cleckley, the leading scholar in the study of psychopathy is Canadian psychologist Dr. Robert Hare, who also created an assessment tool, the Psychopathy Checklist-Revised, that is the most widely used instrument to assess psychopathy in criminal justice systems worldwide.[10]

The Psychopathy Checklist-Revised contains twenty items in which individuals are scored as zero, meaning the feature does not characterize the individual, are scored as one if there is some evidence that the feature characterizes the individual, and are scored as two if the feature definitely characterizes the individual. In other words, the scoring is equivalent to "not at all," "somewhat or sometimes," and "definitely or very much." The twenty items correspond to one of four factors or subthemes of psychopathy in his instrument known as interpersonal, affective, lifestyle, and antisocial. Two items, promiscuous sexual behavior and many short-term relationships, do not correspond to any of the four factors, but are used in producing the total score, which ranges from zero to forty. Those who score twenty or higher are considered moderately psychopathic and those who score thirty or higher are considered clinically psychopathic.

Many are curious whether they have psychopathic traits. The most likely answer is an emphatic no. Survey research on the general population, for instance, reported the prevalence of psychopathy is less than one percent. In addition, seventy-one percent of those in the general public have zero symptoms of the disorder.[11] When there are indicators of psychopathy among individuals in the general population, they generally pertain to impulsivity and irresponsibility, which can cause economic stress and consternation, but usually are not severe enough to produce behavioral dysfunction in a clinical sense. Understanding that most people have zero symptoms of psychopathy puts into perspective how behaviorally different serious offenders like Little, Alcala, and Bundy are relative to the general population.

On the interpersonal and affective dimensions of the Psychopathy Checklist-Revised, Bundy was a complete psychopath. In terms of the interpersonal dimension, the four indicators are glibness and superficial charm, grandiose self-worth, pathological lying, and conning/manipulation. Much of the popular allure about Bundy's personality functioning relates to these interpersonal features, such as his facile ability to impress and influence others with his charm. Coinciding with his attractiveness and verbal intelligence, Bundy's interpersonal prowess facilitated his procuring of victims, and he accomplished this by also employing a variety of ruses where he would feign injury to portray that he needed assistance. The serial murderer character Buffalo Bill in the film *The Silence of the Lambs* engaged in similar behavior during a kidnapping, and the scene was a historical allusion to Bundy's conduct.

Bundy would also approach women and engage in lighthearted and flirty conversation during which he would request a need for assistance to lure the woman away from a crowd so that he could assault and abduct her. The combination of his looks, charming confidence, and sometimes convincing repartee frequently made this move successful.

Importantly, the apparent interpersonal skill is not genuine, it is parroted and fake. Multiple women who Bundy approached at Lake Sammamish on July 14, 1974, the day Bundy murdered both Janice Ott and Denise Naslund, for instance, articulated that Bundy appeared unnatural and nervous, and that his story that he needed help removing his sailboat from his car seemed rehearsed.

There are witness reports immediately prior to other documented Bundy homicides where young women expressed that Bundy approached them with a rehearsed story that the women rather easily saw through and, fortunately, did not go with him. Thus, the interpersonal acumen of the psychopath is contrived and superficial.

The gulf between Bundy's outwardly presented interpersonal prowess and his private beliefs in his ability to relate to others was voluminous. For all of his glibness and the various ruses he employed to approach women, he was ultimately able to kidnap them not because of his guile but because of his use of a tire iron or similar blunt tool to incapacitate the woman with a blow to the head.

Despite his apparent skill at getting along with others, Bundy reported significant difficulty in relating to other people and this was especially true of his ability to relate to women. The interpersonal ineptitude facilitated his lifelong proclivity for voyeurism that ranged from peeping into windows as a juvenile to the extensive stalking and sexually motivated observation that Bundy performed while on the hunt. His discomfort with others was distressing to Bundy. Indeed, one of my more novel assertions is that Bundy exhibited signs of schizoid personality disorder especially when considering his necrophilic sexual behavior.

The pathological lying feature of Bundy's psychopathy was in an odd way one of the motivations for writing this book. When talking to criminal psychopaths, one quickly recognizes that truthful statements often occur in the midst of minimizations, lies by omission, embellishment, and absurd tall tales that even a child would see through. Acknowledgment of one's crimes, even one's murders, follow this same pattern and investigators must deal with the frustration of being told multiple and often wide-ranging estimates of criminal activity.

That was certainly the case with Bundy where murders for which there was incontrovertible evidence of his guilt were denied, and, in rare moments of vulnerable honesty, he would admit to killing far more victims than authorities knew. This also places analysts of Bundy's offending career into somewhat of a conundrum where they must simultaneously disbelieve much of what he said while also zeroing in on the offhand admissions that appear true and consistent with other circumstances in his life.

On the affective dimension of the Psychopathy Checklist-Revised, the four indicators are lacks remorse or guilt, shallow affect, callous and lacks empathy, and fails to accept responsibility. Ted Bundy personified the affective deficits of psychopathy. Throughout his criminal career, he exhibited no sense of remorse, guilt, embarrassment, or shame for his violent transgressions. That coldness and callousness were on display during his court appearances and media interviews where Bundy draped himself in a resplendent cloak of denial and indignation, as if it would be outrageous to expect him to take responsibility for his criminal acts.

The affective deficits are the heart of psychopathic personality. Across interviews with many serious offenders, some display the superficial shtick that Bundy did, but other psychopathic offenders do not exhibit this behavior at all, and instead respond to questioning with chillingly cold yet brutally honest answers. In these cases, the affective deficits effectively overtake the interpersonal dimension, and offenders describe their criminal conduct in a manner not unlike how a clinician would do it: precise and dispassionate. There is an unsettling tone of unfeeling to their answers as is seen in Samuel Little's confession videos.

The chapter's opening quotation from Bundy illustrates psychopathic unfeeling perfectly because it shows the absence of concern and empathy void for other human beings. To Bundy, the scores of women he murdered across the country were insignificant in the broader scheme of the total population, and, in the event the victim was killed while traveling or hitchhiking, would likely not be missed. He was that cold. When journalist Stephen Michaud interviewed Bundy on death row, he inquired about the manner or method that a killer like Bundy would use to actually cause the death of the victim. He wanted specifics about the act of murder. In response to the query, Bundy became visibly annoyed and agitated, and responded, "I don't know. Strangle her. Stab her…something."[12] That is how little the victims' lives meant to him.

The affective deficits in Bundy's psychopathy are brought into shocking focus when one considers that he viewed his life's work as abducting, sexually defiling, and murdering women. To him, women were a receptacle to be dominated, destroyed, and further exploited after death. That several of his victims were decapitated so that he could use their heads and bodies for sexual gratification shows the depths of his callousness and depravity.

On the lifestyle dimension of the Psychopathy Checklist-Revised, there are five indicators: sensation seeking, impulsivity, irresponsibility, parasitic orientation, and lack of realistic goals. Collectively, these lifestyle factors of psychopathy more accurately typify his adult behavioral functioning than the common narrative that Bundy was a generally successful person. In terms of sensation seeking, Bundy enthusiastically used marijuana and alcohol and used the latter substance to prime himself prior to many of his homicides. He continued to use these substances even when on death row. His crimes themselves encapsulated behaviors that were extraordinarily risky, dangerous, and rife with grave consequences if caught in the act. These required daring, fearlessness, and insouciance.

Impulsivity is easy to misidentify with psychopathic sexual homicide offenders because of the extensive planning and premeditation that their crimes require. On the surface, an instrumental offender like Bundy appeared anything but impulsive. Yet it is better to examine the broader behaviors to see that Bundy often acted on impulse and this tendency contributed to his occupational insecurity, his spotty educational performance, and his lack of follow-through with personal commitments. Regardless of his conventional plans for the day, Bundy frequently veered from those plans to engage in criminal activity or perform trial runs for later criminal activity. These same deficits substantiate his irresponsibility. He could never be counted on due to his time commitment to sexual violence.

Although it appeared Bundy wanted to complete law school and become an attorney, and perhaps later a politician, his conduct contraindicated those goals. His lifestyle deficits significantly damaged his functioning in school, work, and relationship domains. The amount of time that was expended engaging in crime and scouring the environment for more potential victims was considerable and occupied time that Bundy would otherwise be in school or at work. For example, his attempts as a law student in Utah were ill-fated from the start. As Bundy researcher and author Kevin Sullivan observed, "Bundy's reason for an almost perfect lack of attendance was actually quite simple. During the time between September 20 when he returned to Salt Lake City, and the eighth of November, he would abduct and murder at least four young women, all in under a six-week period."[13]

To compound matters further, his remaining free time was spent trying to give the appearance of a normally functioning man who was working to complete an educational degree, perform at work, or maintain the semblance of a normal personal relationship. In conversations with his longtime girlfriend Elizabeth Kendall, Bundy admitted that he tried to suppress his dark urges, which were taking up a substantial portion of his time that precluded his investment in law school. Specifically, Bundy told her, "My time was being used trying to make my life look normal. But it wasn't normal. All the time I could feel the force building in me."[14]

Poor behavioral control, early behavior problems, juvenile delinquency, revocation of conditional release, and criminal versatility constitute the antisocial dimension of the Psychopathy Checklist-Revised. For most serious offenders, these indicators are a natural part of their extensive criminal career and history of noncompliance with the criminal justice system. Ironically, these factors are less straightforward to measure in Bundy's life history due to his keen ability to avoid police detection for the preponderance of his offending career.

My personal approach with psychopathy assessments is to be as conservative as possible when rating individuals on the items and only assign a two where there is pervasive and overwhelming evidence of the trait or symptom. As such, if employing a strictly conservative approach, Bundy would score a one on both early behavior problems and juvenile delinquency. To be sure, there is evidence across childhood and adolescence of an assortment of conduct problems and delinquent acts spanning assaults, burglary, theft, and even potential homicides as this book will explore, but Bundy was not an incorrigible delinquent with dozens of police contacts, placements in detention, and commitments to confinement facilities as seen in comparison to the most serious, violent, and chronic delinquents.[15] Compared to offenders in my research and practitioner experiences who had fifty or more police contacts during their childhood and adolescence, Bundy's official juvenile record was rather tame, but did include justice system interventions for burglary and auto theft.[16]

Beyond juvenile delinquency, Bundy fully met the other criteria evidenced by his versatile criminal acts spanning murder, rape, sodomy, assault, motor vehicle theft, theft, burglary, credit card fraud, escapes from custody, flight to avoid detention, and perpetration of additional crimes while under correctional and judicial supervision. Indeed, his statuses as a jail escapee and prisoner within the Utah Department of Corrections were some of the aggravating circumstances in his Florida capital trials.[17]

Criminal versatility is meaningful because it indicates that an individual engages in antisocial behavior irrespective of context, and thus is an important indicator of a person's criminal propensity as discussed in the prior chapter. To illustrate, the most common criminal offenses that a "normal" or normatively behaved person commits are low-level alcohol violations, such as underage use of alcohol, public intoxication, or drunk driving. In this way, their entire range of criminality is rather limited to a specific form of conduct: the overconsumption of alcohol. Aside from alcohol violations though, a "normal" person does not commit violent, property, drug, or firearms violations, their criminality is circumscribed and mostly benign.

In contrast, a criminally versatile offender has such high antisocial propensity, such as Little, Alcala, or Bundy, that virtually any situation is construed as an opportunity to inflict criminal harm. For example, a remarkable feature of Bundy's poor behavioral control is his abduction of Debby Kent on the same day just hours after being thwarted in his attempt to abduct Carol DaRonch.

Once initiated to perpetrate sexual homicide, Bundy thought nothing of targeting multiple women on the same day usually within mere hours of each other. The velocity of his homicidal conduct is incredible. Among the multitude of career criminals in my consulting and research experiences, most have zero, one, or usually at most, two murders on their rap sheet despite the broader extent of their offending history. On paper, their murder is the culmination of their life of crime. For Bundy, that degree of criminal activity was achieved or exceeded in a matter of hours.

Diagnostically, where does Bundy score on the Psychopathy Checklist-Revised? Applying the conservative approach mentioned earlier, Bundy could be scored one for many short-term relationships, early behavior problems, and juvenile delinquency. Again, the latter two scores are in comparison to incorrigible delinquents whose arrest activity starts in early childhood and whose justice system involvement spans their entire adolescence. That did not typify Bundy. All other items Bundy would score two and on most was extraordinarily psychopathic. At minimum, he scores a thirty-seven, which places him in the 99.5th percentile of offenders in North America. On the other hand, given the evidence for his disturbing early life externalizing and delinquent behaviors, it is also reasonable to assign a score of two for early behavior problems and juvenile delinquency, pushing his score to thirty-nine, which is the 99.9th percentile. In the latter scenario, the only item for which Bundy would score one is for many short-term relationships.[18]

Even that item could reasonably be scored as a two. Throughout his relationship with Elizabeth Kendall, Bundy was unfaithful and engaged in multiple sexual relationships with women in a dating context or a short-term sexual encounter. And these events pertain to women with whom the sexual relationship was consensual and does not even count the myriad women who Bundy sexually assaulted and murdered. If one were to score Bundy a two on the many short-term relationships, indicative of his low affiliation, low attachment, and indifference to the feelings of others, his score is a perfect forty, the 100th percentile. Forensically, psychologically, and behaviorally, Bundy's psychopathy is orders of magnitude worse than virtually anyone else in the population save other serial sexual homicide offenders, such as Rodney Alcala or Samuel Little, murderers who also likely killed more than one-hundred people.

Bundy's offense behavior is entrenched in psychopathy. He was a life-long thief and stole from stores and individuals with a strident sense of entitlement and purpose, at times daringly walking into stores, grabbing items that he wanted, and simply walking out of the store. Although his girlfriend Elizabeth Kendall was slow to warm to other forensic aspects of Bundy's conduct, she immediately recognized that nearly all of Bundy's possessions were stolen or obtained via some degree of deception. Many times, the thefts were unnecessary as if they were perpetrated merely for the sake of committing crime. One time when Kendall confronted Bundy about his compulsive acts of theft, he physically grabbed her arm and told her, "If you ever tell anyone about this, I'll break your fucking neck."[19]

Relative to his other crimes, theft has an air of triviality to it, but the basic act of taking something that is not yours also encapsulates the elemental features of psychopathy. Theft is selfish, often impulsive, and indifferent to the victim's property rights. It is an instrumental act that involves the taking and possession of an object that the offender wants. The same logic of his psychopathy extended to Bundy's homicides where he instrumentally abducted women who were so objectified that they were his possession. And Bundy had very specific plans for that possession: incapacitate her, force her to undress, and rape and sodomize her from behind while strangling the life from her. With no remorse, upon completion of his sexual violence, Bundy was already contemplating the next attack.

When considering the assorted features of psychopathy, it is clearly a devilish recipe for crime and violence, one that comports perfectly to Bundy's life and behavioral functioning. It also provides a heuristic for interpreting his maddeningly inconsistent accounts of his murders and the likely significance of his dark figure of crime. On the morning of his execution, for instance, Bundy met with investigator Jim Barton and confessed to two additional murders, of Susan Curtis, age fifteen, from the campus of Brigham Young University in June 1975 and of Denise Oliverson in Colorado in April 1975. When Barton asked that if there were additional victims, Bundy denied there were and asked for a cigarette, to which Barton told Bundy there were additional law enforcement inquiries about unsolved homicides in Illinois and New Jersey. Bundy responded, "Well, let's just deal with whatever is outstanding like that. I can say without any question there is, no, uh, nothing for instance that I was involved in in Illinois or New Jersey."[20] Shortly thereafter, Bundy also denied any killings in Vermont, Texas, and Miami, Florida. Approximately twenty minutes later, the State of Florida executed Ted Bundy.

Dissecting this exchange with Barton highlights multiple features of Bundy's psychopathy. Although he was moments away from his electrocution complete with shaved head and calf to facilitate the electrical current, Bundy still felt he was in control of the situation and could manipulate the investigator by interrupting to ask for a cigarette and dictating the terms of the conversation. If Bundy did not actually commit any murders in these jurisdictions, the answer to the question should have been a quick, easy, and emphatic "no." Instead of replying no, if that were at all truthful, Bundy offers the convoluted answer "let's just deal with whatever is outstanding," suggesting that many other murders in these and other jurisdictions would not be discussed, and "I can say without any question there is, no, uh nothing for instance that I was involved in…" Bundy was obviously lying, and his lie complete with filler interjection, awkward pausing, and external locus of control (i.e., "that I was involved in.") was the final example of a lifelong pattern of untruth, manipulation, and remorselessness.

Cleckley's *Mask of Sanity* conveys the idea that psychopaths present a façade of normalcy that shields their private pathology from others, and it was an effective mask for Bundy, for even astute observers of criminal behavior such as true crime scribe Ann Rule were initially shocked when the allegations of Bundy's crimes emerged during the mid-1970s. A façade is an outward appearance that is maintained to conceal a less pleasant reality, and in Bundy's case, his psychopathic interpersonal functioning superficially allowed him to tread the waters of normal behavioral functioning with louder displays of grandiosity, chattiness, and charm.

But it was all a lie. In truth, Bundy was unsuccessful, inadequate, and insecure, and by his own admission really did not understand how to relate to other people. He couldn't because his emotional life was dominated by violent sexual desire that he knew would reveal the horrifying depths of his cruelty and unfeeling.

Bundy's psychopathy was apparent since childhood. As an explanatory framework, it clarifies his overall behavioral functioning, such as the velocity with which he would lose jobs, enroll and withdrawal from university, and appear rudderless in the pursuit of goals, as well as illuminates the disturbing and creepy incidents across his life. These events, such as pulling mice apart while playing in the woods, prowling neighborhoods, or attempting to drown acquaintances while swimming or boating as a malevolent desolation overtook his eyes appeared with far more regularity than is commonly believed.

In contemporary forensic research, there are many measures of psychopathy each of which takes a slightly different approach and focuses on specific features or facets of the disorder. Some of these were developed to measure psychopathic personality functioning among those in the community, that is, not among correctional clients, jail inmates, or prisoners. Despite the extremity of Bundy's offending career, the majority of it was offline in the sense that he was not caught by police until very late in his homicide career. In an odd way, these alternative measures of psychopathy are also relevant to Bundy. One is known as the Psychopathic Personality Inventory that contains self-report items that bear on eight dimensions that are theorized to encapsulate the psychopathic personality. These are Machiavellian egocentricity, social potency, coldheartedness, carefree nonplanfulness, fearlessness, blame externalization, impulsive nonconformity, and stress immunity.[21]

Machiavellian egocentricity is a highly self-involved and self-interested interpersonal style that comes at the expense of others and typifies someone who is calculating, shrewd, and ruthless. Social potency is the notion that one can affect and influence others with relative ease and control any situation. Coldheartedness is the callous disregard for others' feelings along with lack of guilt or remorse for one's own conduct. Carefree nonplanfulness is the lack of attention to the consequences of one's behavior and problems with long-term commitments. Fearlessness is the absence of fear and a proneness for risky, dangerous endeavors. Blame externalization is the tendency to blame others for one's conduct and to rationalize one's antisocial behavior. Impulsive nonconformity is a disregard for social norms and desire for immediate gratification. Stress immunity is the lack of physiological or psychological reaction to typically stress-inducing situations or circumstances.

Although this measure was developed to examine psychopathic features among the non-criminal population, its various dimensions nevertheless correlate with reports of antisocial behavior and are relevant to criminal outcomes among the offender population. A variety of studies substantiate these psychopathic features as significant drivers of severe conduct problems and violence.[22] Moreover, those who work in criminal justice settings likely immediately recognize some of these features, especially coldheartedness, blame externalization, and impulsive nonconformity among arrestees, jail inmates, prisoners, probationers, and parolees.

Bundy's personality functioning exhibited all of these features, and it is important to recognize that his psychopathy manifested similarly across different behavioral contexts. For example, consider how frightening and stressful his typical offense behavior would be to an individual who is not a psychopath. By ruse, hitchhiker contact, or casual conversation, the notion of contacting a woman to then temporarily distract her in order to hit her in the head with a crowbar, to then handcuff her for abduction is extraordinarily stressful. The impending use of violence would produce a cascade of anxiety and fear in a person with normal personality functioning. The potential for detection and arrest is still another massive stressor. Indeed, most people in the population abstain from criminal offending because of the mere existence of the justice system and the prospect of jail or prison confinement. It is a considerable deterrent. The prospect of committing abduction, rape, and murder is thus beyond the realm of behavioral possibility for most people with normal personality functioning.

Now consider the effects Bundy's conduct had on the victim during the course of the crime. The victim experienced profound pain, disorientation, stress, fear, confusion, sadness, anger, and hypervigilance. During conversations with his defense attorney Polly Nelson, Bundy described in vivid detail the entire sequence of abducting a woman, forcing her to remove her clothing, often taking pictures of her, then raping her while strangling her with a noose or some other ligature. Nelson indicated that Bundy had a warm glow about him as he recounted the step-by-step increments of the crime. After, he informed Nelson that he drove the now deceased woman to a remote location in another state where he dismembered her body.[23] His victims experienced an unimaginably painful and stressful ordeal before their death, and their pain and suffering was precisely what he needed to satiate his sadistic urges.

Among those who survived their encounter with Ted Bundy, the physical injuries, psychiatric burden, and post-traumatic stress disorder symptoms are lifelong. The recognition of these emotions by a normal person would also cause significant distress. Owing to his troubling personality admixture of Machiavellian egocentricity, social potency, coldheartedness, fearlessness, impulsive nonconformity, and stress immunity, Bundy engaged in these acts with effectively no sense of danger or anxiety, and certainly no concern about the victims.

The same brazen traits are also seen in his interactions with the criminal justice system where Bundy's massive ego contributed to his poor decision to attempt *pro se* representation, to his absurdly daring jail escapes, to his utter refusal to recognize the legal jeopardy he was in especially during the Florida prosecutions where he faced and ultimately received the death penalty. His frustrating tendency to report very different numbers of murder victims to investigators and defense counsel, especially during his eleventh-hour confessions immediately before his execution highlights his Machiavellian egocentricity, social potency, carefree nonplanfulness, and profound blame externalization.

I am not alone in the recognition of Bundy's psychopathic features during his interactions with criminal justice practitioners. For example, Dr. Emanuel Tanay, who was an expert witness during his Florida proceedings, had this observation about Bundy's behavior toward criminal justice practitioners. "My impression was that it was typical behavior of a psychopath who likes to defy authority, who has a need, who is driven to defy authority—and that includes lawyers, psychiatrists, law enforcement, judges—and that was more important to him than saving his own life. He was typically responding to a gratification of the moment."[24]

A final conceptual model of psychopathy is known as the triarchic model, which asserts that boldness, meanness, and disinhibition are the core of the disorder.[25] From this perspective, Boldness is an assertive, socially dominant interpersonal style and venturesomeness where the individual is able to recover quickly from stressful situations, is self-assured, and has a high tolerance for unfamiliarity and danger. Meanness encompasses callous, cold, cruel, aggressive features of psychopathy and is consistent with the angry, hostile, aggressive, and violent aspects of the disorder. Meanness is seen in many behavioral manifestations including arrogance and verbal derisiveness, defiance of authority, physical cruelty and various forms of aggression, destructiveness, and the targeted exploitation of others for gain.

Disinhibition relates to impulsivity, irresponsibility, impatience, and a general tendency to fail to inhibit one's conduct. It broadly captures the notion that psychopaths have severe self-regulation deficits and are unable to adequately control themselves in a variety of contexts. Researchers have produced considerable support for the triarchic model of psychopathy especially regarding the linkages between disinhibition and meanness (not as much for boldness) and various forms of antisocial behavior.[26]

Of these dimensions, meanness is the most colloquial of the terms and is broadly understood, but the familiar concept of meanness also truly captures the spirit of psychopathy especially as seen in Bundy's baleful conduct. In contrast to the likeable sheen that Bundy appeared to present to the world, he was an incalculably mean individual whose conduct was as uncaring, violent, and depraved as any offender in American history.

Those with the most direct contact with Bundy had the clearest view of the depths of his meanness. Elizabeth Kendall, her daughter Molly, and various collateral interviewees from Dr. Carlisle's psychological assessment told very similar stories about the hateful, mean, misanthropic behaviors that Bundy would engage in periodically during their acquaintanceship. Even those who worked in criminal law for a living were appalled by the emotional depravity of his personality and behavior. Upon hearing Bundy describe his offense conduct during the course of a murder, his attorney Polly Nelson described the horror. "It was the absolute misogyny of his crime that stunned me, his manifest rage against women, that left me no place to return to. He had no compassion for the victim at all."[27]

When on death row, Bundy acknowledged that Janice Ott was still alive when he returned with the abducted Denise Naslund so that he could murder one of the women in front of the other woman in order to inflict maximum terror. During one of his capital appeals in 1984, the legal prose itself revealed the sheer meanness of his crimes:

> Lisa Levy and Margaret Bowman were killed by strangulation after receiving severe beatings with a length of a tree branch used as a club. Margaret Bowman's skull was crushed and literally laid open. The attacker

also bit Lisa Levy with sufficient intensity to leave indentations which could clearly be identified as human bite marks.[28]

One of the aggravating circumstances in Bundy's Florida convictions that helped to secure a death sentence was the especially heinous, atrocious, and cruel nature of his Chi Omega crimes. Specifically, that the victims were murdered while sleeping in their beds and subjected to bludgeoning, strangulation, and sexual assault, each of which has court precedence establishing it as an indicator of heinousness, equates to meanness on a legal level. Not surprisingly, Bundy objected to this claim and insisted that the trial court erred because the Chi Omega murders were not, in his opinion, particularly heinous, atrocious, or cruel.

That Ted Bundy was a psychopath is indisputable, and even his legal defenders including John Henry Browne and Polly Nelson struggled at times when recognizing they were representing a defendant who was to them the personification of evil. The contours of Bundy's offense history and the specific features of his criminal acts comport perfectly with diagnostic criteria for psychopathy. This too is generally uncontroversial.

Less commonly discussed is that psychopathy is a largely heritable construct and that the more extreme its manifestation, the stronger its genetic origin, and the earlier its behavioral expression. This means it is highly unlikely, even implausible, that Bundy was able to nullify his psychopathic wants until its putative official emergence in 1974. He was too psychopathic for that to be true. The notion that his criminal activity, including additional murders began far earlier is all the more likely when considering that psychopathy was just one of the extreme psychological conditions that Bundy exhibited.

Notes

1. Michaud and Aynesworth (2019, p. 140).
2. American Psychiatric Association (2013).
3. Michaud and Aynesworth (2019, p. 260), italics in original quotation.
4. American Psychiatric Association (2013).
5. Wright et al. (2021).

6. Viding et al. (2005); Viding et al. (2008); Larsson et al. (2006).
7. Nelson (2018, p. 155).
8. DeLisi et al. (2010).
9. Michaud and Aynesworth (1999, p. 55).
10. Cleckley (1941); Hare (1991).
11. Coid et al. (2009).
12. Michaud and Aynesworth (2019, p. 137).
13. Sullivan (2009, p. 91).
14. Kendall (2020, p. 176).
15. Wolfgang et al. (1972); Trulson et al. (2016); Vaughn et al. (2014); DeLisi, Drury, & Elbert (2021).
16. Rule (1980).
17. *Bundy v. State,* 455 So. 2d 330 (1984).
18. In his psychological assessment, Dr. Carlisle described Bundy as somewhat psychopathic on this item after Bundy divulged that he was cohabitating with Kendall, sexually involved with his prior girlfriend Marjorie, and having sex with two women he worked with. Bundy typified this behavior as the "typical bad guy thing".
19. Kendall (2020, p. 63).
20. Michaud and Aynesworth (1999, p. 325).
21. Lilienfeld and Andrews (1996).
22. Kruh et al. (2005); Vaughn et al. (2008); DeLisi et al. (2014).
23. Nelson (2018).
24. Nelson (2018, p. 200).
25. Patrick et al. (2009); Patrick (2010).
26. Sleep et al. (2019).
27. Nelson (2018, p. 254).
28. *Bundy v. State,* 455 So.2d 330 (1984, p. 3).

References

American Psychiatric Association. (2013). *Diagnostic and statistical manual of mental disorders (DSM-5®).* American Psychiatric Publishing.
Bundy v. State, 455 So.2d 330 (1984).

Cleckley, H. M. (1941). *The mask of sanity: An attempt to clarify some issues about the so-called psychopathic personality*. The C. V. Mosby Company.

Coid, J., Yang, M., Ullrich, S., Roberts, A., & Hare, R. D. (2009). Prevalence and correlates of psychopathic traits in the household population of Great Britain. *International Journal of Law and Psychiatry, 32*(2), 65–73.

DeLisi, M., Angton, A., Vaughn, M. G., Trulson, C. R., Caudill, J. W., & Beaver, K. M. (2014). Not my fault: Blame externalization is the psychopathic feature most associated with pathological delinquency among confined delinquents. *International Journal of Offender Therapy and Comparative Criminology, 58*(12), 1415–1430.

DeLisi, M., Drury, A. J., & Elbert, M. J. (2021). Psychopathy and pathological violence in a criminal career: A forensic case report. *Aggression and Violent Behavior, 60*, 101521.

DeLisi, M., Vaughn, M. G., Beaver, K. M., & Wright, J. P. (2010). The Hannibal Lecter myth: Psychopathy and verbal intelligence in the MacArthur violence risk assessment study. *Journal of Psychopathology and Behavioral Assessment, 32*(2), 169–177.

Hare, R. D. (1991). *Manual for the psychopathy checklist-revised*. Multi-Health Systems.

Kendall, E., with a contribution from Molly Kendall. (2020). *The phantom prince: My life with Ted Bundy* (updated and expanded edition). Abrams Press.

Kruh, I. P., Whittemore, K., Arnaut, G. L., Manley, J., Gage, B., & Gagliardi, G. J. (2005). The concurrent validity of the Psychopathic Personality Inventory and its relative association with past violence in a sample of insanity acquittees. *International Journal of Forensic Mental Health, 4*(2), 135–145.

Larsson, H., Andershed, H., & Lichtenstein, P. (2006). A genetic factor explains most of the variation in the psychopathic personality. *Journal of Abnormal Psychology, 115*(2), 221–230.

Lilienfeld, S. O., & Andrews, B. P. (1996). Development and preliminary validation of a self-report measure of psychopathic personality traits in noncriminal population. *Journal of Personality Assessment, 66*(3), 488–524.

Michaud, S. G., & Aynesworth, H. (1999). *The only living witness: The true story of serial sex killer Ted Bundy*. Authorlink Press.

Michaud, S. G., & Aynesworth, H. (2019). *Ted Bundy: Conservations with a killer: The death row interviews*. Sterling.

Nelson, P. (2018). *Defending the devil: My story as Ted Bundy's last lawyer*. Echo Point Books & Media.

Patrick, C. J. (2010). Conceptualizing the psychopathic personality: Disinhibited, bold, ... or just plain mean? In R. T. Salekin & D. R. Lynam (Eds.), *Handbook of child & adolescent psychopathy* (pp. 15–48). The Guilford Press.

Patrick, C., Fowles, D., & Krueger, R. (2009). Triarchic conceptualization of psychopathy: Developmental origins of disinhibition, boldness, and meanness. *Development and Psychopathology, 21,* 913–938.

Rule, A. (1980). *The stranger beside me.* W. W. Norton.

Sleep, C. E., Weiss, B., Lynam, D. R., & Miller, J. D. (2019). An examination of the Triarchic Model of psychopathy's nomological network: A meta-analytic review. *Clinical Psychology Review, 71,* 1–26.

Sullivan, K. M. (2009). *The Bundy murders: A comprehensive history.* McFarland and Company.

Trulson, C. R., Haerle, D. R., Caudill, J. W., & DeLisi, M. (2016). *Lost causes: Blended sentencing, second chances, and the Texas youth commission.* University of Texas Press.

Vaughn, M. G., Howard, M. O., & DeLisi, M. (2008). Psychopathic personality traits and delinquent careers: An empirical examination. *International Journal of Law and Psychiatry, 31*(5), 407–416.

Vaughn, M. G., Salas-Wright, C. P., DeLisi, M., & Maynard, B. R. (2014). Violence and externalizing behavior among youth in the United States: Is there a severe 5%? *Youth Violence and Juvenile Justice, 12*(1), 3–21.

Viding, E., Blair, R. J. R., Moffitt, T. E., & Plomin, R. (2005). Evidence for substantial genetic risk for psychopathy in 7-year-olds. *Journal of Child Psychology and Psychiatry, 46*(6), 592–597.

Viding, E., Jones, A. P., Frick, P., Moffitt, T. E., & Plomin, R. (2008). Heritability of antisocial behaviour at 9: Do callous-unemotional traits matter? *Developmental Science, 11*(1), 17–22.

Wolfgang, M. E., Figlio, R. M., & Sellin, T. (1972). *Delinquency in a birth cohort.* University of Chicago Press.

Wright, N., Pickles, A., Sharp, H., & Hill, J. (2021). A psychometric and validity study of callous-unemotional traits in 2.5-year-old children. *Scientific Reports, 11*(1), 1–10.

5

The Entity

The need, the thought, the feeling, the excitement of harming, of getting some sort of sexual gratification at harming someone, was absolutely paramount.[1]

Ted Bundy

In addition to its early emergence, developmental stability, and consequences for behavioral impairment, another important feature of clinical disorder is the condition usually does not exist in isolation, but instead coincides with other clinical disorders and forensic characteristics. This is known as comorbidity. The more clinical disorders an individual has, the greater and more expansive their psychopathology.[2] Psychopathology is the study of mental and behavioral disorders, and is an umbrella term meant to describe all of the clinical features and conditions that typify an individual.

As a general rule of thumb, persons in the general population have relatively low psychopathology and are high functioning in the sense that they successfully complete school and work responsibilities, have generally healthy and meaningful relationships, and engage in prosocial activities without much difficulty. Thankfully, most people are

© The Author(s), under exclusive license to Springer Nature Switzerland AG 2023
M. DeLisi, *Ted Bundy and The Unsolved Murder Epidemic*,
https://doi.org/10.1007/978-3-031-21418-9_5

fairly well-adjusted and handle the challenges of life with their mental and physical health intact. A significant proportion of the population contributes very little to various social problems including criminal activity.[3] But even behaviorally "normal" individuals are not immune from exhibiting psychopathological features. Fairly common examples of psychopathology in the general population, again among those who are still rather high functioning, include anxiety symptoms, depressive symptoms, and substance use that is usually limited to alcohol and marijuana.

In sharp contrast, offender or correctional populations have significantly higher, more severe, and more comorbid psychopathology, and this is particularly the case among those who commit sexually oriented crimes. Here, offenders not only have much more pernicious and pathological conditions, but also have multiple conditions that exacerbate their antisocial tendencies and worsen their behavioral functioning.[4] For sexual homicide offenders, such as Samuel Little, Rodney Alcala, and Ted Bundy, the nefariousness of their crimes is consistent with their underlying psychological and psychiatric dysfunction.

In addition to his psychopathy, Bundy had multifaceted psychopathology that included pervasive homicidal ideation, personality disorder disturbance with antisocial and schizoid features, and multiple paraphilic conditions spanning sexual sadism, biastophilia, necrophilia, and pedohebephilia. Collectively, these conditions helped drive Bundy's murderous sexual violence that mostly targeted adult females, but also involved pubescent and prepubescent girls. In isolation, any of these conditions is extreme and can contribute to problematic behaviors, which puts into perspective how critically dangerous Bundy's psychological functioning was.

Several definitions are useful for concepts in this chapter. According to the American Psychiatric Association, a paraphilia is any intense and persistent sexual interest other than sexual interest in genital stimulation or preparatory fondling with phenotypically normal, physically mature, consenting human partners. In common parlance, a paraphilia is sexual deviancy that exists outside the confines of normal sexual interests and sexual activity. Bundy was wholly consumed with his paraphilias since childhood and much of his private life centered on his deviant sexual interests, which he referred to variously as his psychopathology, or "the entity."

Whereas paraphilia is the interest, a paraphilic disorder is a paraphilia that causes distress or impairment to the individual, or a paraphilia whose satisfaction entails personal harm, or risk of harm to others.[5] Paraphilic disorder translates the prurient interest into sexual harm. The diagnostic conditions for paraphilic disorder clearly apply to Bundy as much of his adolescent and adult functioning was stunted by the sheer amount of time and energy devoted to preparing for and engaging in sexual violence and murder.

Moreover, the paraphilic disorders caused Bundy considerable distress throughout his life. For example, after his final capture in Florida in 1978, Bundy negotiated with law enforcement to use the telephone and call his former girlfriend Elizabeth Kendall. During that conversation in an effort to help her understand his paraphilic violent conduct, Bundy stated that he wished he could have a private conversation with her where he could describe the depths of his psychopathic need for sexual violence.[6] No one should feel pity for Bundy because of his paraphilic disorders, but this statement puts into perspective how overpowering his sexual drives were, how completely he contemplated murder as a means to satisfy those sexual urges, and the sheer energy that was expended to process his psychopathology.

Additional biographical accounts document both the extensive amount of time and travel that Bundy's sexual violence consumed. To illustrate, after she had become suspicious that Bundy might be involved in the disappearance of multiple young women in Washington, Kendall searched his vehicle and was shocked by the thick stack of gas receipts that Bundy kept above the sun visor in his car, evidence of the extent of his canvassing of victims far above and beyond what would be a normal amount of travel.[7]

He constantly traveled with no explanation for where he went. According to Robert Keppel, Bundy had a compulsion to travel by vehicle that drove his relentless searching for victims. When he was in this perseverative mode of traveling for victims, he would not rest until he murdered. This constant driving behavior puts a travel perspective to the likely geographic spread and extent of his undiscovered and unknown murders. As Keppel advised, "He became, especially when he was acting out the behaviors leading up to an abduction and murder, like the walking dead. There was no emotion except for the compulsion to possess someone else, to inflict upon her a crippling blow that would deliver her into his control. He was chilling in his single-mindedness to kill."[8]

Others also noticed the voluminous and seemingly unexplained distances that Bundy traveled as well as his demeanor after likely engaging in that violence. For instance, Sybil Ferris, an elderly former acquaintance of Bundy who had a critical albeit rather accurate assessment of him, described his aimless existence where it appeared to her that he was pathologically preoccupied with something. Unbeknownst to her, his pathological preoccupation was his paraphilic interests. According to Ferris, "He left the area on a plane one time. He said he was going to Colorado to be a ski instructor there. Something happened and he came back. He went to Pennsylvania and drove his uncle's Cadillac and came back flat broke looking for a job. All in all, he's just a very weird boy."[9] Later in her conversation with Dr. Al Carlisle who was interviewing collateral witnesses for his psychological assessment of Bundy in 1976, Ferris noted, "He told me he was going on trips. *He would be gone all these hours and would come back all hepped up…*I thought he might be trafficking dope."[10]

Bundy obviously was not trafficking narcotics, but was engaging in far more serious criminal conduct. Moreover, the hyperarousal that Ferris observed was him coming down from his exhilaration and hyperarousal after perpetrating sexual homicide. His murderous conduct also meets the second criteria for paraphilic disorder: the satisfaction of his sexual appetites entailed harm to myriad victims.

Within this psychiatric framework are paraphilic disorders reflecting specific sexual desires and the one most applicable to serial sexual homicide offenders including Little, Alcala, and Bundy is sexual sadism disorder. Sexual sadism disorder is defined as recurrent and intense sexual arousal from physical or psychological suffering of another person as manifested by fantasies, urges, or behaviors and which the individual has acted on these sexual urges with a nonconsenting person, or the sexual urges or fantasies cause clinically significant distress or impairment in social, occupational, or other important areas of functioning.[11] Not all individuals who exhibit sexual sadism disorder are known sexual offenders, or known sexual homicide offenders; however, the prevalence of it and other disorders among offender groups is far greater than among those in the general population as is the case with psychopathy.[12]

Assorted criminal acts and crime scene indicators provide important evidence of sexual sadism disorder, and forensic researchers have developed scales of diagnostic items that broadly pertain to Bundy's offense behaviors and presumed motivational factors. These scales include items, such as intense and recurring sexual fantasies involving sexual violence, post mortem sexual activity, marks of violence on erogenous zones, insertion of objects into body cavities, sexual arousal to sadistic acts, strangling and choking the victim, abduction of the victim, and the infliction of gratuitous violence beyond what is necessary to cause the victim's death.[13] The implication is the presence of these aberrant behaviors is not random, nor do they suggest mental illness in the manner of psychosis. Instead, they are manifest indicators of a paraphilic disorder that is effectively congruent with sexual homicide offending.

Sexually sadistic homicide offenders also practice a forensic awareness that shows their acumen at throwing off investigators. A study of 350 sexual homicide offenders, for instance, found greater evidence of forensic awareness among sadistic as opposed to non-sadistic sexual homicide offenders. Nearly two of three sadistic sexual murderers engaged in forensic awareness, and they were significantly more likely to remove or destroy evidence from the body, act upon or manipulate the body or environmental proximal to the body, and take other forensic precautions. Sadistic killers were also more likely to have their cases remain unsolved, in part due to the forensic care that was used during its perpetration.[14] They intentionally engage in behaviors that will help ensure they get away with murder.

Bundy's criminal conduct and consensual sexual history are replete with evidence of sexual sadism. Within consensual relationships, Bundy pressured women to engage in bondage, pressured women to engage in sodomy, and inflicted physical violence in the manner of choking them, attempting to smother them, and attempting to strangle them. Indeed, his sexual behaviors within these dating relationships were at times so coercive and violent that they effectively challenge whether the sexual relations were consensual at all.

During his criminal acts, numerous features of Bundy's behavior vividly highlight his sexual sadism. In multiple cases, Bundy not only raped and sodomized the victim, but also inserted foreign objects into their vagina or rectum. His arrest for possession of "burglary tools" in Utah included what were in fact the tools to perpetrate sexual homicide. The contents of his murder kit included an ice pick, screwdriver, ski mask, crowbar, panty hose mask, rope, trash bags, flashlight, and a belt. The passenger seat of his Volkswagen Beetle was intentionally removed so that the bound and unconscious woman he had just abducted could not be seen from outside the vehicle. The items in his murder kit chillingly reveal the violence he intended to inflict on women he kidnapped, which as the chapter's opening quotation explicitly indicates, was paramount to him.

Bundy decapitated some of his victims with a hacksaw,[15] and estimates are that at least a dozen victims were beheaded in order for him to use their body and head for sexual gratification. By any estimation, this is the nadir of sexual depravity. During his prosecution for the Chi Omega crimes in Florida, the nature of Bundy's sexually sadistic behavior qualified as especially heinous, atrocious, and cruel, which is one of the aggravating circumstances needed to justify capital punishment.[16] During a conversation with his defense counsel John Henry Browne in 1977, Bundy admitted that the excitement of stalking, controlling, and choosing which women to murder sexually aroused him.[17] By any criteria, Bundy was as wholly sexually sadistic as he was psychopathic.

Although Bundy was clearly sexually sadistic and generally preferred to rape adult females, he also exhibited evidence for pedohebephilia, which is sexual attraction to prepubescent and pubescent children as seen in the murders of Lynette Culver, age twelve, in Idaho in 1975 and Kimberly Leach, age twelve, in Florida in 1978. In her contribution to her mother's memoir about dating and living with Ted Bundy, Molly Kendall describes recurrent events during her early childhood where Bundy would engage in sadistic and abusive behaviors toward her, and at times these events involved predatory sexual behavior.

One potentially fatal event occurred when she was just seven years of age when Bundy attempted to "play" with her while he had an erection. As he contemplated whether to sexually assault her, Bundy laid in her bed and ejaculated as he laid behind the terrified child, a similar position he preferred when murdering many of his victims. The terrified child did not understand ejaculation and remarked to Bundy that he had urinated.

Kendall expressed that Bundy had an aggressive, malevolent look in his eyes during this event and seemed to be in a state of hyperarousal. Kendall also mentions recurrent times where Bundy would surreptitiously fondle her vagina even in plain view of others.[18] These incidents substantiate that Bundy viewed seemingly normal interaction patterns as opportunities to sexually aggress and toward a category of victims different from adult females.

However, for at least two reasons, it is unlikely Bundy was strongly attracted to juvenile females enough to warrant a formal pedophilia or hebephilia diagnosis. First, had Bundy been clinically pedophilic, the majority of his sexual homicide victims would have been children, not adults. He was not the type of offender to deprive himself of those who he truly wanted to sexually abuse and kill.

Second, his occasional sexual violence against children and adolescents was likely a function of his extreme psychopathy and sexual sadism where these antisocial conditions effectively "spilled over" into targeting non-adult females for his sexual gratification.[19] In other words, situational and opportunity factors played an important role when Bundy targeted juveniles for homicidal child sexual abuse. This was likely the scenario when Bundy approached 14-year-old Leslie Parmenter in Jacksonville, Florida in order to abduct her, but the contact was foiled because her brother was near. That event occurred just one day before he kidnapped and murdered Kimberly Leach.

As extraordinarily depraved as Bundy's offending career is, it is critical to recognize that a large scientific literature about sexual homicide offenders exists, and many of the features of Bundy's psychopathology and offending behavior are consistent with research based on samples of sexual murderers. Shockingly, his conduct is frankly no more severe than the behaviors of some of his contemporaries, like Little and Alcala, who also murdered throughout the United States during the middle to late twentieth century.

Regarding the circumstances of the Leach murder, a forensic study of 136 cases of homicidal child sexual abuse and 646 cases of non-homicidal child sexual abuse is revealing. The study utilized an analytical technique known as conjunctive analysis of case configurations, which allows the researcher to analyze all possible interaction terms to determine the odds that an event, in this case, homicidal child sexual abuse, would occur based on the offender's characteristics. Each variable is measured as a dichotomy, it was either present or absent. The variables in their study are applicable to Bundy's offense conduct in the Leach case. In one model using the following mix of variables, whether he was a loner, had prior convictions, used alcohol before the crime, and had paraphilic behaviors, the odds of committing a homicidal child sexual abuse were nearly eighteen times higher than offenders who lacked these characteristics.

In other statistical models in the study, the odds of the sexual murder of a child were vastly higher based on Bundy's characteristics. For instance, an offender with used alcohol, who vaginally or anally penetrated the victim, employed a weapon during the crime, and beat the victim was nearly 104 times more likely to murder the child. Overall, the study found that offenders like Bundy who kidnap, rape, and murder children are extremely instrumental in their behavior and capitalize on opportunities to inflict violence.[20]

These scientific findings are consistent with Bundy's own description of some of his crimes. "[t]here was this driving need to have everything happen in a flash, like first the taking possession or control, and then stripping the victim, and then some sort of sexual activity, and then it would happen so quickly; beating, oftentimes."[21] The frenzied and frenetic offense conduct means that Bundy was able to sexually assault and murder victims in the blink of an eye, or in his words, in a flash.

Beyond these horrifying conditions, Bundy displayed other paraphilic disorders to a considerable degree including necrophilia, or sexual activity with corpses, and biastophilia, or sex with a nonconsenting partner, also known as a preference for rape. At certain points of his murder career, it appears that Bundy's primary motivation was necrophilia as he would abstain from sexual activity with the victim until she was deceased. According to Robert Keppel, Bundy exuded considerable embarrassment that he engaged in postmortem sexual activity.[22]

Bundy's postmortem sexual activity with some of his victims comports with forensic studies of other necrophilic sexual murderers. Consistent with Bundy's conduct, necrophilic sexual homicide offenders are likely to kidnap their victims, engage in premortem sexual acts, cause death by strangulation or beating, and employ wooded areas as an environment to perpetrate crimes and dispose of bodies.[23]

The issue of "wooded areas" or forests is interesting. Bundy once indicated that he disliked the crowded and dirty conditions in Philadelphia, Pennsylvania where it is believed he perpetrated some of his earliest murders. The other point of dislike that Bundy had for Philadelphia is that it did not have a forest,[24] thus depriving him of a preferred milieu to murder and discard of bodies. This suggests that Bundy recognized the forensic value of disposing of bodies in the wilds of nature rather early in his homicidal development.

Not all necrophilic sexual murderers engage in the same behaviors. A study of more than one-hundred cases of necrophilic sexual homicide indicated heterogeneity or subvariants of postmortem sexual contact that included opportunistic, experimental, preferential, and sadistic subtypes. Bundy's offense conduct had similarities with the experimental and sadistic typologies, both of which involved necrophilic conduct after antemortem rape, antemortem sodomy, foreign object insertion, and use of asphyxiation and strangulation as the method of killing. Moreover, sadistic necrophilic sexual homicide offenders are more likely to employ a con approach strategy and are forensically aware to avoid police detection primarily by concealing or destroying the victim's body.[25] According to these criteria, Bundy was the quintessential sadistic necrophilic sexual homicide offender.

Forensic study of hundreds of adult male sexual offenders that included eighty-five sexual homicide offenders is also revealing. The study compared the sexual homicide offenders, criminals like Bundy, to control groups of other serious offenders including sexual offenders who had not killed, and sexual offenders who had not murdered, but had committed other serious violent offenses. The group of sexual homicide offenders were very similar to Bundy in terms of their use of alcohol prior to the crime, victim selection, use of weapon to control (or immobilize) the victim, and intrusive sexual acts. Sexual homicide offenders also had evidence of schizoid personality disorder, one of the odd and eccentric disorders characterized by a preference for isolation, coldness, and difficulty/disinterest in getting along with others.

Some with schizoid personality disorder abstain from sexual activity their entire life because the degree of contact and intimacy inherent to sexual activity is repellent to them. They are functionally asexual. But others with schizoid features, like many sexual homicide offenders, are not asexual and harbor a deep sexual desire for others; however, they are conflicted and even befuddled about how to achieve it. These offenders have extensive fantasy life, use pornography, and fixate on their sexual appetites.

During their sexual murders, these offenders instrumentally rape, sodomize, and kill the victim usually with their hands, and are less interested in humiliating the victim or forcing the victim to perform sexual acts on them. They have a sort of schizoid conflict where they are entirely in control of the sexual activity because sexual interaction, even when forced under duress, and the emotional connection that might arise from that interaction are repulsive for the offender.[26]

An anecdote from Bundy's life reveals how this schizoid sexual conflict manifested. During the summer of 1972, Bundy interned with a woman named Kimberly at the Harborview Mental Health Center, and the two began dating. In her conversation with Dr. Carlisle during his data collection to prepare his forensic assessment, Kimberly recounted a time when she and Bundy went swimming, and Bundy repeatedly shoved her head under water, as if "playfully" attempting to drown her. He also repeatedly attempted to remove her swimsuit top. Sometime after this aggressive behavior, once they were on shore, the couple engaged in sexual intercourse. Kimberly advised that although consensual it felt more like rape. This was her description of it:

> Very intense, very aggressive. It was as though I really didn't think he was conscious of what he was doing because it wasn't a bonding situation. I was just a body lying there is all. It wasn't as if we were doing something

together. Something was being done to me. It was sheer terror. It flashed in my mind that nobody else was around here.[27]

Kimberly also reported to Dr. Carlisle about incidents where Bundy appeared in a trance while they were having sex, as if he was wholly in a fantasy world that interested him more than their actual intimate contact. When in this mood, he would also choke her, and forcefully place his arms onto her throat as if to crush it. Many times, she could not breathe. Other women who Bundy dated during this era similarly reported his highly aggressive, dissociative behaviors during sexual intercourse. It is also worthwhile noting that all of these relationships were examples of infidelity to his relationship with Kendall, another feature of his psychopathy.

A final important insight from Kimberly is that Bundy would drive with her in the secluded hills around Lake Sammamish. It was as if he was on a reconnaissance mission for murder disposal sites. He was. When Kimberly would ask why they were aimlessly driving around seemingly in the middle of nowhere, Bundy would tell her he was looking for his aunt's house even though there was not a residential area in sight. It was one of the countless lies Bundy would tell her that contributed to the end of their relationship.

Bundy's psychopathology was complex and involved deep-seated insecurity and conflicted feelings of inadequacy, insatiable sexual desire, and, an equally powerful but diametric hostility toward others, especially women. He wanted sexual contact with women in the form of raping and sodomizing them, but also wanted to kill them, and he knew the latter act was the only way he could have the pure freedom necessary to inflict his violence. Thus, Bundy's paraphilic disorders were both antisocial and asocial, hypersexual and schizoid. He lusted for women, but did so according to his own conditions: incapacitate the women with a blow to the head, engage in sexual activity, kill them, and occasionally engage in additional sexual acts postmortem. Sometimes he would vary this approach and reserve all sexual activity until the victim was deceased.

The complexity and frank weirdness of Bundy's sexual behavior is gleaned from his conduct at the Florida State University bar Sherrod's just hours before his attack of the Chi Omega women and Cheryl

Thomas. Several female witnesses recount seeing Bundy at the bar standing with his arms crossed, scanning the young women on the dance floor, and staring at them with a disconcerting, menacing air. Although his sexual attraction to the young women was apparent, it was also clear that he had no idea how to appropriately and normatively express that sexual interest to them.

He did not know how to approach them.

Instead, Bundy stood there with his psychopathic blunted affect and his unstable mixture of antisocial, asocial, hypersexual, and schizoid thoughts. According to witness Connie Hastings, who saw Bundy at the bar in the hours before the Tallahassee attacks, "it was like a cold stare. It was strange, no expression on his face. You know, a lot of times when you go out if a guy looks like he's interested in you he will smile at you, acknowledge you, not stare at you."[28]

His haywire psychosexual development is fully consistent with other sexual homicide offenders who compared to other violent and sexual types of offenders show specific aberrant sexual behaviors in childhood that suggest a strong need for sexual gratification. During childhood, sexual homicide offenders engage in a diverse mix of problem behaviors, some overt and others covert that span animal cruelty, weapons fixation, chronic lying, angry or poorly moderated temperament, and periodic recklessness. Relative to other violent and sexual offenders, sexual homicide offenders engage more frequently in daydreaming, and display a compulsion for sexual fantasy that moves them further away from their peers and deeper into the prurient images in their mind.[29] Like other sexual murderers, many of these developmental stepping-stones appear in Bundy's background.

Dr. Carlisle's psychological assessment in 1976 unearthed important information about Bundy's psychosexual development that supports my overall view of his psychopathological profile. Dr. Carlisle's work also intimates that Bundy's potentially first murder in 1961 solidified his complex, paraphilic sexual appetites.[30] Carlisle conducted a 90-day evaluation of Bundy after his conviction for aggravated kidnapping in the case involving Carol DaRonch. During his conversations with Bundy, Dr. Carlisle noted the infrequency with which Bundy discussed his mother, whom Bundy thought was his sister until middle adolescence, and a disposition characterized by disappointment, shyness, and inadequacy. In terms of sexual development, Bundy engaged in relatively normative sexual behavior with girls such as kissing and petting, but this behavior ceased when Bundy was fourteen, when he became withdrawn and, in Bundy's assessment, "individualist." In fact, Bundy would not date until late in his senior year and even that relationship was platonic. He would not have consensual sexual intercourse until his early twenties.

As he conversed with Carlisle, Bundy had no explanation for the sudden change in his sexual behavior and social behavior, nor did he intimate any knowledge about Ann Marie Burr who many believe, including me, was potentially his first homicide victim. The disappearance of Burr in August 1961 was a signal event in their community and frontpage news in the local community newspaper, a paper that Bundy delivered on his paper route that took him by Burr's home. Yet when Carlisle inquired about Burr, Bundy's response was awkward, stammering, verbose, and, clearly untrue.

The potential murder of Ann Marie Burr and many others is explored in greater detail in the next chapter; however, the importance of Bundy's potential killing of her when he was age fourteen would be the triggering event or "red flag" that Carlisle identified as altering Bundy's sexual and social development. Once experiencing murder and whatever sexual elements were involved in it, Bundy lost his taste for normal adolescent dating behavior and sexual activity. Instead, he retreated into a world of pornography consumption, voyeurism of the next-door neighbor whose bathroom was visible from his bedroom, and unceasing rumination about sexual violence. Incidents in the first years of his life, such as arranging knives around female relatives as they slept were not aberrations, but early emerging behavioral signs of his psychopathology. And that psychopathology, constantly modified by his social ineptitude and the vicissitudes of adolescence worsened.

Prior to his execution, Bundy spoke at length about the putative causal effects that pornography had for his violence. Irrespective of any validity to his claims, there is no question that Bundy's pornography proclivities closely mimicked his offense conduct. According to Bundy, "I became something of a connoisseur of these kinds of photos and I knew where to get pictures of crime scene photographs. I also became very adept at going into medical school libraries and getting their autopsy texts, especially photographs of autopsies and crime scenes involving young women who had been murdered. This was the sort of thing I got into. That was an interest that was part of the phase of my life before I ever harmed anyone."[31]

As alluded to earlier, there are multiple reports of Bundy attempting to drown acquaintances during leisure activities, and these potential victims were not exclusively adults. Molly Kendall describes recurrent events in her early childhood where Bundy would engage in sadistic and abusive behaviors toward her including incidents of "training" her how to swim by nearly allowing her to drown. Molly recalls these events as moments of sheer terror in which Bundy would appear to relish the event as his cold, unfeeling eyes consumed her panic.[32]

These events underscore homicidal ideation as a consistent feature of Bundy's emotional and cognitive life. Defined as thoughts about perpetrating lethal violence toward specific or non-specific targets regardless of actually attempting a homicide, homicidal ideation is an important forensic concept especially when it is present among individuals who ruminate about killing other people. Homicidal ideation is a robust forensic feature that has versatile effects on behavior, it is not exclusively related to homicide, but also is associated with other forms of violent crime, property crime, and related antisocial behavior. It also strongly relates to behavioral disorders, such as the antisocial and schizoid personality disorder features that Bundy exhibited, with forensic studies reporting estimates of 571% to an astonishing 2,406 percent increased odds of homicidal ideation when presenting with these conditions.[33] The very nature of Bundy's personality functioning was conducive to homicide.

Criminological research indicates that homicidal ideation is strongly correlated with many different forms of criminal behavior and justice system involvement, and among the homicide offenders in those studies, which are generally limited to offenders who killed one or sometimes two victims, homicidal ideation is strongly significant. As a baseline risk factor for violence, homicidal ideation is formidable, and among offenders like Bundy, Little, and Alcala who murdered dozens of victims, it is an overpowering forensic feature.

When offenders are acutely psychopathic and sexually sadistic, not to mention other paraphilic conditions including necrophilia, the idea of murdering another human is not only present as a result of their homicidal ideations, it is also a requisite condition for their sexual tastes. For instance, if an offender is in a necrophilic phase of their homicide career where sexual activity with corpses is coveted, a murder is necessary to procure the victim. If an offender enjoys inflicting extraordinary pain and suffering during the course of a sexual assault, a degree of pain and suffering up to and including death, the homicidal thoughts are intimately connected to their conduct. To some, sexual motivation is murder motivation.

Some serious and violent offenders exhibit homicidal ideation as early as age three years often in the form of homicidal statements and threats to kill. In these cases, the usual target of the homicidal ideation is the child's mother who is usually the primary caregiver. In addition to articulated threats to kill, this precocious homicidal ideation also co-occurs with very poor emotional and behavioral regulation involving severe tantrums as well as cruelty toward and abuse of animals. In these cases, the animal abuse is a byproduct of the homicidal ideation: the young offender wants to see what the homicidal thoughts feel like in practice by killing something. Bundy's disturbing age three knife displays likely reflected his earliest behavioral attempts to process his homicidal ideation.

Throughout adulthood, Bundy's homicidal ideation recurrently simmered below the surface. In the days prior to his double murder at Lake Sammamish State Park on July 14, 1974, Bundy aggressively pushed his girlfriend Elizabeth Kendall into the river during a boating trip in one of the many "pranks" in which he would place a person in harm's way in water or physically attempt to drown them. When Kendall frantically surfaced and attempted to get back into the boat Bundy had shoved her from, she was struck by the blank, unsettling, odd look on his face.[34] It appears his homicidal ideation was strongly primed in the build up to the murders of Ott and Naslund, and his aggression toward Kendall was likely a sign that the homicidal ideation was soon to translate into homicidal conduct.

In the days and hours before his abduction of Susan Rancourt, Bundy approached multiple young women while carrying a large stack of books and feigning injury so to encourage sympathetic contact with them. Something about Bundy's request for the woman to accompany him to a dark area of the parking lot where his car was parked triggered these women to not comply with him, instinctual feelings that saved their lives. Unfortunately, Bundy's homicidal motivation did not dissipate with an unsuccessful abduction approach, and he would simply move on to the next target.

The full extent of the degree to which Bundy contemplated and perpetrated murder is apparent in several insightful passages from Kendall's book about her life with Bundy from 1969 to approximately September 1974 when Bundy moved to Salt Lake City to begin law school.[35] With the benefit of hindsight, her memoir reveals the frequency with which Bundy was thinking about and planning murder, and what seemed like strange observations at the time are now compelling circumstantial evidence of his crimes.

On the first night they met, Bundy informs Kendall that he recently returned from Philadelphia where he had an unsuccessful academic experience at Temple University (Bundy of course did not refer to it in those negative albeit accurate terms). We now recognize this east coast sojourn as containing some of his earliest murders (complete with his indignation that there was not an appropriate forest to discard victims). Indeed, Dr. Carlisle identifies the murders in the Philadelphia area as an important part of Bundy's developmental history in his psychological assessment. From their earliest conversations, Kendall was unbeknownst to her talking to a man who had very recently killed multiple women.

While socializing with Bundy in his apartment, Kendall observed a set of crutches even though Bundy had not incurred any injury and thus had no need for them. We now know that crutches were used as a ruse at various times to procure victims. Kendall also noticed a large meat cleaver in Bundy's kitchen, which he instructed was used to slice vegetables. More likely, the meat cleaver was used to dismember women after killing them. During an outing with Bundy and her daughter Molly, Elizabeth was looking for her daughter's sock under the seats in Bundy's vehicle. Instead, she nearly cut her fingers on the blade of a hatchet. Once again, Bundy told a silly lie to explain why a hatchet was under the seat of his car, in this case, he informed her that he had cut down a tree at his parents' cabin. It too was likely used for dismemberment of his victims.[36]

After Bundy was a prime suspect for the various missing women in the Pacific Northwest and under investigation from multiple agencies, a law enforcement agent inquired to Kendall if Bundy ever had a metal rod or crowbar with its handle taped. In shock, Kendall recalled that Bundy had taped the handle of a crowbar in 1970, and explained it was good to use for a weapon should she ever be attacked during the civil unrest of that time period.

Around the same era, circa 1969–1970, Kendall told the investigator that Bundy had once left her home to go study, but shortly thereafter she heard a noise in the hallway as if someone was trying to walk quietly so to avoid detection. Kendall opened the door and found Bundy who had just retrieved a crowbar from under the radiator in the hallway. According to Kendall, he had a very strange, disquieting look on his face. She also noticed that Bundy's pockets were bulging, and reached into his pockets to find surgical gloves.[37] In retrospect, the entire expanse of his relationship with Kendall contained incidents where she observed or discovered pieces of evidence of materials used to facilitate his crimes, suggesting that throughout their relationship he was acutely and actively homicidal.

Bundy's destructive psychopathology facilitated his forensic awareness that undoubtedly allowed him to stay off the radar of law enforcement for years. His uncanny ability to avoid detection is striking despite the audacity that he displayed in the final years of his offending career by using his own name when approaching potential targets and continuing to drive the Volkswagen Beetle that was mentioned in police alerts. These foolish behaviors showed how his grandiose sense of self at times outweighed prudent attempts to conceal his identity.

But other features of Bundy's offending behavior revealed considerable forensic cunning. For instance, there is no evidence that he used firearms or ever murdered a victim by shooting although he brandished a small handgun during his attempted abduction of Carol DaRonch.[38] Avoiding guns served multiple purposes for Bundy. It allowed for quiet, surreptitious criminal conduct without the loud noise of a gunshot and attendant witness reports. There was never a need to retrieve bullet casings, to destroy and procure new firearms, to worry about gunshot residue on his person, or to allow a ballistic linkage between his crimes.

However, the main reason that Ted Bundy did not shoot his victims to death is that manner of death would be completely unsatisfying to his underlying psychopathology. A gunshot is easy, impersonal, and can be done at a distance. In contrast, Bundy wanted to use his hands to beat and strangle the victim. He wanted the sexual murder to be involved, to be personal (to the degree that his personality functioning permitted such), to be close, and to be, from his distorted perspective, intimate. Death by firearm was incompatible with his paraphilic drives and broader psychopathology.

Bundy's mobility and variable disposal methods meant that he was often passing through an area, would perpetrate a sexual homicide and dump the body, and within hours would be hundreds of miles away often in another state. In other cases, bodies were dumped at locations where he knew that animals and the weather would degrade the bodies to such a degree that potentially inculpatory evidence, such as semen or blood would never be found. His use of a vehicle to abduct, transport, and attack his victims, and then transport the victim's body is consistent with research which shows these factors as the strongest predictor of sexual homicide offenders who show the greatest mobility.[39]

It is one thing to understand that Ted Bundy was clinically psychopathic and that his psychopathology contained a variety of paraphilic disorders, personality disturbances, and other forensic risk factors that enabled his prodigious criminal activity. An overly clinical presentation of this information unfortunately sometimes obscures the human impact of these antisocial conditions, and more importantly, their effects on Bundy's victims. The girls and women he murdered suffered unimaginable cruelty and incurred gratuitous physical and sexual violence inflicted simply for the sake of being evil. The initial blow to the head from a tire iron or similar blunt tool rendered the women unconscious prior to the sexual assault, but the beatings that Bundy inflicted often continued and involved breaking the victim's jaw in multiple places, destroying their teeth, and producing other extremely painful injuries about the head and body.[40] He absolutely delighted in raping and killing them.

Amidst this incredible violence coupled with the duress and terror of the victim, Bundy is physiologically unphased, and, matter-of-factly sexually abuses the women in multiple ways while strangling them with nylons, a necklace, or his hands. All the while, Bundy is sexually aroused and completes sexual acts on the victim, which speaks to the extremity of his paraphilic disorders.

Reportedly after his final arrest in Florida in February 1978, Bundy uttered the famous self-assessment that he was "the most cold-hearted son of a bitch you'll ever meet."[41] He truly was, and his pathological set of psychiatric and paraphilic conditions set into motion one of the most violent and extensive criminal careers in American history.

Notes

1. Nelson (2018, p. 288).
2. Caspi et al. (2014).
3. Caspi et al. (2016).
4. Vaughn et al. (2015); DeLisi et al. (2015); Fox and DeLisi (2018).
5. American Psychiatric Association (2013, pp. 685–686).
6. Kendall (2020, p. 173).
7. Kendall (2020).
8. Keppel and Birnes (2005, p. 418).
9. Carlisle (2020, pp. 64–65).
10. Carlisle (2020, p. 68), italics added.
11. American Psychiatric Association (2013, p. 695).
12. Eher et al. (2019); Fedora et al. (1992); Baur et al. (2016).
13. Proulx et al. (2006, pp. 107–122); Healey et al. (2013).
14. Reale et al. (2020).
15. Bundy confessed this to Keppel just prior to his execution.
16. *Bundy v. State*, 455 So. 2d 330 (1984).
17. Browne (2016, p. 113).
18. Kendall (2020, pp. 200–204).
19. Holt et al. (1999); DeLisi, Drury, et al. (2017); Darjee (2019).
20. Chopin et al. (2021).
21. Nelson (2018, p. 289).
22. Keppel and Birnes (2005, p. 209).

23. Stein et al. (2010).
24. Sullivan (2009, p. 57).
25. Chopin and Beauregard (2021).
26. Beauregard and DeLisi (2021).
27. Carlisle (2020, p. 97).
28. Michaud and Aynesworth (1999, p. 211).
29. Beauregard and DeLisi (2018); Briken et al. (2006); Mokros et al. (2011).
30. Carlisle, A. (2020).
31. Carlisle (2020, p. 187).
32. Kendall (2020, pp. 200–204).
33. DeLisi, Tahja, et al. (2017); Carbone et al. (2020); Vaughn et al. (2020).
34. Kendall (2020, p. 50).
35. Kendall (2020).
36. Kendall (2020, p. 59, p. 62).
37. Kendall (2020, pp. 102–103).
38. Kendall (2020, p. 126).
39. Martineau and Beauregard (2016).
40. Sullivan (2017).
41. Bundy reportedly uttered this to law enforcement officers in Florida in February 1978 after his last arrest.

References

American Psychiatric Association. (2013). *Diagnostic and statistical manual of mental disorders (DSM-5®)*. American Psychiatric Publishing.

Baur, E., Forsman, M., Santtila, P., Johansson, A., Sandnabba, K., & Långström, N. (2016). Paraphilic sexual interests and sexually coercive behavior: A population-based twin study. *Archives of Sexual Behavior, 45*(5), 1163–1172.

Beauregard, E., & DeLisi, M. (2018). Stepping stones to sexual murder: The role of developmental factors in the etiology of sexual homicide. *Journal of Criminal Psychology, 8*(3), 199–214.

Beauregard, E., & DeLisi, M. (2021). Unraveling the personality profile of the sexual murderer. *Journal of Interpersonal Violence, 36*(7–8), 3536–3556.

Briken, P., Habermann, N., Kafka, M. P., Berner, W., & Hill, A. (2006). The paraphilia-related disorders: An investigation of the relevance of the concept in sexual murderers. *Journal of Forensic Sciences, 51*(3), 683–688.

Browne, J. H. (2016). *The devil's defender: My Odyssey through American criminal justice from Ted Bundy to the Kandahar massacre.* Chicago Review Press.

Bundy v. State, 455 So.2d 330 (1984).

Carbone, J. T., Holzer, K. J., Vaughn, M. G., & DeLisi, M. (2020). Homicidal ideation and forensic psychopathology: Evidence from the 2016 Nationwide Emergency Department Sample (NEDS). *Journal of Forensic Sciences, 65*(1), 154–159.

Carlisle, A. (2020). *The 1976 psychological assessment of Ted Bundy.* Carlisle Legacy Books.

Caspi, A., Houts, R. M., Belsky, D. W., Goldman-Mellor, S. J., Harrington, H., Israel, S., Meier, M. H., Ramrakha, S., Shalev, I., Poulton, R., & Moffitt, T. E. (2014). The p factor: One general psychopathology factor in the structure of psychiatric disorders? *Clinical Psychological Science, 2*(2), 119–137.

Caspi, A., Houts, R. M., Belsky, D. W., Harrington, H., Hogan, S., Ramrakha, S., Poulton, R., & Moffitt, T. E. (2016). Childhood forecasting of a small segment of the population with large economic burden. *Nature Human Behaviour, 1*(1), 1–10.

Chopin, J., & Beauregard, E. (2021). Patterns of necrophilic behaviors in sexual homicide: A criminological perspective. *International Journal of Offender Therapy and Comparative Criminology, 65*(15), 1676–1699.

Chopin, J., Beauregard, E., & DeLisi, M. (2021). Homicidal child sexual abuse: Identifying the combinations of factors predicting a lethal outcome. *Child Abuse & Neglect, 111*, 104799.

Darjee, R. (2019). Sexual sadism and psychopathy in sexual homicide offenders: An exploration of their associates in a clinical sample. *International Journal of Offender Therapy and Comparative Criminology, 63*(9), 1738–1765.

DeLisi, M., Drury, A., Elbert, M., Tahja, K., Caropreso, D., & Heinrichs, T. (2017). Sexual sadism and criminal versatility: Does sexual sadism spillover into nonsexual crimes? *Journal of Aggression, Conflict and Peace Research, 9*(1), 2–12.

DeLisi, M., Tahja, K., Drury, A. J., Caropreso, D., Elbert, M., & Heinrichs, T. (2017). The criminology of homicidal ideation: Associations with criminal careers and psychopathology among federal correctional clients. *American Journal of Criminal Justice, 42*(3), 554–573.

DeLisi, M., Vaughn, M. G., Salas-Wright, C. P., & Jennings, W. G. (2015). Drugged and dangerous: Prevalence and variants of substance use comorbidity among seriously violent offenders in the United States. *Journal of Drug Issues, 45*(3), 232–248.

Eher, R., Rettenberger, M., & Turner, D. (2019). The prevalence of mental disorders in incarcerated contact sexual offenders. *Acta Psychiatrica Scandinavica, 139*(6), 572–581.

Fedora, O., Reddon, J. R., Morrison, J. W., Fedora, S. K., Pascoe, H., & Yeudall, L. T. (1992). Sadism and other paraphilias in normal controls and aggressive and nonaggressive sex offenders. *Archives of Sexual Behavior, 21*(1), 1–15.

Fox, B., & DeLisi, M. (2018). From criminological heterogeneity to coherent classes: Developing a typology of juvenile sex offenders. *Youth Violence and Juvenile Justice, 16*(3), 299–318.

Healey, J., Lussier, P., & Beauregard, E. (2013). Sexual sadism in the context of rape and sexual homicide: An examination of crime scene indicators. *International Journal of Offender Therapy and Comparative Criminology, 57*(4), 402–424.

Holt, S. E., Meloy, J. R., & Strack, S. (1999). Sadism and psychopathy in violent and sexually violent offenders. *Journal of the American Academy of Psychiatry and the Law, 27*(1), 23–32.

Kendall, E., with a contribution from Molly Kendall. (2020). *The phantom prince: My life with Ted Bundy* (updated and expanded edition). Abrams Press.

Keppel, R. D., with Birnes, W. J. (2005). *The riverman: Ted Bundy and I hunt for the Green River killer.* Pocket Books.

Martineau, M., & Beauregard, E. (2016). Journey to murder: Examining the correlates of criminal mobility in sexual homicide. *Police Practice and Research, 17*(1), 68–83.

Michaud, S. G., & Aynesworth, H. (1999). *The only living witness: The true story of serial sex killer Ted Bundy.* Authorlink Press.

Mokros, A., Osterheider, M., Hucker, S. J., & Nitschke, J. (2011). Psychopathy and sexual sadism. *Law and Human Behavior, 35*(3), 188–199.

Nelson, P. (2018). *Defending the devil: My story as Ted Bundy's last lawyer.* Echo Point Books & Media.

Proulx, J., Blais, E., & Beauregard, E. (2006). Sadistic sexual offenders. In J. Proulx, E. Beauregard, M. Cusson, & A. Nicole (Eds.), *Sexual murderers:*

A comparative analysis and new perspectives (pp. 107–122). John Wiley & Sons.

Reale, K., Beauregard, E., & Martineau, M. (2020). Is investigative awareness a distinctive feature of sexual sadism? *Journal of Interpersonal Violence, 35*(7–8), 1761–1778.

Stein, M. L., Schlesinger, L. B., & Pinizzotto, A. J. (2010). Necrophilia and sexual homicide. *Journal of Forensic Sciences, 55*(2), 443–446.

Sullivan, K. M. (2009). *The Bundy Murders: A Comprehensive History*. McFarland and Company.

Sullivan, K. (2017). *The Bundy secrets: Hidden files on America's worst serial killer*. Wildblue Press.

Vaughn, M. G., Carbone, J., DeLisi, M., & Holzer, K. J. (2020). Homicidal ideation among children and adolescents: Evidence from the 2012–2016 Nationwide Emergency Department Sample. *The Journal of Pediatrics, 219*, 216–222.

Vaughn, M. G., Salas-Wright, C. P., DeLisi, M., Maynard, B. R., & Boutwell, B. (2015). Prevalence and correlates of psychiatric disorders among former juvenile detainees in the United States. *Comprehensive Psychiatry, 59*, 107–116.

6

Timeline

But the police are saying that the murders started in 1969—that's the year we met.

What was it that made it start in '69?

Elizabeth Kendall

The police are years off.[1]

Ted Bundy

An offender with psychopathology as extensive as Bundy's would by definition experience impairments in social functioning and face difficulty achieving the milestones of success that a normatively behaved adult would. His biography makes this clear. Born on November 24, 1946, Bundy graduated from high school in the spring of 1965 at an age-appropriate eighteen years, but his educational career thereafter experienced a number of starts and stops. The intermittency and arrested development of his early adult education was not due to cognitive impairment for Bundy had adequate intelligence and academic skills to handle the rigors of university education. Instead, Bundy struggled to manage his sexually homicidal desires and spent a considerable

© The Author(s), under exclusive license to Springer Nature
Switzerland AG 2023
M. DeLisi, *Ted Bundy and The Unsolved Murder Epidemic*,
https://doi.org/10.1007/978-3-031-21418-9_6

amount of his time stalking potential victims, and in other cases, actually attacking, sexually assaulting, and murdering women.

During his early adulthood, the 1965–1969 period in Bundy's life is peripatetic, unfocused, and stalled as if some tremendous force was holding him back from reaching normal milestones. Immediately after completing high school, Bundy attended the University of Puget Sound for one year then transferred to the University of Washington for the fall 1966 term. There he initiated his first and potentially most impactful intimate relationship with Stephanie Brooks (referred to as Marjorie in Dr. Carlisle's psychological assessment) who ultimately ended the relationship due to Bundy's listless, seemingly stuck-in-gear existence.

By 1968, Bundy severed his schooling and worked in a variety of relatively inconsequential service or retail jobs. It was also during this era of his life that Bundy traveled extensively for a variety of personal, leisure, educational, and undisclosed reasons including, as indicated previously, a brief stint as a student at Temple University (where he likely perpetrated multiple homicides and disliked the city because it did not have adequate forested areas). During this period, he is known to have been in Arkansas, California, Colorado, Florida, Pennsylvania, New York, New Jersey, and Vermont, not to mention states in between these destinations. After this period of wanderlust, Bundy drifted back to the Pacific Northwest and reenrolled at the University of Washington for the fall 1969 term.

More than four years after completing high school, the meandering Ted Bundy was an unsuccessful student and had yet to complete an undergraduate degree. This fact is important on two fronts. It counters the notion about his life of alleged achievement and powerful intellect. He was simply more intelligent than the average violent criminal. More importantly, the delay in his educational training and the myriad unexplained absences establishes that he was doing something else throughout this period of his life. I am not alone in my critical assessment of Bundy's intellectual and educational achievement. Polly Nelson, his attorney during his capital appeals in Florida, advised, "One of the enduring Bundy myths is that Ted was 'brilliant.' He was not. Superficially he appeared about as intelligent as a fair-to-middling college undergraduate...But Ted had real deficits in judgment, awareness, and deeper thinking. He could talk and write, but he couldn't comprehend or respond."[2]

In 1969, Bundy initiated the other pivotal intimate relationship of his life with Elizabeth Kendall and by outward appearances achieved a sort of domesticity that continued through September 1974, prior to the early stages of Bundy's official contacts with the criminal justice system in 1975. As Kendall herself observed, Bundy likely used the relationship to demonstrate a façade of adult functioning and normalcy that provided appropriate cover for his clandestine antisocial acts. Indeed, it was a perfect cover for him to compartmentalize his sexual murders from the outside world.[3] With her, he could enjoy his personal world of murder while remaining tethered to the outside world.

Although the relationship with Kendall provides a signpost upon which to document much of Bundy's time, it is also clear from her memoir that Bundy was highly undependable and would seemingly disappear for stretches of time without plausible explanation for his whereabouts and activities. At times, these disappearances were interspersed among other normal activities and social events they had planned. Over time, Kendall became increasingly annoyed and concerned with Bundy's absurd lies to account for and justify his absences, but this era of his life provides tangible evidence about the extensive amount of time where Bundy's location and behaviors are unknown.

That is an important observation. Law enforcement officials in the Pacific Northwest believe that Bundy's murders began in 1969, although as the chapter opening quotation from Bundy suggests, that estimate itself is wildly inaccurate. In addition, during the years with Kendall from 1969 until his arrests and detention, there are innumerable times when Bundy simply disappeared with no good explanation for where he was and what he was doing.

These periods of undocumented time where Bundy's activity and whereabouts are uncertain are all the more remarkable given the extremity of his psychopathology. He could move about the country at will. He was floridly psychopathic and constantly ruminated about procuring, incapacitating, raping, bludgeoning, and strangling women. Bundy's homicidal ideation was overpowering. His time was not consumed working or competing with school responsibilities although he would finally complete his undergraduate bachelor's degree in psychology in 1972 when was more than twenty-five years old. Something far more nefarious consumed his time.

Before articulating my central thesis that Bundy's homicide career began far earlier and was more expansive than commonly reported, it is important to provide a chronology of Bundy's "semi-official" criminal career that spanned the January 1974 to February 1978 period in terms of his criminal activity and terminated in January 1989 with his execution. Some caveats are in order. There is scholarly and investigative disagreement about the victims who are attributable to Bundy during the 1974 to 1978 period, and extant records vary in terms of dates and even occasionally of the names and spelling of the names of specific victims. To protect the status of victims and afford them anonymity, the use of pseudonyms in the Bundy literature is common.

Another reason for this dissensus relates to the sheer volume of sexual assaults and sexual homicides that Bundy committed. It is frankly difficult to keep track of the number of people he killed especially during years where his location and movements are unclear. To provide the most conservative timeline and victim information of his semi-official criminal career, I utilized multiple sources and included only those where there is considerable confidence that Bundy was the killer (i.e., he was convicted in court, he confessed, or there is significant circumstantial evidence of his involvement).[4] Bundy usually raped and sodomized his victims, but the broader term of sexual assault is used here because it is not always known which specific form of sexual violence he inflicted, and whether the sexual abuse occurred premortem, perimortem, postmortem, or all of these.

On January 4, 1974, Bundy physically and sexually assaulted Joni Lenz, also known as Karen Sparks, in her residence in Seattle, Washington. She survived the attack. Twenty-eight days later on February 1, 1974, Bundy assaulted, kidnapped, sexually assaulted, and murdered Lynda Ann Healy in Seattle, Washington.[5] About six weeks later on March 12, 1974, Bundy kidnapped, sexually assaulted, and murdered Donna Manson in Seattle, Washington. These sexual assaults and murders occurred within the same general geographic area.

About 107 miles away and six weeks later on April 17, 1974, Bundy kidnapped, sexually assaulted, and murdered Susan Rancourt in Ellensburg, Washington. Approximately 303 miles away and nineteen days later on May 6, 1974, Bundy kidnapped, sexually assaulted, and murdered Kathy Parks, also known as Roberta Parks in Corvallis, Oregon. Roughly 250 miles away and twenty-six days later on June 1, 1974, Bundy kidnapped, sexually assaulted, and murdered Brenda Ball in Burien, Washington. Ten miles away and ten days later on June 11, 1974, Bundy kidnapped, sexually assaulted, and murdered Georgann, also known as Georgeann, Hawkins in Seattle, Washington.

Twenty days later on July 1, 1974, Bundy showed his prodigious geographic mobility and kidnapped, sexually assaulted, and murdered Sandra Weaver in Salt Lake City, Utah, which is 830 miles from the Hawkins murder. More than 814 miles away and thirteen days later on July 14, 1974, Bundy kidnapped, sexually assaulted, and murdered Janice Ott and Denise Naslund in Issaquah, Washington. More than 180 miles away and nineteen days later on August 2, 1974, Bundy kidnapped, sexually assaulted, and murdered Carol Valenzuela in Camas, Washington. Her remains were located in October 1974 along with the remains of an unidentified female who it is believed Bundy also murdered.

After this spate of murders, Bundy moved to Utah for his ill-fated attempt as a law student. On October 2, 1974, Bundy kidnapped, sexually assaulted, and murdered Nancy Wilcox in Holladay, Utah, which was 761 miles away from the Valenzuela murder. Sixteen days later on October 18, 1974 and just nine miles away, Bundy kidnapped, sexually assaulted, and murdered Melissa Smith in Midvale, Utah. Nineteen miles away and thirteen days later on October 31, 1974, Bundy kidnapped, sexually assaulted, and murdered Laura Aimee, also known as Aime, in Lehi, Utah. About 21 miles away and eight days later on November 8, 1974, Bundy kidnapped and assaulted Carol DaRonch in Murray, Utah who survived the assault and escaped from Bundy's vehicle. For this crime, Bundy was convicted of aggravated kidnapping on March 1, 1976 and sentenced to an indeterminate 1–15 years sentence on June 30, 1976. On the same day as the DaRonch crime and 18 miles away,

Bundy kidnapped, sexually assaulted, and murdered Debby, also known as Deborah or Debra, Kent in Bountiful, Utah.

Approximately 405 miles away and 60 days later on January 12, 1975, Bundy kidnapped, sexually assaulted, and murdered Caryn Campbell in Snowmass, Colorado. About 87 miles away and over two months later on March 15, 1975, Bundy kidnapped, sexually assaulted, and murdered Julie Cunningham in Vail, Colorado. Over 147 miles away and 22 days later on April 6, 1975, Bundy kidnapped, sexually assaulted, and murdered Denise Oliverson in Grand Junction, Colorado. Nine days later on April 15, 1975, Bundy kidnapped, sexually assaulted, and murdered Melanie Cooley in Nederland, Colorado, which is 242 miles away.

More than 581 miles away and 21 days later on May 6, 1975, Bundy kidnapped, sexually assaulted, and murdered Lynette Culver in Pocatello, Idaho. Roughly 206 miles away and nearly two months later on June 28, 1975, Bundy kidnapped, sexually assaulted, and murdered Susan Curtis in Provo, Utah. Over 473 miles away and just three days later on July 1, 1975, Bundy kidnapped, sexually assaulted, and murdered Shelley (also known as Shelly) Robertson (also known as Robinson) on July 1, 1975 in Golden, Colorado. Approximately 517 miles away and just three days later on July 4, 1975, Bundy kidnapped, sexually assaulted, and murdered Nancy Baird in Layton, Utah. On August 16, 1975, Bundy was arrested for possession of burglary tools when discovered prowling a neighborhood in Granger, Utah, which is 29 miles away. That arrest almost assuredly prevented another sexual homicide.

On June 7, 1977, Bundy escaped from Pitkin County law library in Vail, Colorado and was shortly thereafter recaptured. On December 30, 1977, Bundy escaped from the Garfield County Jail in Glenwood Springs, Colorado and absconded out of state. Over 1,744 miles away and about two weeks later on January 15, 1978, Bundy sexually assaulted and murdered Lisa Levy, murdered Margaret Bowman, attempted to murder Kathy Kleiner, attempted to murder Karen Chandler, and attempted to murder Cheryl Thomas in Tallahassee, Florida.

For the murders of Levy and Bowman, Bundy was convicted on July 23, 1979 and sentenced to death on July 31, 1979. Twenty-five days after the Chi Omega crimes on February 9, 1978, Bundy kidnapped, sexually assaulted, and murdered Kimberly Leach in Lake City, Florida. The Leach murder was 106 miles away from the Tallahassee murders and attempted murders. Leach's body was found 57 days after her disappearance. For these crimes, Bundy was convicted on February 6, 1980, sentenced to death on February 9, 1980, and executed by electrocution on January 24, 1989.

My confidence that Bundy murdered far more prolifically and for longer duration is supportable by evidence from those who knew him best and those who spent extensive time interviewing him. If an advantage to being an honest person is that one never has to remember anything, Bundy placed himself into logical quandaries because he constantly lied to those in his life and certainly to those investigating his crimes. But the lies were so convoluted, overlapping, and varied in their motivation, it was impossible for Bundy to keep them straight.

Thus, an admission about the origins of his homicide offending or some other important chronological or forensic detail would change depending on who was talking to him, depending on the context of that interaction, and depending on whatever duplicitous mood he was in. Invariably; however, Bundy would also occasionally provide accurate, even forthright descriptions of his behaviors, at times in vivid and highly informative forensic detail.

During an interview on February 21, 1978 between Major Nick Mackie, Detective Robert Keppel, and Elizabeth Kendall, she reported several key pieces of information about Bundy's psychopathology and his homicidal impulses—in addition to her observation of crutches, a meat cleaver, crowbars with a taped handle, and other implements of murder described in the prior chapter. In one instance, Bundy admitted that he previously attempted to murder her in 1973 by obstructing the fireplace chimney flue to cause her asphyxiation. She also provides a unique first-hand perspective on his criminal activities that predated the presumed 1974 onset.

According to Kendall, Bundy acknowledged that his "sickness" was taking up increasingly larger amounts of his time circa 1970–1973, and that his attempts to moderate his sickness distracted him from his educational responsibilities. Moreover, Bundy would call Kendall from out of state during times that coincided with the disappearances of young women as if to establish an alibi by connecting with her.[6] Importantly, he *never* had an alibi for the murders for which he is suspected.[7]

During the aforementioned 1970–1973 period when Bundy would call Kendall late at night from out of state to "check in," these occasions directly corresponded to unsolved disappearances of young women, and there are unconfirmed but likely Bundy sexual homicides in Arlington, Pullman, Seattle, Spokane, and Tumwater, Washington; Creswell, Eugene, Portland, Springfield, and West Linn, Oregon; and Oroville, Santa Clara, and San Francisco, California.

In his legal memoir, defense attorney John Henry Browne provided some of the most revelatory information about the precocious onset of Bundy's homicide career, its geographic spread, and the staggering roster of victims. During a meeting in jail with Browne in 1977, Bundy admitted to, in his estimation, "countless" homicides including all of the ones for which he was suspected in Washington in addition to murders in California, Oregon, Idaho, Utah, and in states all along the East Coast.

In a rare mood when Bundy was not coy about his crimes and was actually honest with his attorney, he recited to Browne that he murdered Lynda Ann Healy on January 31, 1974, Donna Manson on March 12, 1974, Susan Rancourt on April 17, 1974, and Roberta/Kathy Parks sometime in May 1974. Bundy confided to Browne that he murdered Brenda Ball on June 1, 1985, Georgann Hawkins on June 11, 1974, and both Janice Ott and Denise Naslund on July 14, 1974. He also confessed to another murder in August 1974 of a female victim in Vancouver, Washington, but was unable to recall her name.

As Browne digested the body count, Bundy also informed him that he murdered at least eight women in California in 1972 and 1973.[8] The latter point is all the more remarkable because there is little evidence in the Bundy literature of homicide activity in California let alone potentially eight murders. Another equally important point is that much of this homicidal activity that Bundy confessed to predated the 1974 official phase.

According to Browne, Bundy divulged that his first murder occurred as a young teenager, an age was unspecified, when he killed a boy in the woods while the two played a sexual exploration game. Browne noted that Bundy also confessed to him that the stalking of women and deciding which ones he would murder and which ones he would "only" rape and let live excited him sexually. That bears repeating. The hunting of women and the decision-making process of whether to rape a woman and let her go or rape and murder her was sexually arousing to Ted Bundy.

According to Bundy, the hunting process was comparable to his childhood behavior of buying a box of mice and allowing some of them to live by freeing them in the woods, while killing others with his hands. During these acts of animal cruelty, Bundy would obliterate the mice by pulling them apart. Browne also noted, "Ted said that he was not certain of the exact number of individuals he had killed, but it was over one-hundred. He told me that he took people's lives in almost every western state as well as the Northeast, Florida, and some Midwestern states."[9]

In 1988, as his various capital appeals process was ending, Bundy's attorney Polly Nelson directly confronted Bundy about the extent of his homicide career. Bundy was cryptic and unable to describe his first killing and he divulged neither the date nor the victim's name. He also scoffed at the notion that he had murdered over one-hundred people. However, his putative denial that he killed one-hundred persons was, true to his manipulative bearing, odd. According to Nelson, Bundy laughed at the one-hundred victims estimate and stated, "They have no idea what it takes to do one, what it takes out of you." Later in the conversation, Bundy admitted to Nelson that he murdered thirty-five women, although he was merely confirming the quantitative estimate of killings that Nelson had mentioned to him.[10] By agreeing with the data estimate she already provided, Bundy could ingratiate himself to his attorney with his apparent sincerity while also depriving her of the actual information she wanted.

Additionally, in 1988 during conversations with psychiatrist Dr. Dorothy Otnow Lewis, who served as a defense expert in his Florida cases, Bundy acknowledged likely homicidal activity in 1969 during his time in Philadelphia, New Jersey, and New York, but later in the same conversation suggested the first killing was in 1971 in Seattle. Either way, his murders predated 1974, "years off" as Bundy once suggested.

Bundy also challenged the conventional wisdom at the time that his Florida murders represented a behavioral deterioration or devolving of sorts where his conduct was portrayed as sloppily executed, increasingly violent, and almost animalistic in its ferocity. He described the Florida murders as a frenzy, and told Dr. Lewis that he had killed in these frenzied episodes previously. When she asked if the police were aware of these previous frenzied murders, Bundy indicated the police do not know what happened and have no idea about these and other prior murder cases.[11]

This point is critical on two grounds. First, Bundy uncharacteristically provides an admission of prior murders that had a highly pejorative manner in terms of the extremity of the violence and the youthfulness of the victim (Leach), both of which were aggravating circumstances of the murders. It is surprising that he would admit to Dr. Otnow Lewis that he had engaged in this degree of brutality before, and moreover that he had done so on multiple occasions.

Second, his disclosure that he had committed many previous frenzied murders that the police are completely unaware of is also an insight into the sheer brutality of his murders throughout his offending career. The Florida killings were not a portrait of a seasoned serial murder in decline or deterioration, they were just one variant of the sexual violence he had committed for years upon years.

In the first edition of *The Stranger Beside Me*, perhaps the masterwork in the Ted Bundy canon, Ann Rule described an exchange between Detective Norm Chapman of the Pensacola Police Department and Bundy in 1978. After hearing that Bundy might be responsible for thirty-six murders, Chapman asked Bundy if that was true, to which he replied, "Add one digit to that and you'll have it."[12] Of course, the question then becomes did he kill 136 or did he kill 360?

In 1980, journalist Hugh Aynesworth recounted this conversation to Bundy, who confirmed that he nodded his head in affirmation to the notion that he killed "three digits," meaning at least one-hundred people.[13] Bundy disputed that he murdered "four digits" of victims. During his conversations with FBI Special Agent William Hagmaier just prior to his execution in 1989, Bundy described his earlier murders as impulsive and amateurish, a sharp contrast to his "prime predator" period of killing beginning in 1974. Without admitting as much, the obvious implication is that Bundy killed far earlier than the mid-1970s, and that by his own assessment, these early murders lacked the expertise and precision of his later crimes.

How does one reconcile so many conflicting quantitative estimates of Bundy's murder career? To what extent are the denials and minimizations of various estimates of his homicide total accurate, and to what degree are they merely another indication of his psychopathic lying? In the rare disclosures of murdering one-hundred or more victims, to what degree were these exaggerations, also indicative of psychopathic lying, and to what extent was Bundy actually being honest with his attorneys and other investigators?

To provide answers to these questions, it is best to triangulate evidence from multiple sources including law enforcement data and other investigators, such as correctional officials and the media, Bundy's historical behavior where his regular failures at school, work, and relationships suggest some hidden, time- and labor-intensive activity, and Bundy's own statements about his murder career especially statement that appear offhand and not germane to the current conversation, suggesting they are true utterances. There is also important circumstantial evidence about unsolved cases where the modus operandi is very similar to Bundy's crimes and his location is a geographic match to the crime, and, last but not least, the pathological constellation of clinical disorders he instantiated. With this evidence in mind, here is the first part of my thesis.

I strongly suspect that Bundy first murdered during the latter part of his childhood in the late 1950s, approximately 1958 or 1959, or early adolescence in the early 1960s, approximately 1960 or 1961. His first killing would be rash, quickly but sloppily perpetrated, and would involve a younger child victim. It would represent a human extension of the animal cruelty he had been perpetrating for several years. The first murder would not appear as a homicide, but likely would present as an accident, such as a drowning, fall, or accidental blow to the head. For instance, it would appear that a small child had fallen and hit their head on a rock. It is likely Bundy's first attempts to murder another human being were unsuccessful and thus were attempted murders, but he would quickly learn from his mistakes and not only ensure that the next attack was fatal, whether by drowning or surreptitious blow to the head, but also ensure that the death did not appear suspicious. His forensic awareness was keenly developed even as a child.

The crime would be an opportunity for Bundy to understand the mélange of powerful, taboo thoughts and feelings at the time including his interest in weapons (where the display of knives had occurred approximately a decade earlier), his unfocused, but vibrant violent sexual thoughts about women, his indignation about the contrast between his grandiose, superficial, but fraudulent self-identity and his poor relatedness to others, the perceived problems within his family, and his percolating homicidal thoughts.

To reiterate, because the killing would be experimental and likely appeared as an accident, it went undiscovered as a homicide. It would be another shadow in the dark figure of crime. It likely occurred in a remote location, such as the woods, and qualitatively would resemble the behavior of Gary Ridgway, the infamous Green River Killer about whom Bundy would later provide consultation, who around age fifteen years stabbed a 6-year-old boy in his neighborhood to see what it felt like. (Ridgway would not begin his "official" murder career of females until his early thirties). If Bundy's admission to his lawyer John Henry Browne is accurate, the first victim was another young boy, and the interaction had sexual overtones.

During this phase of his life, Bundy likely engaged in sexual activity with other children, much of it exploratory in nature and some of it predatory in nature. True to his criminal versatility, Bundy would also engage in other delinquent offenses he was keen to obscure from his parents and other adults in his neighborhood.

That Bundy's first murder was a sexually experimental event in the woods with another boy is consistent with his subsequent awkwardness and discomfort, or sheer refusal, in discussing the event. To his defense counselors Browne and Nelson, Bundy displayed uncharacteristic shame and embarrassment and refused to provide details of his first murder. To investigator Robert Keppel, Bundy plainly stated there were some murders he was unwilling to discuss especially those that involved young victims and were proximate to his home.[14]

During the interaction between Bundy and Browne, it appeared that Bundy was emotionally overwrought and he spoke with a rare degree of candor and honest self-assessment. In rapid succession, Bundy divulged information about murders already linked to him in addition to crimes that no one had previously considered, and in states where it was not previously known that Bundy had killed. As an interviewer, this is an important detail from Browne's book because during conservations with criminal psychopaths, there are usually occasions where the offender will uncharacteristically engage in honest disclosure. It is a riff of decency in a conversation that is otherwise colored by deception.

Bundy told Browne that he was a really bad person ("I want to be a good person. I am just not."),[15] a true but astonishing understatement, and admitted that the triple digit victim total was accurate. It was as if Bundy temporarily looked in the mirror and caught a real glimpse of the depths of his psychopathy, sexual atrocities, and homicides, and this caused him genuine distress. It is during these rare moments when severe psychopaths "come clean" that an interviewer can extract revealing truths about the offender, something I have personally experienced.[16] But these moments are short-lived. Shortly after his disclosures to Browne, the familiar Ted Bundy with his absurd, cajoling bullshit was back, and the honest self-assessment of his offending career was over.

Whereas details are limited about Bundy's confession to Browne about murdering another male child for his homicidal onset, more circum-stantial evidence exists regarding Bundy's potential killing of Ann Marie Burr on August 31, 1961, when he was age fourteen years. Burr's body was never found. Bundy lived near the Burr home, approximately ten blocks away, and may have interacted with Burr or observed her via her proximity to his uncle's home.

Throughout his interactions with clinical and investigative figures, Bundy exhibited odd, often stammering responses to any inquiries about his involvement in the Burr case. In a conversation with Robert Keppel, Bundy offered this response to the simple question of whether he murdered Burr:

No. Absolutely not. That's one of the few I wish that people would believe. They believe everything else except my answer, which is no—on that one, you know, and that's very sad. But it's also so ludicrous because I don't know if you ever looked at it in the course of your studies. It's all the way across town, really, from where I—as a kid—hung out and had my paper route. The inference was, for instance, my paper route came close to or included the Burr home. Well, my understanding is it's, you know, for a kid, where the Burrs lived, as it relates to where I lived, it was in a different part of the world. That was a pretty long ways away. Different schools, different high schools. Never went to that area. Never had any occasion to go there. It was just, just another part of the forest. And—agh—I was only like thirteen, fourteen years old, or less.[17]

Like me, Keppel did not believe a single word of this passage, which reflects the pathological lying, conning, and manipulation that define the interpersonal features of psychopathy. To anyone who had the experience of riding a bicycle during childhood, traveling ten blocks or more is nothing, and is done numerous times each day. The distancing of himself from Burr and any connection to her home is interesting, as is the flimsy evidence that they attended different schools. Of course, they did, they were six years apart in age. The mentioning of "another part of the forest" is a non sequitur in the sentence, but perhaps Bundy is conflating the murder of Burr with the murder of the other child that occurred in the forest at least according to his jail cell allocution to John Henry Browne. Even when trying to recall the homicidal activity of his youth, Bundy apparently had difficulty keeping the victims straight.

Bundy's unconvincing denial of involvement in the Burr case does not end there. Bundy denied to Dr. Carlisle about even knowing about the case despite its prominence in his community in 1961, and the evasiveness with which he discussed it emerged as a clinically meaningful forensic insight in Carlisle's assessment. In fact, the murder of Burr coincides with the fundamental change in social functioning that Carlisle discovered about Bundy during his investigation of his childhood. Dr. Carlisle strongly suspected that Bundy had murdered Burr.

During his conversations with criminologist Dr. Ronald Holmes, Bundy discussed the Burr case in the third person and intimated that this "third person" was likely responsible for a much earlier killing of a child of Burr's age.[18] In the 2018 edition of *The Stranger Beside Me*, Ann Rule indicated that Donald Burr, the victim's father, is convinced he saw Bundy near a construction site at the University of Puget Sound on the day Ann Marie disappeared and that her body was likely buried at the site. Moreover, an anonymous woman contacted Rule years later and indicated that when Bundy was a ninth-grade student, he asked the young woman if she would like to see where he had buried a young girl's body years earlier.[19]

At times, the earliest indicators of pathological antisocial behavior are the truest harbinger of who an offender will become. For instance, in the course of my consulting and research experiences, I am aware of an offender who was first contacted by police at the age of two years and ten months when he was discovered playing with gasoline and matches at a park after wandering away from his home. In his late twenties, this individual was convicted of arson and had multiple fire setting incidents in his developmental history and offending career. Over the course of his life, this offender experienced lifelong suicidal ideation, attempted suicide several times during childhood and adolescence, and also has evidence of self-injurious behaviors, dissociative experiences, and thought disturbances. His lifetime diagnoses include ADHD, pervasive developmental disorder, major depressive disorder, bipolar I disorder, oppositional defiant disorder, schizoaffective disorder, cannabis dependence, and antisocial personality disorder. Although his mix of criminal charges is versatile and spans many types, his most frequent police contacts involved setting fires.

This brief profile of another serious offender puts into context how one can interpret Bundy's early conduct, and it is not difficult to imagine that his precocious displaying of knives around his female relative as she slept while observing them in a hypnotic, seemingly dissociative, and foreboding manner was itself a bizarre and unsettling example of his latent sexual violence. That simmered for approximately a decade until the incubation period was over, and he was ready to act.

Bundy's denials about murdering Burr especially to Drs. Carlisle and Keppel are outrageous lies, and it is important to recognize that both interviews occurred when Bundy was in custody, thus the ever-calculating Bundy knew that nothing good would come from him confessing to homicides for which he could subsequently be prosecuted. Another reason for Bundy's refusal to acknowledge his earliest murders likely centers on his own negative assessment of those crimes, which prior to his execution, he referred to as the impulsive works of an amateur. Although his strong psychopathic features largely shielded him from normal self-conscious emotions, such as shame, embarrassment, remorse, and guilt, Bundy internally likely experienced considerable embarrassment about his earliest murders in terms of their execution, in terms of how poorly the crimes comported with his fantasies, in terms of his sexual performance and sexual enjoyment during the criminal event, and in terms of his overall satisfaction with the execution of the murder.

As an older child or young adolescent, did Bundy experience a sense of revulsion and anger that he had to murder a child when his true target was the young adult women in his pornography repository? Did he lose his nerve and kill the child before he was able to dabble in the behaviors that his sadistic desires craved? If his first killing was of another male within a sexual context, did he shudder at the homosexual contact when there is no subsequent evidence of similar behavior?

Conversely, were Ted Bundy's first murders very much representative of his later ones, the majority of which involved a victim whose body was never found, and, absent of his death row confessions, would have never been resolved? That Ann Marie Burr and the other unnamed child victim disappeared without a trace is phenotypically consistent with the behaviors of a killer who would scatter bodies in the woods to be degraded, decomposed, and disappeared by animals, weather, and the passage of time. The burglary of the Burr home to contact Ann Marie is also consistent with the delinquent offenses of burglary and auto theft that Bundy had police contacts for in 1965 prior to his graduation from high school, justice system contacts that are often overlooked.

It is of course unknown how frequently Bundy murdered after the initiation of his homicide career, which from my perspective occurred circa late 1958–1961, but some criminological factors are important to consider. Middle to late adolescence is the peak of antisocial behavior in the life course which dissipates throughout adulthood, a phenomenon known as the age-crime curve, thus from approximately 1960–1965 Bundy would be at the greatest risk of antisocial behavior as a function of age.[20] As he aged and continued along his antisocial development, he would also increase his mobility, his access to resources, his ability to access victims, and his ability to approach and constrain a broader range of victims beyond the younger children of his own childhood.

It is also very likely that Bundy's first murders were generally dissatisfying especially when compared to his peak offending behavior in the mid-1970s. My confidence that the first murders were not satisfying is supported by Bundy himself. During a conversation with journalist Steven Michaud, Bundy provided the following third person assessment of what an offender's first murders were like:

> The individual would reflect on the quality of the act, to a degree, but not a great deal of reflection as a means of preserving it for the sake of gratification. Because it wasn't a totally satisfying experience, you know. Once the condition began to reassert its force, it didn't look back. It looked forward. Didn't want to dwell on the preceding event, but began to plan, anticipate, contemplate the next. Of course, things would be learned. Experience teaches in overt and subtle ways. And over a period of time, there would be less panic, there would be less confusion, there would be less fear and apprehension. There would be a faster regeneration period.[21]

My hypothesis that Bundy first murdered during late childhood or early adolescence is consistent with the behavioral change Dr. Carlisle described in his psychological assessment of Bundy in 1976, where he asserted that the potential killing of Burr would set this change into motion. Once initiated, the murders were not going to stop. When Bundy asked Carlisle if he thought Bundy had murdered all of the women in the Pacific Northwest, Carlisle replied, "I don't know, but if you did, I believe you will do it again."[22] The notion that Bundy was killing after his graduation from high school in 1965, and killing at a frequently escalating pace would go a long way toward contextualizing the poor academic performance, odd behaviors, frequent travel, and arrested development that pervaded his life at the time.

Considering Bundy's psychosexual development and functioning as a recent high school graduate are also critical for anticipating his likely offense behaviors. His psychopathy would continue to metastasize, his consumption of violent pornography would persist, and his violent, paraphilic sexual urges would continue to build. At this point in his adulthood, Bundy had yet to engage in sexual intercourse and that sexual frustration was made all the more potent given his psychological functioning.

In his own words, Bundy was dissatisfied sexually, less panicky, and more strident in his sexual violence, and each additional crime engendered a faster regeneration period. As such, during his youth, Bundy spends considerable time prowling neighborhoods, committing theft, stalking young women, and deciding which course of violent action would prove most cathartic. These criminal endeavors are the anti-matter to the conventional behaviors he should be practicing and explains his poor functioning during this era.

Bundy's murders during the 1960s and early 1970s would be more episodic and varied as he refined his paraphilic tastes and practiced a lethal form of trial and error. As Bundy stated, "things would be learned." Some of the killings would involve bludgeoning, others strangulation with ligatures, others manual strangulation, and others stabbing. The mix of sexual violence would include rape, sodomy, or both, and these acts would occur premortem, perimortem, postmortem, or all three. Some killings would involve biting, undressing of victims, photographing of victims, beating, or dismemberment, and in other murders, these features or some combination of them were absent.

The fluidity with which Bundy murdered and the various rituals and signatures embedded within each killing are consistent with forensic research. For instance, a study of thirty-eight serial sexual homicide offenders who collectively murdered 162 victims found that contrary to criminological lore, most did not engage in the same rituals and leave unique signatures at every one of their crime scenes. Instead, those murderers engaged in a host of ritualistic behaviors including orifice penetration, binding, overkill, beating, posing, mutilation, dismemberment, foreign object insertion, torture, biting, gagging, necrophilia, and photographing to memorialize the event. Murderers of this scale mix it up.

Although murderers have preferences or tastes for some of these behaviors, they would also mix some of these behaviors and engage in some depending on events or physical features in the environment where they killed. The murderers in their data also exhibited multiple themes during their murders depending on the qualitative mixture of ritualistic behaviors at the crime scene. The most prevalent themes were "power, control, and domination," "rage and revenge," and "degradation and humiliation." Nearly one in five murders displayed multiple themes during their crimes.[23]

Some of his potential crimes; however, would already have the hallmarks of the Bundy murders during his "prime predator" phase. The June 23, 1966 bludgeoning of Lonnie Trumbull, who died from the beating, and Lisa Wick, who narrowly survived the attack, in Seattle, Washington is widely attributed to Bundy. That case denotes several parallels to the attacks at the Chi Omega sorority in Tallahassee, Florida in January 1978, a case that conventional wisdom suggests is indicative of Bundy in deterioration based on the depravity of his conduct in that event, such as biting the buttocks of Lisa Levy, and thus, uncharacteristically leaving forensic evidence and sodomizing her with a foreign object. Alternatively, the latter case did not represent a deterioration or devolving at all, instead it was indicative of the ferocity with which he wanted to destroy his victims and a cruel forensic insight into the offense conduct of a malevolent psychopath.

On June 30, 1969, Susan Davis and Elizabeth Perry were discovered fatally stabbed in a forest in the greater Philadelphia area near Somers Point and Ocean City, New Jersey. The targeting of two victims on the same day is consistent with Bundy's conduct, but the stabbing is an example of variable killing methods Bundy likely engaged in during this time. Based on his evaluation, Dr. Carlisle identifies these Philadelphia-area murders as perhaps Bundy's first.[24] Bundy himself describes the Philadelphia period of the late 1960s as the time where he "reached the point of acting out."[25] As indicated previously, Bundy disliked the urban environment in Philadelphia due to its lack of forested areas.

The period spanning the late 1960s to early 1970s represents a flood of murders with differential evidence that Bundy is involved, and some of which he frankly admitted to. These include the rape and murder of Rita Curran on July 19, 1971 in Burlington, Vermont, where she was killed in her residence, approximately seven murders in Oregon between May 1972 and November 1973, and the eight homicides in California during 1972 and 1973 that Bundy admitted to his attorney Browne.[26]

Bundy was likely alternating his murders across these two states, Oregon and California, prior to the greater Seattle, Washington murders in early 1974, his official onset. The potential Curran homicide is forensically interesting because it represents a hybrid of the fatal bludgeoning of victims in their homes (e.g., Seattle and Tallahassee) and the sexual homicides that usually occurred in remote locations with even more remote body disposal.

Even when considering the pathological velocity with which Bundy murdered particularly during 1974 and 1975, when murders would span mere weeks or days apart, sometimes across state lines, and would occasionally involve two attacks on the same day, there are lingering, interdependent substantive points to reconcile. The one-hundred or more victim count could not have been achieved during the 1974–1978 period especially when considering the amount of time that Bundy spent in custody following his arrest for the DaRonch attack, subsequent commitment to prison in Utah, extradition to Colorado and assorted jail stints, escapes, and recaptures, and his final attacks in Florida that concluded in February 1978.

A longer span of time was needed to murder many victims, and the evidence of a first murder occurring circa 1960 certainly provides a more logical timeline. Consistent with criminological and forensic science and Bundy's own descriptions of his psychopathology and homicidal motivation, the first decade or so of Bundy's homicide career would be unsatisfying, experimental, harried, diverse, unprofessional, impulsive, and amateurish. With each murder, unfortunately, Bundy's acumen would sharpen, his resolve would increase, and the latency between kills would reduce.

He would become a veritable killing machine.

The evolution of Bundy's homicidal activity from its origins in the late 1950s or early 1960s to its culmination in 1978 is fully consistent with forensic research on compulsive homicides and within that typology the unplanned and planned forms of compulsive homicide. Compulsive homicides are those where sexual activity and violence are fused and the murder is sexually gratifying to the offender. The erotization of the violence produces powerful urges that compel the offender to seek victims to kill.

Within the compulsive homicide type are unplanned and planned variants. In unplanned compulsive homicides, the compulsion to kill is present for years and sadistic fantasy is also present, but in a simple, undifferentiated form. The motivation to kill is sexual, the murder includes sexual assault and other sexually ritualistic acts, and there are usually ominous warning signs in the offender's background that are seemingly predictive of sexual violence. In planned compulsive homicides, the compulsion to kill builds for years and the sadistic fantasy is elaborate but not in reference to a particular person. In this variant, nearly any victim suffices. Planned compulsive homicide offenders also exhibit ominous warning signs years before their offense conduct is known and given their planning and criminal sophistication, they usually murder for a long period before detection and apprehension.[27]

Based on this typology, we can envision that the murders of Bundy's youth were unplanned, often spontaneous, and heavily dependent on situational dynamics that presented contact with a child or young female and a brief window within which to commit the sexual homicide offense. As he learned from each offense, the compulsivity remained and the premeditation and execution transitioned from unplanned to planned.

As his relationship with Kendall progressed and as Bundy struggled to balance the demands of his clandestine sexual murdering with the demands of being a boyfriend, father figure, occasional employee, law student, and apparently normal citizen, he finally had enough and submitted himself entirely to his homicidal desires. Seemingly in a midlife crisis, Ted Bundy acknowledged to himself who he was and went with it.

Thus the 1974 murders, construed as the official beginning of Bundy's criminal career, actually represent the apotheosis of his criminal activity and the most full-fledged expression of his psychopathy and paraphilic drives. Regarding the murder of Lynda Ann Healy, allegedly his first, considers this description of the police response to that crime. "it was almost beyond comprehension to them that anyone would be so bold as to enter a house where others were sleeping, attack and render unconscious a woman, hang up her nightgown, gather up clothes, grab a backpack, meticulously make the bed and then carry the victim up a flight of stairs and out into the night."[28] Borrowing from their description, it is beyond comprehension to believe that a first-time murderer would exhibit such confidence in perpetrating a sexual homicide, but it is entirely likely if Bundy had already been killing for nearly fifteen years.

If Ted Bundy had not murdered one-hundred or more victims, why did so many law enforcement investigators believe that he did when they inquired about unsolved crimes that were nearly identical to his known offenses? In a rare moment of full disclosure to his defense counsel, information that is potentially guarded by attorney-client privilege, why did Bundy tell John Henry Browne that he murdered one-hundred or more victims in addition to other previously unknown details about his offending trajectory? Why did Bundy tell law enforcement officials after his ultimate capture that his murder victim total was in the triple digits, and why did he repeat this claim to investigative journalists once on death row?

When his longtime girlfriend, and arguably the person who had the most extensive and intimate knowledge about Bundy asked why his murders began in 1969, itself a full five years before the "official" estimate of his murder onset, why did Bundy reply that the police are years off? Despite the volume of sexual homicides that Bundy finally would confess to prior to his execution, why did he tell multiple law enforcement and media investigators there were many additional murders that he simply was never going to discuss? Even a madman can tell you the time of day, and even the most forensically resourceful, inveterate psychopaths like Ted Bundy can on occasion reveal the truth.

This chapter contained the names of many victims, most of whom whose disappearance and likely location and date of death could be ascertained. Many other girls and women in the United States during the 1960s and 1970s were not so easy to locate, were in transit, and in a seemingly more nostalgic era, were unfortunately eager to accept a ride from a courteous, handsome, and conversationally slick young man driving a Volkswagen Beetle. The social and cultural features of American life in the middle to the late twentieth century, which provided ample opportunities to procure, murder, and dispose of victims, are examined next.

Notes

1. Kendall (2020, p. 177).
2. Nelson (2018, p. 61).
3. Kendall is a pseudonym which I also use since her memoir is published under the last name Kendall.
4. Michaud and Aynesworth (1983); Ramsland (2013); Sullivan (2009). Readers might also consult the FBI files on Ted Bundy, which also contain suggestive information about additional homicides in multiple states: https://vault.fbi.gov/Ted%20Bundy%20/view.
5. Of all his known victims, Lynda Healy is the only one where there is evidence Bundy would have had contact with her prior to her murder. According to Robert Keppel, Bundy and Healy took some of the same undergraduate courses in psychology at the University of Washington. See Keppel and Birnes (2005, p. 81).
6. Michaud and Aynesworth (1999, pp. 237–240).
7. Keppel and Birnes (2005).
8. Browne (2016).
9. Browne (2016, p. 114).
10. Nelson (2018, pp. 252–253).
11. Nelson (2018, p. 288).
12. Rule (1980, p. 271).
13. Michaud and Aynesworth (2019, p. 191).
14. Keppel and Birnes (2005).
15. Browne (2016, p. 111).
16. DeLisi et al. (2021).
17. Keppel and Birnes (2005, p. 399).
18. Sullivan (2009, pp. 1–3).
19. Rule (2018).
20. Hirschi and Gottfredson (1983); Farrington (1986); Moffitt (1993).
21. Michaud and Aynesworth (2019, p. 96).
22. Carlisle (2020, p. 152).
23. Schlesinger et al. (2010); Koeppel et al. (2019).
24. Carlisle (2020, p. 187).
25. Nelson (2018, p. 276).
26. Keller (1989); Browne (2016).
27. Schlesinger (2007); Schlesinger (2004).
28. Sullivan (2009, p. 20).

References

Browne, J. H. (2016). *The devil's defender: My odyssey through American criminal justice from Ted Bundy to the Kandahar Massacre.* Chicago Review Press.

Carlisle, A. (2020). *The 1976 psychological assessment of Ted Bundy.* Carlisle Legacy Books.

DeLisi, M., Drury, A. J., & Elbert, M. J. (2021). Psychopathy and pathological violence in a criminal career: A forensic case report. *Aggression and Violent Behavior, 60,* 101521.

Farrington, D. P. (1986). Age and crime. *Crime and Justice, 7,* 189–250.

Hirschi, T., & Gottfredson, M. (1983). Age and the explanation of crime. *American Journal of Sociology, 89*(3), 552–584.

Keller, L. (1989). *Confessed mass murderer Ted Bundy…South Florida Sun Sentinel,* retrieved May 27, 2021 from https://www.sun-sentinel.com/news/fl-xpm-1989-01-24-8901040963-story.html.

Kendall, E., with a contribution from Molly Kendall. (2020). *The phantom prince: My life with Ted Bundy* (updated and expanded edition). Abrams Press.

Keppel, R. D., with Birnes, W. J. (2005). *The riverman: Ted Bundy and I hunt for the green river killer.* Pocket Books.

Koeppel, S., Schlesinger, L. B., Craun, S. W., Keel, T. G., Rubin, D., & Kum, J. (2019). Foreign object insertions in sexual homicide. *International Journal of Offender Therapy and Comparative Criminology, 63*(9), 1726–1737.

Michaud, S. G., & Aynesworth, H. (1983). *The only living witness.* Signet.

Michaud, S. G., & Aynesworth, H. (1999). *The only living witness: The true story of serial sex killer Ted Bundy.* Authorlink Press.

Michaud, S. G., & Aynesworth, H. (2019). *Ted Bundy: Conservations with a killer: The death row interviews.* Sterling.

Moffitt, T. E. (1993). Adolescence-limited and life-course-persistent antisocial behavior: A developmental taxonomy. *Psychological Review, 100*(4), 674–701.

Nelson, P. (2018). *Defending the devil: My story as Ted Bundy's last lawyer.* Echo Point Books & Media.

Ramsland, K. (2013, Fall). The many sides of Ted Bundy. *The Forensic Examiner, 2013,* 18–25.

Rule, A. (1980). *The stranger beside me.* Norton.

Rule, A. (2018). *The stranger beside me: The shocking inside story of serial killer Ted Bundy*. Gallery Books.

Schlesinger, L. B. (2004). *Sexual murder: Catathymic and compulsive subtypes*. CRC Press.

Schlesinger, L. B. (2007). Sexual homicide: Differentiating catathymic and compulsive murders. *Aggression and Violent Behavior, 12*(2), 242–256.

Schlesinger, L. B., Kassen, M., Mesa, V. B., & Pinizzotto, A. J. (2010). Ritual and signature in serial sexual homicide. *Journal of the American Academy of Psychiatry and the Law, 38*(2), 239–246.

Sullivan, K. M. (2009). *The Bundy murders: A comprehensive history*. McFarland and Company.

7

The Open Road

She was hitchhiking. Yeah, I never heard anything more about her…The person I used to be would get into a fit and just drive. And people have trouble relating to that. You sort of lose orientation. You sort of lose track of where you've been. You just get lost.[1]

Ted Bundy

An individual's psychopathology does not exist in isolation, it is continually enmeshed in environmental contexts that can attenuate or exacerbate the underlying conditions. No offender, even one as pathological as Bundy, can perpetrate crime without restraint. Instead, the conditions to abduct a victim must be right both in terms of immediate environmental factors, such as is there anyone around to deter the crime and in terms of the broader environmental milieu, such as being in a remote location on an isolated highway. The decision whether to pick up a young woman traveling along a remote road and murdering her was just as much a function of whether Bundy saw another vehicle in his rearview mirror as it was his vicious, relentless psychopathology. Environmental factors matter greatly, and a highly motivated offender exploits environmental opportunities to victimize others.

© The Author(s), under exclusive license to Springer Nature Switzerland AG 2023
M. DeLisi, *Ted Bundy and The Unsolved Murder Epidemic*,
https://doi.org/10.1007/978-3-031-21418-9_7

The middle to later decades of twentieth-century America provided a relatively fertile environmental context to engage in a broad range of behaviors, including crime, and many offenders like Bundy, Little, and Alcala took full advantage.[2] These opportunities unfolded from broad societal and sociological factors that typified the country during this era. Structurally, the interstate highway system provided a vast interconnected roadway network in the contiguous United States that greatly enhanced the ability to travel by automobile. The vast mobility that Bundy exhibited, driving hundreds to thousands of miles and recurrently crossing jurisdictional boundaries, would not have been possible in prior eras. Although the interstate highway system "shrunk" the United States in the sense that its geographic massiveness was now connected, it is important to recognize that outside of major urban areas, the majority of the country is rural and remote especially in the years that Bundy was actively killing.

The structural benefits that the interstate system provided for personal travel and commerce also facilitated a broader societal ethos of freedom, opportunity, and leisure that had begun with the creation of the Lincoln Highway and U.S. Route 66 decades earlier. The open road was a symbol of the manifest destiny of the United States where individuals could pick up and move, usually West, to pursue greater opportunities and presumably greener pastures. There was a communal sense of potential and excitement with traveling about, and this sentiment is seen in the idealism of hitchhiking where young people would stand on the side of the road, their hand extended and thumb out, eager to wait for a ride from a passing stranger.

Popular music offered many songs during this era including Marvin Gaye's "Hitchhike," Joan Baez's "The Hitchhiker Song," Chuck Berry's "Route 66," and Nat King Cole's "(Get Your Kicks On) Route 66" that spoke to the perceived innocence, fun, and possibility of hitchhiking and traveling the open roads of the United States. The risks of hitchhiking that are so obvious in the contemporary era were not broadly appreciated then, although still other songs like The Doors' "Riders on the Storm" chronicled the violent dark side of the road with lyrics that eerily evoke the types of homicides that serial sexual homicide offenders committed.

This broader sense of freedom and idealism pervaded other social institutions during this era as well. Those reared in the middle to late decades of the twentieth century experienced a degree of autonomy, freedom, and limited supervision that is wholly foreign to the helicopter parenting and structured activities overcommitment of the modern age. Historically, parents provided their children with a much greater range of freedom to play and socialize outside of the family home and generally outside of their reach. The phrases "be home for supper," and "be home by the time the street lights come on" convey a form of parenting where children could experience the social world without constant monitoring, evaluation, and sanctioning from adults. This was not neglectful parenting, but an acknowledgement that autonomy and discovery were important parts of socialization and maturity. Indeed, research has shown that historically more liberal and autonomous types of parenting were not the main reasons for increases in crime.[3]

For most, this era of childhood and adolescence was idyllic and those who experienced it look back on the innocence of bike riding, hide-and-go-seek, flashlight tag, backyard football, slumber parties, kick the can, pickup basketball, and related fun with their friends with warm nostalgia. Scores of television shows (e.g., *Happy Days*, *What's Happening!!*, and *The Jeffersons*), movies (e.g., *American Graffiti*, *House Party*, *Stand by Me*, and *Grease*), and songs (e.g., "I Wish" by Stevie Wonder, "Memories" by the Temptations, "Old Days" by Chicago, "Keeping the Faith" by Billy Joel, and "Night Moves" by Bob Seger) of the latter twentieth-century document the Americana, adolescent fun, and freedom of this era.

It was not just parents who had a more relaxed perspective on monitoring and surveillance. Technologically speaking, American society of the middle to the late twentieth century was extremely limited in terms of knowing the precise location of an individual, especially if one compares that to today where cell phones and other electronic devices provide a moment-to-moment chronology of a person's activities and whereabouts. In prior eras, for instance, the telephone was very limited and one only knew that another person was home if they answered a call on their home landline. How many telephone calls were never heard because someone was using a vacuum cleaner? Although there were ubiquitous public pay phones, one effectively could not be located if they were not at home responding to a phone call. In the event that a person was home but already using the telephone, a third party attempting to call them would receive a busy signal and would have to try to call later or drive to the person's home to contact them.

At the time, innovations like call waiting and answering machines felt like otherworldly technological advances. Of course, there was also no texting or social media during this era and instead of e-mail, the primary means of written communication was via letter or postcard that was dependent on the U.S. mail. In terms of broader surveillance, there was limited use of close circuit television, and contemporary forms of video monitoring including traffic cameras, home security systems, and doorbell cameras were virtually non-existent or had yet to be invented. For many years, the United States was an open, remote, and disconnected society.

The resources of the criminal justice system were equally primitive especially in terms of dissemination of information about wanted subjects and missing persons, and the sharing of information across jurisdictions within and across state lines. The National Crime Information Center, or NCIC, which is the computerized clearinghouse of information for criminal justice system organizations and practitioners, did not exist prior to 1967, and in its first two decades had limited capacity in terms of how quickly information could be sent in automated or computerized format to law enforcement.

At its inception, the NCIC contained only 350,000 criminal record files. Today, it processes fourteen million records each day.[4] There were no sexual offender registries or notification systems and in yet another example of the nostalgia of this era, the only way people were aware of serious offenders was by seeing FBI or police most wanted flyers at the local community post office. Until relatively recently, law enforcement officers in the field did not have access to computers, thus for most of the twentieth century, police were unlikely to receive information about potential suspects, missing persons, or victims while on patrol. They could not send or receive information about criminal offenders in real time.

When suspects were booked into jail and fingerprinted, their fingerprint card was mailed to a state agency for matching and identification and the first Automated Fingerprint Identification System, known as AFIS, did not emerge until approximately 1984, long after Bundy was already in confinement in Florida and awaiting execution. This means that for the entirety of Ted Bundy's offending career, the criminal justice system was woefully underequipped to locate, arrest, detain, or frankly, to even identify him.

His longtime girlfriend Elizabeth Kendall contacted law enforcement officials in Seattle in 1974 and Salt Lake City in 1975 to report her concerned suspicion that Bundy was involved in the numerous missing women in these jurisdictions only to be informed that Bundy had already been investigated and cleared.[5] The ease with which he escaped from jails in Colorado further attests to the informality and lax security of this era. Even his final capture and apprehension in Florida revealed the poor technology and information flow as it took time to disconfirm Bundy's aliases of Chris Hagen and Kenneth Misner and determine his real identity.

Notwithstanding nostalgic sentiment about the middle to late decades of the twentieth century, many societal indicators during this era indicated that American society was actually much worse than today. Our memory of a winsome time period obscured gritty realities. Based on objective societal indicators, the era was far different from its perceived innocence. Mortality from motor vehicle-related injuries between 1950 and 1980, for instance, was more than twice as high as today due largely to more safely designed vehicles and the mere fact that seatbelts were rarely worn in prior eras.[6] American life expectancy in 1960 was less than seventy years, today it is nearly eighty years.[7]

In part due to the looseness of American society, demographic changes, the breakdown of informal social control mechanisms, and the broad limitations of the criminal justice system, the latter twentieth century experienced an unprecedented crime boom that began in 1965 and that did not relent until the mid-1990s. The incidence of crime was in direct contrast to the perceived innocence of this era among the general population. In 1960, for instance, the homicide rate in the United States was 5 per 100,000. By 1970, it was 8.8 per 100,000 and would reach its zenith in 1980 at 10.4 per 100,000.[8] Between 1960 and 1980, the same era of Bundy's homicide career, the national homicide rate more than doubled and sexual homicide was also at unprecedented levels. For example, a study of thirty-two years of data from the FBI Supplementary Homicide Reports indicated a fivefold reduction in adult perpetrated sexual homicide between 1976 and 2007. The first decade of those data from the mid-1970s to mid-1980s accounted for fifty-six percent of all sexual homicides in the United States.[9]

Serial murder, the repeated killing of two or more victims with periods of downtime, or a "cooling off" period also reached its peak during the middle to late twentieth century, coinciding with Little, Alcala, and Bundy's offense history.[10] Criminologists have estimated that the prevalence of serial murder victimization during Bundy's era was likely underestimated by a factor of ten, and that similar to the incidence of sexual homicide, the incidence of serial murder has also declined sharply since this time. The reasons for this are many and include increased effectiveness of law enforcement, increases in sentencing and prison incapacitation, and technological changes in American society that exponentially increased the ability of individuals, businesses, and governments to conduct surveillance and monitor the activities and movements of individuals.[11]

Bundy's adolescence and adulthood coincided with a historical era in American history characterized by the liberalization of social and interpersonal mobility, comparatively low parental monitoring, and limited enforcement and surveillance capacity of the criminal justice system. Aside from his arrest while prowling at night in Utah in 1975, there is no evidence that Bundy was contacted by law enforcement for prowling, stalking, and attempting to procure victims despite the countless hours for which he was actively engaging in these activities in the community. (The details of his juvenile justice system contacts for burglary and auto theft are not available.)

That is an incredible streak of luck. His stalking and driving encompassed years of his time and innumerable situations where he was engaging in felonious conduct and yet there were no police reactions to his conduct until 1975. If my estimates of his actual homicide career are accurate, this equates to more than fifteen years of criminal activity before a police contact, which is quite a dark figure of crime.

In this respect, Bundy's offending career was as serendipitous as it was pathological.

Physically and metaphorically, the vast interstate highway system permitted unprecedented travel and the transportation means for an offender to engage in extraordinary geographic spread in their criminal offending. Numerous serial sexual homicide offenders spanning the 1960s–1980s including William Bonin, Randy Kraft, Patrick Kearney, Randall Woodfield, Rodney Alcala, and Samuel Little either directly utilized the interstate system as a means to abduct, transport, and dispose of their homicide victims, or indirectly used it by their itinerant criminal activity across dozens of states. The open road was so conducive to murder that an entire genre of highway killers emerged to troll the nation's highways during this time.

Interview data with Samuel Little illustrate the importance of the open road to serial sexual homicide offenders. During his confession to a 1993 murder in Las Vegas, Nevada, Little described that he murdered the victim as he was leaving town to travel to California. Little rolled the victim's body down a large slope similar to a ravine. In describing the area, Little informed investigators, "But I was on the very outskirts, the very outskirts. There was a couple of motels I remember, the gas station there. It was scattered dot, dot, dot, dot. Because it was getting thin, population, as you go further out."[12] His description of the desolation of the environment puts into perspective how easily a murder victim could be killed and dumped, never to be seen again.

During his confession to a murder in 1982 in New Orleans, Louisiana, Little told investigators, "We stopped at a gas station. We was on Highway 1, and uh, going toward Slidell. I seen the sign that said Little Woods. So I cut off. I took off the exit. And we went and that, sure enough, was a road leading me into the woods. And we went in and park."[13] The remote vastness of the open road was a great advantage to these offenders.

Throughout his offending career, Bundy exhibited incredible mobility and he astutely moved across states once the public notice of disappearing young women became potentially problematic. To illustrate, during his conversations with investigators from the Idaho Attorney General's Office, Bundy described two murders in that state, one of which was an unknown female he picked up hitchhiking. In that incident, Bundy described that he was driving from Seattle, Washington to Salt Lake City, Utah, which by car is more than 826 miles and entails nearly fifteen hours of drive time. Bundy described that he spent three or four hours with the victim, raped and murdered her, and dumped her body in a river.[14]

During the course of his conversations with journalist Stephen Michaud while on death row, Bundy described the seemingly endless hours of drive time on the highway system as a "luxury" to provide adequate time to think about additional crimes to commit and where to dispose of the body once he was done. This tendency was not unique to Bundy. Seminal forensic research on sexually sadistic criminals found that forty percent of them engaged in excessive driving.[15]

Given the amount of time he was on the road, it is highly probable that Bundy murdered additional women he encountered while driving or in other contexts as he trolled for victims. During the same conversation with the investigator from the Idaho Attorney General's Office, for instance, Bundy was asked if there were additional murders to which Bundy replied, "No, oh, oh, wait a minute, ya. I should just give that a little bit more thought, I could have. I thought you meant before, on that particular trip, which was the only trip that I made to Pocatello from Salt Lake."[16]

That quotation reflects the reflexive deception that Bundy exuded across life; in his mind, the query about homicides in the area was parsed to a specific trip in which he had already murdered. Upon reflection, Bundy provided a negative, then positive, then speculative answer. Perversely in his defense, there were likely so many abductions, rapes, and murders across the sparsely populated Western states that Bundy could not keep them straight. But the quotation also shows how frequently he lied about the extent of his homicide offending, and how patently unbelievable those lies usually were.

The panoramic geographic spread of his violence was unaffected by his legal status. Even after his final jail escape from Colorado, Bundy spent time in Chicago, Illinois, Ann Arbor, Michigan, and Atlanta, Georgia before making his way to Tallahassee, Florida, all while he was the most wanted criminal in the United States. In fact, Bundy confessed to his attorney John Henry Browne that he stalked a woman during his brief stint in Ann Arbor, Michigan, and was going to rape and murder her, but decided against it at the last minute.[17] That was likely a half-truth: Bundy likely did stalk a woman in Ann Arbor, Michigan, but unlike what he told Browne, he probably murdered her as well.

A macroscopic look at American society during this era is useful to contextualize the copious opportunities that Bundy had to abduct, rape, and murder, and the likelihood that many of these victims and their final locations remain unknown to the present day. This is a critical point. With one exception, the unknown female who was buried along with Carol Valenzuela, the roster of women who Bundy killed that appears in the previous chapter are known, not unidentified missing persons.

An individual who is missing faces an exponential high risk for foul play. Moreover, the risk of homicide victimization generally and sexual homicide victimization specifically is not equally distributed throughout the population, but instead shows clear age, race, and sex differentials. Overall, adolescents and younger adults relative to older adults, nonwhites especially African Americans relative to whites, and males relative to females are more likely to be murdered; however, the sex effect is flipped for sexual homicide where females are much more likely than males to be killed.

A study of homicide victimization by age and sex among missing persons similarly reveals these sharp differentials. Among women ages 19–24, which was the most common age range of Bundy's victims, the risk of a missing person report resulting in homicide was one in 1,000. Among females ages 14–18, which encompassed some of Bundy's other victims, the risk of a missing person report resulting in homicide was one in 13,000. To put these estimates into comparative perspective, the risk of a male ages 14–18 years who was missing resulting in homicide is one in 169,300.[18]

A follow-up study focused on missing cases that had been cancelled because the person was either no longer missing, such as they were found safe, or conversely had been found dead. The mortality risks were striking. Among males, the overall proportion found dead who were homicide victims was one in 114; for females, the ratio was one in fifteen. Moreover, the age effect reversed. Younger males and younger females were more likely than older males or older females to be homicide victims. Among females ages 14–18 years, the proportion found dead who were victims of homicide was one in four. Among females ages 19–24, the ratio was also one in four. Among females between the ages of 25 and 29, the proportion found dead who were victims of homicide was one in three![19]

These data put the risks for homicide victimization among young female hitchhikers, missing persons, and the missing along the open roads of the United States into sharper context and provide a historical glimpse into the dark figure of murder and how it expanded exponentially throughout the 1960s and 1970s. A hitchhiker on the open road during this era could not be located. They could not be telephoned. They could not receive a telegram. For as long as they remained in traveler status, they were effectively missing. This is important because the epidemiological data make clear that if a young woman was missing and later found deceased, she was likely murdered. When the sociocultural ethos of this era is considered along with the prevalence of hitchhiking, the reasons for the meteoric increase in unsolved murders start to crystallize.

Perpetrating violent sexual crime in one state and then traveling to another state shortly thereafter enhanced Bundy's lengthy homicide career, as did his varied manner of killing that blended strangulation, beating, bludgeoning, and drowning. His forensic versatility is scientifically important. To illustrate, a study of 1,381 multiple homicide offenders in the United States found that killing with multiple methods and killing across state lines were two of the strongest predictors of greater criminal career length.[20] The ways that Bundy murdered helped to ensure that he would murder for a long duration of time, far longer than the relatively short-lived 1974–1978 period.

These multiple forms of killing reveal important details about Bundy's life and the likely expanse of his homicide career in the decade or more before the putative 1974 onset. Foremost, during this era, Bundy was experimenting with how to kill and evaluating in a step-by-step process how to engage in an experience that would satisfy his sexual desires. In terms of the initial approach of the victim, would he rely on a blitz attack, a ruse, or his guile? Were these approach strategies irrelevant given the ample number of young women he encountered hitchhiking across the nation's highways? Did the "natural" approach of giving a stranger a ride build his confidence and permit him to test various ruses or verbal approach scenarios? Did the hitchhiker murders cultivate the confidence that he displayed during the 1974–1978 period?

Did the stranger contacts on the open road have an explicit sexual connotation to them, and if so, to what degree did Bundy engage in consensual sexual activity, nonconsensual sexual activity, or homicidal sexual activity? How often did he mix the range of sexual activity? For contacts that lacked any sexual innuendo or conversation, did this eventuate in the use of the tire iron or blunt tool to incapacitate the victim? A violent weapon attack raises still other issues relating to the amount of force that would incapacitate but not kill, the amount of time the victim's unconsciousness lasted, and whether the injury reduced the sexual valence of the encounter. The latter point is forensically valuable: to what degree did Bundy ever recoil from sexual violence during the course of a crime that was bloody and produced significant injuries?

Were his necrophilic tastes diverse, meaning that he found women in various states of incapacitation, up to and including death, to be sexually attractive? Did he ever have sexual performance problems generally, and specifically because of the violence he already inflicted? Or, in the words of Ann Rule, was his sexual violence simply "rage, hate, animalistic mutilation."[21]

The varied manner and method of killing would likely depend on Bundy's mood at the time of the encounter and whether he was edgy and somewhat agitated, his usual psychopathic malevolent self, or acutely sexually aroused. For instance, Bundy described himself as supercharged and "bestial" during his Florida murders, and the macabre nature of those crimes, such as biting erogenous areas of the victim, the overkill of the bludgeoning, or raping by instrumentation, supports such an assessment. These emotional states and his own sordid self-assessment of his execution of the crimes would likely dictate to what degree he brutalized the victim, discarded the body, or attempted to preserve the victim for postmortem sexual activity.

Other forensic features of his crimes also allowed Bundy to get away with murder for many years. His offense conduct was consistent with forensic research on homicide offenders whose cases are never solved and whose behaviors are typified as either "violent and sadistic" or "forensically aware." Consistent with the violent and sadistic typology, Bundy committed rape, beat the victims, and usually killed by strangulation. Consistent with the forensically aware typology, he did not leave biological evidence that could be collected and most of his cases were unsolved. The open road was a perfect venue for his chameleon-like murderous behavior.

In other respects; however, Bundy's behavior was idiosyncratic and defied typologies derived from research studies of other sexual homicide offenders. Although the preponderance of his cases was never solved, he would take items from the victims, sometimes mutilate the victim, sometimes insert foreign objects into their vagina or rectum, and inflict variable forms of physical violence.[22] He was forensically all over the place, and this heterogeneity coupled with his extensive travel rendered his cases not only difficult to solve, but also difficult if not impossible to ascertain that Ted Bundy had ever met them, let alone murdered them.

It is my belief that the majority of Bundy's homicides, roughly seventy percent or so, occurred during his late adolescence and early adulthood after completing high school from 1965 until 1974 when his murders are better documented. These murders occurred as he traveled across the United States, and most of the victims were hitchhikers, runaways, or other young women who were unfortunately isolated for just long enough for him to strike. These victims would include women who were reported missing and others for whom loved ones would have no reason to believe that the person was missing. Repeatedly during his conversations with investigators Keppel and Reichert while advising about the Green River Killer, Bundy implored the investigators to realize that long-term serial murderers have many additional victims that authorities are not aware of, and that will not be found.

He stated this with strident confidence because he knew it was true from his own experiences.

Many of these murders would occur precisely as Bundy described to media investigators in terms of picking up a woman in his car, sexually assaulting and murdering her, and disposing of the body in some manner. On the issue of the great mobility of young people during his homicide career, Bundy remarked about the disappearance of a young adolescent girl, "We assume she ran away. She had run away before. But what they don't know is that she's in a ditch somewhere. And they may *never* know it."[23]

This quotation is critical for discerning Bundy's narrative even when he is speaking hypothetically or in the third person. What appears to be offhand observations with his forced intellectual cadence were really direct statements about what he had actually done. For years, Bundy travelled across the United States and picked up scores of young females where they talked about her travel plans, whether she was a runaway, whether she was a hitchhiker, and whether her absence or disappearance would be noticed.

With his vile calculus, Bundy knew that females with a particular behavioral history for whom spontaneous travel was common would never be reported missing because their loved ones would have no reason to believe they were. Bundy knew that women could be sexually assaulted, murdered, and thrown in a ditch "somewhere" because he had done it countless times.

One of Bundy's conversations with his defense attorney Polly Nelson substantiates my claim that the preponderance of his murders occurred on the open road and that many to most of the victims were never found. Consider this passage from Nelson's legal memoir:

> He drove across the state line to a secluded place in the woods that he was already familiar with. He led the girl out of the car, assuring her that no harm would come to here. He made her strip and kneel on her hands and knees while he took Polaroid pictures of her. (For Ted, another small miracle had been that when his apartment had been searched upon his first arrest in Utah, the investigators had failed to check the building's utility room. When he was released on bail for the attempted abduction of Carole (sic) DaRonch he retrieved the shoebox of photos he'd hidden there and destroyed the most graphic and conclusive evidence of the true depth of his depravity).[24]

No one knows how many photographs of Bundy's murder victims were in that shoebox. Dozens? Hundreds? Even more? What we do know is that Ted Bundy spent much of his time between 1965 and

1974 driving across the United States and there is evidence that he was in approximately twenty states. He spent much of his time on reconnaissance for isolated places where he could rape, kill, dismember, desecrate, and discard the bodies of his victims. He knew all the places in the woods to do this. And he spent so much time doing this that his domestic, educational, and vocational development were stalled in non-performance.

In describing his conversations with another serial murderer who was on death row in Florida, Bundy informed Keppel and Reichert, "there are huge, enormous gaps at very critical times when he was clearly in a state of mind, based upon my knowledge of how these things go, where he would—more likely drink and engage in that kind of behavior."[25] Without directly telling them what he had done, Ted Bundy told them what he had done.

Another important phenomenon that facilitated Ted Bundy's criminal career occurred during this era: the clearance rate for murder plummeted. A clearance rate is the proportion of cases that are closed by arrest. They are solved cases. At mid-century, about nine out of ten murders were closed by arrest because the circumstances of the killings, and the parties involved, were rather predictable and involved family killings, such as domestic homicide, murders during the course of other criminal activity, such as an armed robbery, and murders occurring between known criminals. These cases were basically quick and easy to solve.

But the large-scale societal changes of the 1960s and the dramatic changes to the sociological framework that once tightly held society together unraveled, as too did the basic nature of the relationships between individuals. By 1970, the murder clearance rate was eighty-five percent, and by 1980, barely seventy percent. Today, it hovers slightly above fifty percent. Among several explanations offered for the sharp reduction of solved murders and the sharp increase in unsolved ones centered on stranger-on-stranger murders where it was difficult to impossible to establish where a person was, who they were with, who caused them harm, and what happened to the offender and victim afterward.[26] It was a perfect environmental context for an apex predator like Ted Bundy, and it was during this era that the dark figure of murder began to grow precipitously.

A fair and straightforward criticism of my assertation that seventy percent of Ted Bundy's murders occurred during his itinerant travels across the United States is this: where is the evidence of these unsolved murders? The evidence is the multiple data sources showing an epidemic of unsolved murders in the United States, where the main question is how large of a problem is it? Based on estimates from the United States Department of Justice, there are 250,000 unsolved murders in the United States, and about six-thousand additional unsolved murders are added to that total each year.[27]

According to Project Cold Case, there were 967,856 murders in the United States between 1965 and 2020 and 636,855 of these were cleared by arrest. This means that slightly more than sixty-six percent of murders were solved across these decades and 331,001 murders remain unsolved.[28] Many of these cold cases have been unsolved for several decades including during Little, Alcala, and Bundy's era of homicidal activity. When one considers the relaxed informal social controls and popularity of hitchhiking during the 1960s and 1970s, the limitations of the criminal justice system, and the relentless predatory hunting that the most pathological offenders like Bundy exhibited, it is reasonable to assert that he and offenders who shared his pathological offending patterns and psychopathology are responsible for a disproportionate share of these crimes.

If Wolfgang and colleagues' research on the Philadelphia birth cohorts is any indication, approximately five percent of the most pathological offenders are responsible for the bulk of these unsolved murders, and given their forensic awareness inherent in switching jurisdictions, altering their modus operandi and manner of death, and targeting people who are the missing , the proportion of murders is probably far greater than the seventy-one percent of murders that the 1945 chronic offenders committed.

It is one thing for infrastructure and cultural features to enable unfettered travel about the United States and provide opportunities to access potential victims, but it is another to have a highly motivated, highly energized, highly opportunistic offender take advantage of those environmental features to commit a crime. During a conversation with his defense attorney Polly Nelson, Bundy offered this description of the events leading up to the Chi Omega attack. "I was walking back, just happening to be walking along the road, and I was just all aroused, full of energy, you know peaked for this. I happened to look over across the street casually and I saw a door open to the sorority house. And I just turned and walked right for the door."[29]

As the quotation indicates, Bundy exhibited a set of psychopathological factors that often put him in a state of heightened physiological and sexual arousal, where mundane environmental contingencies, such as an open door, were all that was needed to initiate an attack. Bundy exuded what criminologists have recently described as criminal energetics.

Criminal energetics is a novel idea that uses the science of energy and human performance to understand the profound individual-level differences in criminal activity.[30] In developing this idea with my colleague Michael Vaughn, we relied on many years of criminal justice practitioner, researcher, and consultant experiences involving direct interaction with thousands of offenders and indirectly, through review of their records and correctional case files, with thousands of others. Although none of these experiences included an offender as criminally prodigious as Bundy, Little, or Alcala at least in terms of sexual homicides, several of these interviews involved offenders who had perpetrated multiple homicides either in the community, in correctional settings, or both, who had highly aggressive psychopathology including antisocial personality disorder and psychopathy, and who had extensive criminal histories spanning decades of offending and including hundreds of arrests, convictions, and prison commitments.

Among the most active offenders, it was common for them to describe, often in vague but colorful language, the intrinsic drives that propelled their criminal activity. These offenders used a variety of terms such as "force," "rage," "anger," "energy," or simply, "thing," which to them was the causal force of their antisocial motivation and criminal acts. Sometimes offenders would attribute this nebulous force to specific incidents in their life, such as a death in the family or some form of abuse, or generalized incidents, such as feelings of persecution about being bullied or otherwise ostracized from their peers.

Still others denied any causal process, and simply reported that for as long as they can remember, they have always been extremely violent, antisocial, and had difficulty controlling their emotional responses and behavior. During a memorable psychopathy assessment with an offender with nearly four dozen violent arrest charges and convictions, he described, "I've been broken for as long as I can remember. It doesn't matter why. It is what it is. And when I decide to do it [engage in violent behavior], I don't have reverse. I don't go back."

Criminal energetics advances the notion that a multitude of cognitive, endocrine, cardiovascular, sexual, motivational, and behavioral features distinguish the most active and reprehensible criminals. This is an important point to emphasize. As indicated in an earlier chapter, there is great diversity or heterogeneity within the criminal population where the majority of offenders are occasional or moderate offenders in terms of the quantity of their crimes and the seriousness of their crimes.

In contrast, across societies about five percent of criminal offenders account for more than half of the crime in a population as well as the majority of serious violent felonies,[31] and criminal energetics delves into that severe five percent to understand what factors drive their extraordinary criminal activity. Other forensic and criminological factors, such as the paraphilic disorders that Bundy exhibited are also theorized to facilitate the most active offending careers.

In Bundy's case, the unique mix of his personality functioning played an important role in his recurrent and prodigious criminal activity. To illustrate, an ingenious survey of seventy-three professional psychologists examined Bundy's personality features based on secondary files and biographical information, not direct examination. Nearly the entire sample, ninety-six percent of professional psychologists, opined that Bundy had antisocial personality disorder, and nearly eighty percent of these professionals considered Bundy a prototypic, textbook case of that disorder.

Other conditions including schizoid and narcissistic personality disorders were also highly rated. In terms of Bundy's personality traits, he rated as highly antagonistic evidenced by his manipulation, deceitfulness, mistrust, arrogance, and callousness. In terms of extraversion, Bundy was rated high on assertive, active, and thrill-seeking, but extremely low on warmth. He was low on all features of neuroticism except angry hostility.

Uniquely for a serious criminal, Bundy was rated as high on conscientiousness factors, such as competence, orderliness, achievement orientation, and deliberateness. Thus, he had the overall dysfunctional personality structure of a serious criminal, but the conscientiousness of a highly productive, even prolific individual, in his case, one who "achieved" many murders as opposed to some non-criminal, constructive outlet.[32]

While he was on death row granting interviews to investigative journalists, Bundy suggested that some of his most daring criminal activities, such as the double abduction, rape, and murder at Lake Sammamish were attributable to irregular fluctuations that were biologically or biochemically based.[33] In periods such as these, he experienced intense arousal and motivation where his psychopathic and paraphilic drives were so strong that he engaged in brazen daylight approach scenarios even using his real name and personal vehicle. It is also probable that his admission to Dr. Otnow Lewis about prior frenzied murders also involved this state of hyperarousal.

Bundy is likely correct that periods of intense criminal arousal during his offending career probably had a genetic, neurophysiological basis, of course, medical data on him are not available. However, an environmental proxy of his criminal energetics can be inferred from his extraordinary travel across the United States scouring local areas for remote places to commit sexual homicide and/or dispose of bodies. For example, while in Florida for his final crimes, Bundy subsisted on stolen credit cards and traveled using stolen vehicles. Prior to the murder of Kimberly Leach, Bundy filled the gas tank of his vehicle three times in a span of twenty-four hours across two days.[34]

This is meaningful because it is well-documented that Bundy was in northern Florida the entire time during this period, and thus reveals the sheer amount of driving he engaged in to attempt and procure young females to murder. Notwithstanding the physiological elevations he experienced, the amount of driving and travel time he engaged in was so extreme that it was almost beyond belief. To him, the open road was the physical infrastructure along which his homicidal sexual drives could go.

A recurrent feature in Bundy's life described by relatives, acquaintances, and women who narrowly evaded his homicidal reach is the seeming metamorphosis that he appeared to undergo immediately prior to and during the midst of his antisocial acts. His blue eyes would appear to darken as his pupils dilated, this is a condition known as mydriasis, and a sense of detached malevolence appeared to overtake his countenance. Although this sounds perhaps farfetched, numerous affective states are exhibited in the eyes, and some conditions, including schizophrenia produce a pronounced darkness in and around the eyes after the onset of the disease.

I once interviewed a severe psychopath who reported involvement in at least ten murders during his decades in prison, and who had the most violent and extensive criminal record of my career, one that began when he was a young boy. This individual had brown eyes that appeared black. He had the most intense, unwavering, and penetrating eye contact I've ever seen, and it would intensify during parts of the interview where he was describing his murders or other violent events.[35] It was as if the affective deficits of his psychopathy created physiological reactions within him, which appeared to affect his eyes.

At other points during his federal supervision, this highly psychopathic offender also told his supervising officer that he would only talk in generalities about his homicide offending. He would not give names, provide dates, or in any way implicate himself to a crime for which he could still be prosecuted. He explicitly told his supervising officer, "I am reluctant to tell you about all the murders and all the orders to murder that I got away with."

His undisclosed self-report of murder and violence was his closely guarded personal dark figure of crime, and he was not going to reveal it. Likely little did he know that his unsolved murders are a small fraction of similarly undiscovered and unsolved homicides throughout the United States.

Notes

1. Keppel and Birnes (2005, p. 397).
2. Of these three serial sexual homicide offenders, Little's travel is the best documented since he has arrest activity in at least twenty states and confessed to ninety-three murders in at least nineteen states. Due to his

recurrent arrest, judicial, and correctional records, we know definitively where he was at certain times. Moreover, Little's confession videos to the Texas Rangers investigator also document the copious travel within and across states before, during, and after his homicide offending. Bundy and Alcala's travels were similarly extensive and itinerant.

3. Collishaw et al. (2012).
4. Retrieved July 8, 2021, from https://www.fbi.gov/news/stories/ncic-turns-50.
5. Kendall (2020, p. 1).
6. https://www.statista.com/statistics/184607/deaths-by-motor-vehicle-related-injuries-in-the-us-since-1950/.
7. https://www.macrotrends.net/countries/USA/united-states/life-expectancy.
8. https://www.statista.com/statistics/187592/death-rate-from-homicide-in-the-us-since-1950/.
9. Myers et al. (2016).
10. https://www.fbi.gov/stats-services/publications/serial-murder#two, Accessed October 6, 2021. A variety of definitions of serial murder are in use and they tend to vary across practitioner, investigative, and academic audiences. In the Protection of Children from Sexual Predator Act of 1998, serial murder was defined as three or more killings. A 2005 symposium on serial murder involving investigators from the National Center for the Analysis of Violent Crime arrived at the current definition of two or more murders.
11. Quinet (2007) and Yaksic (2015).
12. https://www.fbi.gov/video-repository/vicap-samuel-little-confession-las-vegas-1993.mp4/view, Accessed October 6, 2021.
13. https://www.fbi.gov/video-repository/vicap-samuel-little-confession-new-orleans-1982.mp4/view, Accessed October 6, 2021.
14. Sullivan (2017, pp. 122–123).
15. Dietz et al. (1990).
16. Sullivan (2017, p. 135).
17. Browne (2016, p. 114).
18. Newiss (2004).
19. Newiss (2006).
20. Campedelli and Yaksic (2021).
21. Rule (1980, p. 243).
22. Balemba et al. (2014).
23. Michaud and Aynesworth (2019, p. 122, italics in original).

24. Nelson (2018, p. 254).
25. Keppel and Birnes (2005, p. 320).
26. Regoeczi et al. (2008).
27. U.S. Department of Justice. (2020). The crisis of cold cases. Retrieved July 15, 2021 from https://www.ojp.gov/files/archives/blogs/2019/crisis-cold-cases.
28. https://www.murderdata.org/p/blog-page.html.
29. Nelson (2018, p. 287).
30. Vaughn and DeLisi (2018).
31. DeLisi (2005), and Vaughn et al. (2011).
32. Samuel and Widiger (2007).
33. Michaud and Aynesworth (2019).
34. Michaud and Aynesworth (2019, p. 54).
35. DeLisi et al. (2021).

References

Balemba, S., Beauregard, E., & Martineau, M. (2014). Getting away with murder: A thematic approach to solved and unsolved sexual homicides using crime scene factors. *Police Practice and Research, 15*(3), 221–233.

Browne, J. H. (2016). *The devil's defender: My Odyssey through American criminal justice from Ted Bundy to the Kandahar massacre.* Chicago Review Press.

Campedelli, G. M., & Yaksic, E. (2021). Survival of the recidivistic? Revealing factors associated with the criminal career length of multiple homicide offenders. *Homicide Studies.* https://doi.org/10.1177/10887679211010882

Collishaw, S., Gardner, F., Maughan, B., Scott, J., & Pickles, A. (2012). Do historical changes in parent–child relationships explain increases in youth conduct problems? *Journal of Abnormal Child Psychology, 40*(1), 119–132.

DeLisi, M. (2005). *Career criminals in society.* Sage.

DeLisi, M., Drury, A. J., & Elbert, M. J. (2021). Psychopathy and pathological violence in a criminal career: A forensic case report. *Aggression and Violent Behavior, 60,* 101521.

Dietz, P. E., Hazelwood, R. R., & Warren, J. (1990). The sexually sadistic criminal and his offenses. *Bulletin of the American Academy of Psychiatry and the Law, 18*(2), 163–178.

Kendall, E., with a contribution from Molly Kendall. (2020). *The phantom prince: My life with Ted Bundy* (updated and expanded edition). Abrams Press.

Keppel, R. D., with Birnes, W. J. (2005). *The riverman: Ted Bundy and I hunt for the Green River killer.* Pocket Books.

Michaud, S. G., & Aynesworth, H. (2019). *Ted Bundy: Conservations with a killer: The death row interviews.* Sterling.

Myers, W. C., Chan, H. C., & Mariano, T. Y. (2016). Sexual homicide in the USA committed by juveniles and adults, 1976–2007: Age of arrest and incidence trends over 32 years. *Criminal Behaviour and Mental Health, 26*(1), 38–49.

Nelson, P. (2018). *Defending the devil: My story as Ted Bundy's last lawyer.* Echo Point Books & Media.

Newiss, G. (2004). Estimating the risk faced by missing persons: A study of homicide victims as an example of an outcome-based approach. *International Journal of Police Science & Management, 6*(1), 27–36.

Newiss, G. (2006). Understanding the risk of going missing: Estimating the risk of fatal outcomes in cancelled cases. *Policing: An International Journal of Police Strategies & Management, 29*(2), 246–260.

Quinet, K. (2007). The missing missing: Toward a quantification of serial murder victimization in the United States. *Homicide Studies, 11*(4), 319–339.

Regoeczi, W. C., Jarvis, J., & Riedel, M. (2008). Clearing murders: Is it about time? *Journal of Research in Crime and Delinquency, 45*(2), 142–162.

Rule, A. (1980). *The stranger beside me.* Norton.

Samuel, D. B., & Widiger, T. A. (2007). Describing Ted Bundy's personality and working towards DSM-V. *Independent Practitioner, 27*(1), 20–22.

Sullivan, K. (2017). *The Bundy secrets: Hidden files on America's worst serial killer.* Wildblue Press.

Vaughn, M. G., & DeLisi, M. (2018). Criminal energetics: A theory of antisocial enhancement and criminal attenuation. *Aggression and Violent Behavior, 38*, 1–12.

Vaughn, M. G., DeLisi, M., Gunter, T., Fu, Q., Beaver, K. M., Perron, B. E., & Howard, M. O. (2011). The severe 5%: A latent class analysis of the externalizing behavior spectrum in the United States. *Journal of Criminal Justice, 39*(1), 75–80.

Yaksic, E. (2015). Addressing the challenges and limitations of utilizing data to study serial homicide. *Crime Psychology Review, 1*(1), 108–134.

8

Unsolved

If a killer is out there, he's doing stuff. The police have not found them.[1]
Ted Bundy

At 3:15 pm on November 6, 2003, an unknown white adult male entered Superbike Motorsports motorcycle shop in Chesnee, South Carolina and methodically murdered three adult males and one adult female who were the shop's owner, service manager, mechanic, and bookkeeper. All of the victims were shot in the forehead, a detail that was never released to the public. They were coldly, summarily, executed. Although a composite sketch of the suspect was produced and widely distributed, there were no immediate arrests after the quadruple homicide. The case would remain unsolved for thirteen years.

At 8:56 pm on November 25, 1986, a 15-year-old white male kidnapped a 14-year-old white female at gunpoint and commandeered her to his residence in Tempe, Arizona. There, the young man duct-taped the mouth of the young woman, tightly bound her hands with rope, removed her clothing, and raped her. After the sexual assault, the male threatened to murder her and her two younger siblings if she ever

© The Author(s), under exclusive license to Springer Nature
Switzerland AG 2023
M. DeLisi, *Ted Bundy and The Unsolved Murder Epidemic*,
https://doi.org/10.1007/978-3-031-21418-9_8

told anyone about the rape. He escorted the victim back to her residence where she immediately called police who quickly responded to the scene.

Upon contact with law enforcement, the juvenile promptly confessed that he lured her out of her house at gunpoint, committed the sexual assault, and threatened to murder multiple members of her family to potentially cover up the crimes. Pursuant to a plea agreement, the male perpetrator was convicted of kidnapping and a dangerous crime against children in the first degree and served fourteen years in a juvenile confinement facility. He was released and relocated to South Carolina approximately two years before the quadruple homicide in Chesnee.[2]

On November 3, 2016, a 30-year-old white female who had been missing for nearly three months was located alive by law enforcement near Woodruff, South Carolina. The woman was found bound and chained within a storage facility where she had been kept as a sexual slave by the owner of the property, Todd Kohlhepp. The young woman reported that Kohlhepp had murdered her boyfriend during the course of abducting her. Approximately a week later, the remains of another young adult couple were also found on the property. Shortly after his arrest, Kohlhepp confessed to these three murders, kidnapping, criminal sexual conduct, and weapons offenses.

He also stunned investigators when he admitted to perpetrating the quadruple homicide in Chesnee thirteen years earlier. Todd Kohlhepp was also the juvenile perpetrator of the armed kidnapping and rape from Arizona in 1986. He is currently serving seven life sentences in the South Carolina Department of Corrections.[3]

A textbook case of a career criminal, Todd Kohlhepp's extraordinary life of antisocial behavior began very early. A legal affidavit from his juvenile kidnapping-rape case indicates that he exhibited clinically meaningful and severe problems with behavioral and emotional regulation as early as age fifteen *months*. His early childhood evinced an array of highly aggressive and destructive acts including assault, bullying, animal cruelty, property damage, and disparate delinquent acts. Kohlhepp experienced pronounced homicidal ideation throughout his life and threatened to murder his mother several times during his childhood.

Similar to offenders such as Little, Alcala, and Bundy, Kohlhepp had merged violence and sexual behavior and displayed psychopathic and sexually sadistic urges very early in life. In the legal documents pertaining to his armed rape and kidnapping case during his youth, experts advised that he posed an elevated risk for continued violent conduct if released. His litany of criminal acts during adulthood resoundingly supported the forensic prognosis made about him during his adolescence.[4]

Inconsistent with the extremity of his criminal career, it is surprising that Kohlhepp confessed to the four murders from 2003. That is a rare disclosure by an individual with such vivid psychopathic features. Usually psychopathic career criminals are guiltless and refuse to accept responsibility for their actions. Absent that unexpected confession, it is likely those murders would never have been solved and the cases would have remained as cold and without investigative leads as they had for thirteen years.

The case touches on a much broader societal problems about the dark figure of crime and the epidemic of unsolved murders in the United States, and reveals the reality that a disproportionate share of those unsolved murders is the responsibility of the most pathological offenders. These are ones who have murdered numerous times during their offending careers as well as perpetrated other grievous offenses, such as kidnapping and rape. Indeed, since his convictions, Kohlhepp has contacted newspaper media with claims that he has murdered numerous other victims who have not been discovered, and even suggested that his murder total potentially exceeds one-hundred victims.[5]

These claims should not be casually dismissed as the boastful lies of a publicity-hungry offender, but could be the foundation upon which to explore other unsolved murders. As the chapter opening quotation from Bundy asserts, if an active murderer remains in the community, he is murdering and will continue to murder.

As indicated previously, the United States Department of Justice estimates there are at least 250,000 unsolved murders in the United States and other data repositories dedicated to cold cases place the number at greater than 330,000 unsolved murders. The gravity of that number of homicides is difficult to process but can be put into perspective when considering the annual prevalence of homicide offending.

Since 1960, the United States has experienced more than 20,000 murders relatively infrequently, occurring in 1974 and 1975, when Ted

Bundy was likely at the height of his homicide career, 1979 through 1982, 1986 through 1995, in what was an unprecedented decade-long homicide binge, and most recently in 2020 when murder increased approximately thirty percent from the previous year—the greatest one-year increase in murder in U.S. history (Final homicide data for 2021 and 2022 are not available yet). Between 1996 and 2019, there were never more than 20,000 annual murders in the United States. Thus, it is fairly rare. To put the various estimates of unsolved murders into perspective, they are roughly equivalent to twelve to fifteen years with 20,000 murders. Each year, unfortunately, approximately six thousand more unsolved murders are added to the aggregate tally.

It is among the most glaring and appalling failures of the criminal justice systems in the United States.

Unsolved murders impose multiple problems. They deprive the surviving family members and friends of the murder victim, known as homicide covictims, of a dispositive legal response to their victimization. The despair, prolonged grief, and traumatic symptoms that many families of murder victims experience are compounded further by failure to clear the case, which can give the impression that criminal justice authorities do not view the murder as a priority, or at least, as a case they can likely solve. Unsolved murders indefinitely deprive the loved ones of an appropriate funeral and burial, ceremonies that have sacred value in our culture.

Beyond the devastation felt by covictims of homicide, unsolved murder cases fail to hold the offender responsible for their lethal conduct and thus leave the due process and crime control missions of the criminal justice system unfinished and unachieved. Unsolved murders are a blight on the legitimacy and efficacy of the criminal justice system. The inaction of the justice system permits offenders like Bundy, Alcala, Little, and more recently, Kohlhepp, to remain at large. The unsolved murder crisis is epidemic in size, scope, and sustainability, and there are several hypotheses offered to explain why murder, a crime that in earlier eras of American history was much more likely to be solved, frequently remains unsolved.

An obvious and vexing explanation for unsolved murders is seen in cases involving offenders like Todd Kohlhepp. His predatory criminal behavior for kidnapping and rape was clearly known by legal authorities, and he served a lengthy confinement sentence for his Arizona conviction. But he would remain generally off the radar of the justice system until his final capture for predatory criminal behavior for murder, kidnapping, and rape in South Carolina. Had that missing woman not been found, it is unlikely that either her murdered boyfriend or the other murdered young couple would have been found. The discovery of those homicide victims, and the ultimate arrest of Kohlhepp to clear those murders was contingent on the good fortune of locating his victim who was a missing person.

Just as serendipitous was his unlikely confession to the quadruple homicide, four murders that languished at unsolved status for thirteen years. Absent his uncharacteristic acceptance of responsibility for that criminal conduct, they too would likely have remained unsolved. That Kohlhepp has since contacted the media and suggested that he is responsible for many more homicides where the victims remain undiscovered provides more opportunities to potentially solve other cases. But since he is a psychopath prone to manipulation and outlandish lying, investigators are not necessarily keen to interview him despite the potential for resolving cases. Moreover, since he is already serving seven consecutive life sentences, there is little urgency to further investigate his alleged crimes.

Between 1960 and the early twenty-first century, the prevalence of unsolved murders in the United States increased by nearly eighty percent, and according to the most recent data from 2020, just half of the murders are cleared by arrest.[6] To examine the reasons why, criminologist Janet McClellan reviewed studies on the decline in murder solvability and observed several trends during this period. There were changes in the relationship between the murderer and victim that moved from lethal interactions between family members, intimates, and acquaintances to an increasing number of homicide events involving strangers where the connectedness between the killer and the killed is uncertain or unknown.

During both the middle twentieth century and today, homicides are clustered among persons actively involved in criminal behavior, such as gang activity. However, improvements in law enforcement technology, surveillance, information sharing, and size have been offset by reductions in investigative effectiveness, poor relations between the police and subpopulations with the highest homicide offending and victimization, and differential law enforcement responses to certain homicide victims. Specifically, murders involving males, racial and ethnic minorities, persons of lower socioeconomic status, persons in unstable neighborhoods, and perhaps most importantly, persons who are engaged in high-risk lifestyles characterized by substance use, immersion in criminal activity, and transiency are less often solved.

Another factor that McClellan noticed was associated with unsolved status involved murders that were committed in remote locations. Remote locations were the province of offenders, such as Little, Alcala, and Bundy. McClelland's overall assessment on potential improvements in the clearance of murder cases in the United States was not favorable. "There may be little that law enforcement investigators can do about the changing nature of homicides committed in the United States as it portends forces of socio-economic and systemic alterations of culture and national character that are greater than the efforts practical for any individual or department other than to understand, appreciate, and apply its significance in investigative practices."[7]

The data source for homicide that is most closely connected to official arrest data is known as the Supplementary Homicide Reports, which provides incident-level information on all murders and nonnegligent manslaughters that law enforcement agencies report to the Federal Bureau of Investigation. The Supplementary Homicide Reports provide information on the age, race, and sex of the homicide offender and victim, the nature of their relationship, weapon, geographic information, and other circumstances of the homicide event. The Supplementary Homicide Reports indicate the variance in whether homicide cases are solved or remain unsolved across assorted variables of interest. A study of these data spanning 1976–2001 found that the murders most likely to be solved involve very young victims ages thirteen years and under and among cases from rural areas. For both of these variables, only thirteen percent of cases go unsolved.

Aside from those types of cases, the proportion of unsolved cases is frankly disturbing. In terms of age, among adolescent victims ages fourteen to seventeen years, nearly twenty-nine percent are unsolved. Among those eighteen to twenty-four years, nearly thirty-two percent are unsolved, for twenty-five to thirty-four years, over thirty percent are unsolved. More than twenty-seven percent of homicide cases with white victims and nearly thirty-one percent of homicide cases with black victims are unsolved.

Location matters greatly. In large cities, thirty-seven percent of murders are unsolved. This reduces to nearly thirty-one percent in medium cities, and nearly twenty-two percent in small cities, but increases to nearly twenty-six percent in suburban areas. The region of the country generally had no effect on whether murders were solved or unsolved. The proportion of unsolved murders in the Northeast (almost thirty-seven percent), Midwest (thirty percent), South (more than twenty-three percent), and West (nearly thirty-two percent) is disconcertingly high.[8]

In many respects, the unsolved homicide problem in the United States has evolved from one that was primarily rooted in technological and surveillance limitations to a more sociological phenomenon relating to distrust in the legal system and lack of cooperation with law enforcement, factors that both correlate strongly with race. A study of one decade of unsolved homicides in Indianapolis, Indiana between 2007 and 2017 is revealing. Compared to the national homicide clearance rate in 2020 of fifty percent, homicides in Indianapolis during this era ranged from a high of seventy percent in 2008 to a low of thirty-eight percent in 2016.

At every data point across the decade, the clearance rate for murders of white victims far exceeded those for minority victims, the overwhelmingly majority of whom were African American. For instance, the white clearance rate in 2015 in Indianapolis was approximately ninety percent whereas the minority clearance rate was just forty percent. Over the study period, minority victim cases had forty-three percent reduced odds of being solved and cases with male victims had forty-two percent reduced odds of being solved. Resident complaints of community disorder were associated with thirty-one percent reduced odds of being solved. Among murders with African American victims, the homicide clearance rate dropped thirty-six percent between 2007 and 2017.[9]

These data on race differences are consistent with trends in unsolved murders in other large cities in the United States. Relative to whites, blacks have significantly greater homicide offending, significantly greater homicide victimization, significantly worse assessments of police legitimacy, and significantly lower trust in the criminal justice system's ability to solve cases. Among African American males who are adolescents and young adults, homicide is the leading cause of death. These problems are compounded by neighborhood contexts where the animosity toward the criminal justice system coexists with a genuine fear of retaliatory violence from the offender population if one were to cooperate with law enforcement during a homicide investigation.

In Chicago, for instance, approximately ninety-five percent of homicide offenders and homicide victims are black or Hispanic, most of whom are young males. However, homicide risk is not equally distributed across these racial and ethnic groups but instead is heavily concentrated among antisocial segments of these populations especially those involved in gangs. The University of Chicago Crime Lab found that among both homicide offenders and victims, more than half are gang affiliated, nearly eighty percent have prior arrests, and more than half are habitual offenders. In about three of out four cases, murders in Chicago are immediately precipitated by an argument, altercation, or confrontation. In turn, many subsequent murders are retaliation for the preceding murder. Active offenders who are heavily immersed in gang activity have generally negative relations with law enforcement, and offer little cooperation toward solving murders. According to the most recent data in the University of Chicago Crime Lab report, only twenty-six percent of murders are cleared by arrest. For non-fatal shootings, which are effectively attempted murders, a mere five percent of cases are cleared by arrest.[10]

Research indicates that unsolved murders have almost paradoxically increased despite huge improvements in resource allocations to law enforcement, pervasive increases in surveillance, the proliferation of computers to monitor financial transactions and thus an individual's movements, and a general tightening of the informal social controls within society. The *laissez-faire* social norms of the 1960s and 1970s are wholly foreign to today, but we face the contemporary challenge that just five out of ten murders are cleared by arrest. As exemplified by the Chicago data, most of this decline in solvability relates to a subculture of distrust, animosity, and uncooperativeness that exists at both the neighborhood and individual levels. The unsolved murders epidemic in the United States has morphed from a technological resource problem to a social problem rooted in social conflict.

There is an important caveat. Most research on unsolved murders pertains to what could be called normal homicides that stem from common interaction patterns and have relatively straightforward motives. More challenging to solve are abnormal homicides, such as those with a sexual component and offender motivations that are an outgrowth of their rare and clinically significant psychopathology. Thus, when considering the unsolved murder problem, there are at least two broad types spanning the normal and the abnormal.

According to the classic definition developed by profilers within the Federal Bureau of Investigation, a sexual homicide must have at least one of the following characteristics: victim's attire or lack of attire, exposure of sexual body parts of the victim's body, sexual positioning of the victim's body, insertion of foreign objects into the victim's body cavities, evidence of sexual intercourse/sexual activity, or evidence of substitute sexual activity, interest, or sadistic fantasy.[11] Sexual homicides are highly abnormal, and commensurately, quite rare. Study of nearly four decades of FBI Supplementary Homicide Reports spanning 1976–2011 found that slightly less than one percent of all murders in the United States are sexual homicides.[12]

Sexual homicide cases go unsolved or take a very long time to investigate for a variety of reasons. Forensic research on sexual homicides found several modus operandi and criminal investigation factors that influence whether the investigation length of a case is extended and whether the case involves serial murders. In terms of modus operandi factors, premeditation, victim mutilation, and the number of post-homicide precautions that the offender took increased the duration of the investigation or involved serial murder.

Additional factors, such as whether the victim was kidnapped, whether the offender inserted objects into the victim, and whether the victim exhibited sophisticated hiding of the victim's body had either non-significant or negative linkages to case duration or serial status. Several investigation factors, such as if the body was discovered by civilians, whether the body was in a state of advanced decomposition, whether the actual killer was interviewed by police but not held, and poor decision-making by investigators extended the duration of the investigation although only the latter factor was associated with it being a serial murder case.[13]

There are other challenges in abnormal murder cases that also contribute to the remaining unsolved. One is forensic awareness where the offender is careful to avoid leaving evidence at the crime scene or will manipulate the crime scene or the victim's body in some manner. Forensic awareness manifests in behaviors such as cleaning up semen and other biological materials as well as moving, concealing, or dismembering the victim's body. A study of 350 sexual homicides in which 250 cases were solved and one-hundred cases were not reported a strong association for any specific forensic precaution and the case remaining unsolved.[14]

In many cases, and Bundy's offense history contained numerous examples of his efforts to avoid detection, the victim's body is moved during the course of a sexual homicide. Numerous factors including the manner of death, such as stabbing or strangulation, use of bindings, restraints, or gags, evidence of overkill, using a deserted body disposal site, and dumping the body outdoors can impact solvability in these cases. In still other cases, sexual homicide offenders dismember the victim's body as will be explored later in this chapter via Bundy's admissions about his offense conduct.[15]

Dismembering the victim's body creates obvious investigative challenges when parts that are most useful for identification purposes, such as the hands and head are not dumped or buried along with the rest of the body, or have been destroyed altogether. In some cases, different parts of a sexual homicide victim's body are located in multiple states which further complicates the investigation. None of these strange and extraneous features are usually found in normal homicides.

Multiple sources produce knowledge about unsolved murders. A tension within criminology and the forensic sciences centers on the relative value and contributive role of knowledge borne from academic theories and quantitative data analysis compared to the knowledge that is informed by applied experiences with actual criminal offenders. From the experiential, applied perspective, there are other reasons for the unsolved homicide problem in the United States, and some of these insights originate from the most unlikely of sources: Ted Bundy.

In October 1984, Bundy wrote a letter to Robert Keppel, the former homicide detective and member of the Ted Task Force who helped to investigative Bundy's murders in Washington State and offered his knowledge to help in the apprehension of the Green River Killer, who ultimately turned out to be Gary Ridgway, now serving forty-nine life sentences for murder at the Washington State Penitentiary, and similar to Bundy, Little, and Alcala, is believed to have murdered many more victims than his official conviction tally. After some negotiation, Keppel and fellow law enforcement officer Dave Reichert, who would ultimately arrest Ridgway, flew to the Florida State Penitentiary to collaborate with Bundy on the Ridgway case. Keeping with the surreal nature of Bundy's audacious offer and the unlikely pairing of this collaboration, Bundy would offer his perspective on the offender he almost comically referred to as the Riverman.[16]

Bundy's thoughts about the Riverman's mindset, modus operandi, and behavioral patterns prior to, during, and after the killings were valuable to the investigators, but more valuable was the realization that during the course of offering his insights about Ridgway, Bundy would be drawing on his own experiences to speak to Ridgway's crimes. Keppel and Reichert were keenly aware of this: what Bundy told them about Ridgway, he was surreptitiously divulging about himself. Consequently, Keppel and Reichert intentionally used verbiage such as "would you speculate" or "why do you think" to give the conversation a more theoretical, hypothetical valence that would give Bundy the impression that he was distancing himself from his own behavior. The more they made Bundy feel like a university professor or a dispassionate expert witness, the freer he was to reveal himself.

The first insight about why many murders go unsolved is that serial sexual homicide offenders' *raison d'etre* is to abduct, sexually abuse, murder, and often, perpetrate additional sexual violence after death. They are obsessed with this behavior and thus are extraordinarily motivated, engage in epic travel to procure, transfer, and dispose of bodies, usually target strangers, and thrive in remote settings where witnesses are scarce. They routinely change jurisdictions and exploit bureaucratic limitations within and across criminal justice systems. This is qualitatively different from the mundane and normal interaction patterns that engender most normal homicides were some known individual murders another known individual during a conflict and the nature of their association and relationship is clearly established.

In this respect, the unsolved nature of sexual homicides is not exclusively an indictment of the failures of the criminal justice system to adequately investigate a homicide case, develop enough evidence for probable cause to arrest the suspect, sustain the case through successful prosecution, and sentence the offender to a lengthy prison term to incapacitate his ability to harm others. Instead, it speaks to the mastery that the most prolific serial murderers exhibit during the course of their offending career. They know who to target and who to avoid. They know that their various internal drives to rape and murder are equally dependent on external drives or environmental contingencies, and thus, their murdering will exhibit intermittency. Their murderous productivity will have starts and stops just like any other form of behavioral output.

They are experts at trial and error.

They learn how to blend into environments and how to use multiple environmental contexts to obfuscate their criminal conduct and hide their bodies. They learn that stabbing and bludgeoning produce a great deal of blood, which can be avoided with strangulation. But they also know that an extremely violent bludgeoning or stabbing, with volumes of blood at the scene, appears behaviorally distinct from a victim who was bloodlessly strangled. They know how to bury bodies and how to scatter them. They sometimes simply leave bodies at the scene. They learn to dismember some bodies while leaving others intact. They adapt and use fire to destroy evidence and the body of the murder victim. Their extreme psychopathy lends itself to an almost purely instrumental mode of thinking, one that is seen in their highly refined forensic awareness and the dexterity with which they will alter their offense conduct. It is because serial homicide offenders are so good at their craft that confessions are so valuable and essential for closing cases.

According to Bundy, one reason why so many murders remain unsolved is that investigators fixate almost entirely on what he referred to as "front end" issues pertaining to the crime scene or abduction scene and the evidence located there, potential eyewitness information, and theories and speculation about the likely motive of the offender. Although offender profiling is a valuable tool to law enforcement investigators and forensic theorizing, it loses its specificity when considering an offender who frequently changes their modus operandi and offense conduct to throw investigators off the scent of their crimes. On this issue, Bundy suggested that an expert serial murderer, who is intelligent and controlled, will continuously modify their modus operandi to facilitate a longer period of offending.[17] In this way, an undue allegiance to specific theories of crime or motivational models of homicide offender behavior can create a sort of linkage blindness in the investigator's mind that prevents them from appraising a homicide offender's conduct with an open mind.

More meaningful were "back end" issues that centered on the dump site of the murderer's victims. Bundy implored law enforcement to closely surveil fresh dump sites where a victim's body had recently been found because the offender would likely return to the site repeatedly, usually to engage in necrophilic sexual acts. It was at the dump sites where law enforcement officials were much more likely to catch the offender in the act. This was not only critical for making an arrest, but it also critical for furnishing a geographic area where additional bodies, and thus other unsolved murders, could be found.

Keppel and Reichert observed that Bundy employed a professional but staid tone of voice when describing his thoughts about the Riverman, but that tone would change dramatically when Bundy would talk about the Riverman's body dump sites. During those moments of their conservations, Bundy exuded a sense of arousal and excitement that was very different from his business-like approach when discussing abduction sites. There was a fixation, preoccupation, and zeal about the dump sites.[18] Bundy was sheepish in telling them the precise reasons why the dump sites were so exhilarating to him, but it was clearly for postmortem sexual activity and his interview arousal was a proxy indicator for what he experienced at those remote sites.

Bundy's insistence about the importance of the dump sites to the Green River Killer, and by inference about the importance of these locations to his own murders is a revelation about his primary sexual motivation as seen in the case of Georgann Hawkins on June 11, 1974 (and likely dozens of additional murders). In the final days before his execution, Bundy told Keppel that he employed a ruse by using crutches and carrying a heavy briefcase full of books, to which Hawkins offered her assistance to help carry the books to his vehicle. Once they reached Bundy's Volkswagen Beetle, Hawkins momentarily turned her back toward Bundy who immediately seized the crowbar he has stored outside of the vehicle and hit her over the head with it, knocking her unconscious. Bundy promptly handcuffed her, placed her on the passenger side flooring where the seat had been removed and quickly drove away along Interstate 5 and Interstate 90 to a remote wooded area.

Hawkins began to stir as they reached the woods. Bundy told Keppel that he carried her from the vehicle and once again hit her in the head with the crowbar. This blow again knocked her unconscious. Ted Bundy then used a small length of rope to fatally strangle Georgann Hawkins. Bundy moved the body approximately ten yards away to a more hidden area of trees, undressed her, and stayed with the body until dawn. At that point, Bundy left the body and drove away, throwing all of Hawkins' possessions out of the car window as he drove.

Amazingly, Bundy returned to the abduction site on a bicycle as police started their investigation. Highlighting his psychopathic boldness, Bundy maneuvered his bicycle precisely to the spot where his vehicle had been parked and picked up a shoe and earring that had fallen from Hawkins' body during the abduction.

Three days later, Bundy returned to the dump site and had sex with the decomposing corpse of Georgann Hawkins. He then decapitated her with a hacksaw and buried the head in the dirt on a rocky hillside about fifty feet from the road. Her body was dumped elsewhere.

Bundy's description of the killer's activities between abduction sites and dump sites also yielded clues about why so many homicides go unsolved, and how these discrete behaviors reflect considerable forensic awareness. Drawing on his own experiences, Bundy reported that the victim's license or other identification, clothing, and other materials that had been removed from the body would simply be thrown out of the window as the killer was leaving the scene, going to another area within the state, or leaving the state. His advisement on the Riverman's behavior was cribbed from his own murderous behavior.

Thus, if materials from a missing person were found along roads or seemingly in the middle of nowhere, it was likely those materials were proximate to a dump site. Other evidence disposals and destruction methods include burning and burying. In unsolved murders where the body was located at a dump site, Bundy strongly suggested there were additional bodies there that had not been located, but were still more unsolved murders.

Essentially, Bundy had divulged his hypotheses about the Riverman's offense conduct by simply divulging his own behavior. Thus, his "consultation" in 1984 to Keppel and Reichert was in many respects a trial run for his confessions to Keppel in 1989.

Even a seasoned homicide investigator like Keppel was stunned at the admissions of decapitation and the complexity of burying heads in different locations from the rest of the body. At one point, Bundy possessed the heads of four of his victims in his apartment. I am similarly surprised about the importance that Bundy attributed to dump sites as well as his confession about the nature of his sexual abuse of Hawkins.

In many respects; however, Bundy's necrophilia and decapitation are consistent with other sexual homicide offenders who dismember their victims. Analyses of data from the Sexual Homicide International Database found that sexual homicide offenders who dismember their victims are highly organized in their modus operandi and perpetrate the murder with considerable efficiency. Those who dismember are highly paraphilic and their offense behavior reflects the intention to murder the victim, necrophilia, and commission of extreme behavioral acts with the victim's corpse.

In retrospect, it is clear that Ted Bundy was highly polymorphic in his paraphilic drives and sexual conduct during his homicide events. His sexual crimes spanned molestation, rape, sodomy, rape by instrumentation, and necrophilia. At certain points of his homicide career, Bundy's preferred acts involved rape and sodomy while fatally strangling the victim, but at other points, there was no evidence of sexual activity while the victim was alive. In some of his murders, even an unconscious woman was an unappealing sexual target. She would have to be deceased to arouse Bundy. His penchant for necrophilia also supports my contention that his personality was marked not only by antisocial features, but also schizoidal features. The victim's death was required for him to achieve the necessary isolation for sexual activity.

This realization and the perverse sacredness of the dump sites turn the entire criminal career of Ted Bundy on its head because one must consider both the abduction sites and attack sites where bodies were not moved—what Bundy referred to as the front end—and the dump sites where his later sexual violence occurred—what Bundy referred to as the back end. The abduction site, the attack site, the dump site, and, the burial site are collectively all primary crime scenes, which makes these cases significantly more complex, and, as a result, more challenging to solve.

His revelations about the relative importance of front-end and back-end considerations also indicate how extraordinarily versatile Bundy was over the course of homicide career. His mixed methods of murder were so pronounced it was as if he was ten different offenders in one, something that is clinically remarkable given how he would also vary his sexual activity across his crimes just as he would vary moving the body, dismembering the body, or burying the body. Given this variance, how many other homicides did he likely perpetrate where there is not the faintest notion Bundy was responsible?

Finally, drawing on his own horrifying sense of morality, Bundy suggested that the Riverman likely harbored qualitative distinctions about the victims based on their perceived innocence. Thus, the offender would likely talk openly and honestly about the murder of adult prostitutes, but would not talk at all about child victims, or adult victims who were not prostitutes and thus had a higher moral character. In making this point, Bundy *suggested* that a killer may have killed a dozen or so young preadolescent girls perhaps a slip of the tongue about his own offense history including his likely involvement in the case of Ann Marie Burr.

More explicitly, Bundy's sheer unwillingness to discuss his potential involvement in the Burr case is instructive about the variable level of comfort that a killer has in describing his victims. The implication is imperative: unsolved cases that are never discussed would likely forever remain unsolved. That is especially true when there is not a body.

Notes

1. Keppel and Birnes (2005, p. 319).
2. https://www.greenvilleonline.com/story/news/crime/2016/11/05/super-bike-slayings-unsolved-13-years/93377108/,   Accessed   September 23,   2021;   https://www.cbsnews.com/news/todd-kohlhepp-case-48-hours-confessions-of-a-suspected-serial-killer-buried-truth/,   Accessed September 23, 2021.
3. https://public.doc.state.sc.us/scdc-public/inmateDetails.do?id=%200 0372454, Accessed September 23, 2021.
4. *Arizona v. Kohlhepp*, CR-87-00863 (1987).
5. https://www.goupstate.com/news/20171211/serial-killer-todd-koh lhepp-claims-to-have-more-victims/1, Accessed September 23, 2021.
6. https://www.themarshallproject.org/2022/01/12/as-murders-spiked-pol ice-solved-about-half-in-2020, Accessed August 26, 2022.
7. McClelland (2007, p. 65).
8. Fox (2004).
9. Magee et al. (2020).
10. University of Chicago Crime Lab (2017).
11. Ressler et al. (1988).
12. Chan and Beauregard (2016) and Chan (2017).
13. James and Beauregard (2018).
14. Beauregard and Martineau (2014).
15. Chai et al. (2021).
16. Keppel and Birnes (2005).
17. Keppel and Birnes (2005, p. 247).
18. Keppel and Birnes (2005, p. 263).

References

Beauregard, E., & Martineau, M. (2014). No body, no crime? The role of forensic awareness in avoiding police detection in cases of sexual homicide. *Journal of Criminal Justice, 42*(2), 213–220.

Chai, A. M. M., Beauregard, E., & Chopin, J. (2021). "Drop the body": Body disposal patterns in sexual homicide. *International Journal of Offender Therapy and Comparative Criminology, 65*(6–7), 692–714.

Chan, H. C. O. (2017). Sexual homicide: A review of recent empirical evidence (2008 to 2015). In F. Brookman, E. R. Maguire, & M. Maguire (Eds.), *The handbook of homicide* (pp. 105–130). John Wiley & Sons.

Chan, H. C., & Beauregard, E. (2016). Choice of weapon or weapon of choice? Examining the interactions between victim characteristics in single-victim male sexual homicide offenders. *Journal of Investigative Psychology and Offender Profiling, 13*(1), 70–88.

Fox, J. A. (2004). Missing data problems in the SHR: Imputing offender and relationship characteristics. *Homicide Studies, 8*(3), 214–254.

James, J., & Beauregard, E. (2018). How sexual murderers thwart investigations. In J. Proulx, E. Beauregard, A. J. Carter, A. Mokros, R. Darjee, & J. James (Eds.), *Routledge international handbook of sexual homicide studies* (pp. 574–593). Routledge.

Keppel, R. D., with Birnes, W. J. (2005). *The riverman: Ted Bundy and I hunt for the Green River killer*. Pocket Books.

Magee, L. A., Fortenberry, J. D., Tu, W., & Wiehe, S. E. (2020). Neighborhood variation in unsolved homicides: A retrospective cohort study in Indianapolis, Indiana, 2007–2017. *Injury Epidemiology, 7*(1), 1–10.

McClellan, J. (2007). Unsolved homicides: What we do and do not know. *Journal of Security Education, 2*(3), 53–69.

Ressler, R. K., Burgess, A. W., & Douglas, J. E. (1988). *Sexual homicide: Patterns and motives*. The Free Press.

University of Chicago Crime Lab. (2017). *Gun violence in Chicago, 2016*. University of Chicago.

9

No Body, No Crime

Those who have been found were not, and those who haven't been found were buried.[1]

Ted Bundy

Interviewing offenders is a fascinating look at the complexity and quirks of the antisocial personality. In the course of my career, I have interviewed a few thousand offenders who span a broad range on a variety of content areas. These include "normal" people arrested for the first time to those in their mid-eighties whose arrest histories span more than a half century; people who are relatively well-adjusted to those who are profoundly mentally ill and mostly unable to complete the interview; and those who are cordial and behaviorally similar to family, friends, and neighbors to those who are disturbingly antisocial and violent, and who, if the environmental contexts were different, would think nothing of killing me.

Offender responses to being interviewed also vary greatly. First-time and lower risk offenders are generally mortified to be experiencing a criminal justice system contact and their behavior during the interview reflects that. They often cry, have numerous questions, and are highly

© The Author(s), under exclusive license to Springer Nature
Switzerland AG 2023
M. DeLisi, *Ted Bundy and The Unsolved Murder Epidemic*,
https://doi.org/10.1007/978-3-031-21418-9_9

distressed by their legal liability and perceived safety while in custody. First-time and lower risk offenders exude emotion during interviews, especially guilt, remorse, shame, and embarrassment. Chronic offenders couldn't care less about their criminal justice system status. They do not cry nor reveal any semblance of shame. Instead, recriminations are common.

Offenders also vary to a great degree in terms of their amenability to being interviewed. Some offenders belligerently refuse to participate, and their only words to me are a quick mix of profanity and threats. A handful of offenders have told me to go fuck myself. Fortunately, these occurrences are rare. For the most part, offenders are willing to talk to criminal justice practitioners, consultants, clinicians, and other investigators, but how much information they provide depends on the legal context, interview rapport, the amount of collateral information the interviewer has, and other factors. Some offenders participate in the interview but are largely distrustful and cold, and provide basically "yes or no" answers to any question. Those are not effective interviews. Those too are fortunately fairly rare.

In my experience, serious offenders including those who are clinically psychopathic are often more than willing to talk with interviewers, and Bundy was no exception as his many interviews with defense counsel, law enforcement investigators, and media figures substantiates. Although many serious offenders are eager to talk, the basic nature of their antisocial personality features renders the conversation very different than conversations between people with normal personality functioning. Psychopathic offenders like Bundy are usually highly antagonistic, they score low on all facets of the personality feature of agreeableness, and thus they are not terribly compliant with requests for information, queries about prior bad acts, or certainly quantitative estimates of their criminal history including potential murder victims.

It is common for offenders with extensive criminal history to provide dramatic underestimates of their record, for instance reporting five prior arrests compared to the fifty to one-hundred arrests that appear on their rap sheet. During the course of interviews, a frequent tactic is for the offender to provide a vague estimate of their criminal activity and then dismissively point to the large pile of papers on the desk, their criminal record, to tell the interviewer to "look it up." A certain amount of noncompliance is to be expected.

These conversations with serious offenders offer a unique perspective on the large magnitude of crime in their own lives that is unknown and undiscovered, their own personal dark figure of crime. Sitting across from me at the table, the offender is keenly aware of his life history especially involvement in the most serious forms of crime potentially including murder. But he doesn't want to tell me so what unfolds is an interpersonal exchange comprised of overt lying, minimization, refusal to discuss certain cases or crimes, refusal to acknowledge that other crimes even happened, and discomfort in discussing other crimes. In fairness to serious offenders, some of them have perpetrated so much violence there are genuine memory lapse and accumulation errors where it all runs together.

To remedy this, there are several interview strategies that can help build rapport and "free" the interview subject to provide more revealing and honest responses. First, it is important to recognize there is a natural reluctance to discuss prior acts of criminal behavior especially those involving unsolved homicides that denote substantial legal liability for the subject. Offenders also tend to be sensitive in discussing sexually oriented crimes especially those involving child victims, or other offenses that might have a sexual component to them, such as a burglary that involved voyeurism or direct sexual contact.

In the case of Samuel Little, Texas Ranger James Holland observed that Little was first and foremost a murderer, and the sexual components of his crimes, and his status as a rapist, was more sensitive to him and should be less of a discussion point. Consequently, Holland had Little focus on his murders. This subtle tact of interviewer rapport resulted in Little's confession to ninety-three murders.[2] What is remarkable is that prior to his working relationship with Texas Ranger Holland, Little had never confessed to any investigator about any of his crimes.

There are also unsatisfying features of a criminal event that are known only to the offender, and these features can lead to a refusal to discuss that specific event, but a willingness to discuss another criminal event even for the same charges. Thus, an offender might refuse to discuss one murder, but have no qualms discussing prior or subsequent murders because the latter crimes did not contain the embarrassing feature that the other crime did. Throughout his life, there were some murders that Bundy adamantly refused to discuss.

To circumvent this, I will usually tell an offender that I am interested in talking about two versions of the defendant. One of which is the prior version of the defendant that contained all of those prior crimes and the other, newer, seemingly better version where the defendant has improved behavioral functioning, that is, the person is in custody and not actively offending in the community. This strategy allows the defendant to disassociate himself from prior bad acts, and discuss them in more dispassionate and clinical manner. There is also a subtle act of manipulation on my part in doing this because I can simultaneously be praiseworthy of the offender's current functioning while also being critical of their prior conduct, and can encourage the offender to do the same. In a way, this interview strategy allows the interviewer and the interviewee to collectively examine, discuss, and analyze the interviewee's prior life and offense history. This is precisely what investigators Keppel and Reichel did with Bundy when they interviewed him about the Green River Killer case.

Second, although not all psychopathic criminals share Bundy's highly grandiose interpersonal style, many do, and this is a tremendous asset to an interviewer because those with a grandiose sense of self-worth love to talk about themselves. They have considerable pride in their life of crime. In some cases, and this too was true of Bundy, the interview subject feels that they are actually in control of the exchange of information and thus are in control of the interview. In a subtle way, I have relinquished control of the interview to an offender particularly when the offender is highly talkative and providing rich clinical information and other forensic insights into their behavioral functioning. A skilled interviewer should allow the offender's ego to take over only if it facilitates the production of valuable information.

Third, because the purpose of an interview is to gather information, it makes no sense to be antagonistic or judgmental about an offender's conduct even when that conduct is reprehensible. A neutral moral approach is best. Depending on the context of the interview, however, one must alternate between being friendly or praiseworthy of an offender, such as appearing to agree with them, to being challenging and mildly confrontational. Some examples make this clear. When interviewing offenders who have been in prison security threat groups, one can ask an individual how long they were at a particular prison facility before they had to stab another inmate. Notice the question was not "did you ever stab an inmate?" Instead, it is assumed that a highly antisocial and violent person will do this in confinement (especially when the interviewer has correctional records that substantiate such conduct), and thus the interviewer is tacitly agreeing with this behavior, or at least acknowledging that is occasionally must be done. This strategy is also exploiting the callousness of the interviewee.

Other times, an interview needs to see how the subject responds to provocation, and uttering an occasional condescending or judgmental comment will achieve this and trigger an example of how that response to provocation looks. For example, I once interviewed a defendant on federal supervision for armed bank robbery who had spent many years in the Crips street gang in Los Angeles and described to me with considerable pride a shooting where he killed two victims.

After listening to his jovial reenactment of the crime, I intensified my eye contact and in a disgusted tone asked, "If that really something to be proud of?" The offender immediately intensified his eye contact, scowled at me, and sat up straight in his chair, then, seconds later, realized where he was and calmed. Neither of us further discussed this interaction, for I already observed the information I needed.

Psychopaths are highly manipulative individuals and those who have a socially dominant interpersonal style use a range of devices to control and influence others. An example of this is their proneness for lying even when the lie is immaterial to the situation and cannot provide any benefit to them. For instance, on the night they met, Bundy told Elizabeth Kendall that he was writing a book exploring how cultural differences between Americans and the Vietnamese related to the Vietnam War. She was skeptical but considered it such a pointless and random lie that it was irrelevant to her.[3]

But a psychopath's lies are intermixed with statements that are mostly true, some minimized and some embellished, and at other times interwoven with startling acknowledgments about the offender's true offense history or graphic details of specific crimes. It is here where details of their dark figure of crime can emerge. For example, the day after his crimes in Tallahassee, Florida, Bundy talked about the crimes with other residents of The Oak residency where he was staying. After a neighbor characterized the attacks at Chi Omega and of Cheryl Thomas as the work of a lunatic, Bundy disagreed and stated that the crimes were the work of a rational, professional killer who had perpetrated these crimes previously. Bundy also indicated this "professional killer" had likely already departed the area.[4]

Unbeknownst to the neighbor, Bundy, who was using the alias Chris Hagen, had just divulged accurate criminological information about his homicide career punctuated by a false statement about leaving the area. This is why it is imperative that before interviewing an offender, the interviewer has exhaustively read the criminal history and other relevant legal documents, such as presentence investigation reports, prison records, probation and parole records, treatment data, and behavioral assessment data. A well-timed mentioning of information from the offender's legal record can alert him to the fact the interviewer is keenly aware of prior offense history and dissuade lying and other deception from going too far during the interview.

These assorted issues are apparent in Stephen Michaud and Hugh Aynesworth's death row interviews with Bundy that involved more than 150 hours of tape-recorded conversations that were featured in their books *The Only Living Witness* and *Ted Bundy: Conversations with a Killer: The Death Row Interviews*. They employed a "good cop, bad cop" strategy with Michaud adopting an understanding, at times, almost deferential tone with Bundy to encourage rapport and Aynesworth utilizing a more confrontational approach to verbally force Bundy to tell the truth (to illustrate, Bundy lied one minute into their interviews). Aynesworth in particular consistently pressed Bundy to divulge the number of total murder victims, which Bundy in turn repeatedly avoided doing or generally provided coy, deceptive answers.[5]

Their conservations also reveal the strategy of allowing Bundy to in effect distance himself from his conduct. In their initial conversations, Michaud and Aynesworth noticed that Bundy was very guarded and provided limited information about his crimes, psychopathology, or life history. To remedy this, they asked Bundy to speak about the crimes in third person as if he was an expert witness who was providing "hypothetical" information about the crimes, the offender's mindset, and other etiological factors.

The strategy worked.

Unable to keep his ego in check, and certainly challenging any notion of his prodigious intelligence since he so easily fell for the ploy, Bundy bequeathed valuable information on a range of topics that, if interpreted with a criminological lens, supports my notion that Bundy killed far earlier than 1974 and had many more victims. He repeatedly dropped hints about his unknown homicides.

During his musings about his life of crime, Bundy appears genuinely surprised and curious about the etiology of his criminal propensity and his appetite for sexual violence. He is emphatic that no specific trauma triggered his psychopathology, where the earliest evidence of it is the age 3 knife displays toward female relatives, and that for many years the condition was latent. This supports the largely genetic origin of his psychopathy since there were not the usual environmental pathogens in his rearing environment. He was naturally like this.

His inner-life involved a conflict between his developing clinical disorders and his outwardly normal personality and behavioral functioning. He insists that he only thought about sexual murder for many years before finally acting on these impulses. He is self-aware enough to report that he was socially stunted during his adolescence and did not know how to appropriately relate to others. Although Bundy shows self-awareness in providing these insights, he was probably not aware that these developmental characteristics involving a percolating compulsion to kill and undifferentiated, recurrent sadistic fantasy are fully consistent with the developmental sequela of unplanned compulsive sexual homicide offenders.[6]

Bundy is insistent that he never engaged in conduct problems during childhood and adolescence as his psychopathology was, according to him, in its latent development. However, in multiple places, often during a later span of the same interview, he discussed his engagement in various deviant behaviors including theft, prowling, pornography consumption, voyeurism, disabling the vehicles of young women to increase their vulnerability to attack, and frequent alcohol use. It is clear there is an escalation in his conduct, but Bundy is careful not to provide the time period or specific years of his antisocial development. According to Bundy, "while he may have toyed around with fantasies before and made several abortive attempts to, uh, act out a fantasy, it never reached the point where actually he was, uh, confronted with harming another individual, or taking possession or abducting or whatever—which really is ultimate, I suppose: one of the ultimate antisocial acts, as it were."[7]

This sentence is revealing because Bundy is likely both telling the truth and lying simultaneously. The use of "uh" which is linguistically known as filler is commonly an indicator of deception. Bundy had extensive fantasies about sexual violence and made abortive attempts, for instance, where he would disable the vehicles of women, but the event did not result in an abduction. At other times, his attempts to contact women were successful. The words about "taking possession or abducting" are precisely what he did, in fact Bundy refers to the act of killing as a sense of taking possession especially during his conversations with his attorney John Henry Browne.

His description of the crimes, which were specifically kidnapping, rape, and murder, as one of the ultimate antisocial acts is technically correct—these are the crimes of a sexual homicide. His use of the phrase "as it were" is an example of him attempting to add an intellectual sophistication to his personal narrative. In digesting this quotation, Bundy is likely conflating his developmental processes and his actual conduct in becoming a compulsive sexual homicide offender. Although he does not state his age during this part of his antisocial development, his description of it is consistent with the experimentation, uncertainty, and limited confidence of youth. He is clearly not describing his post-1974 conduct when he is approaching thirty years of age.

In his obtuse conversational style, Bundy describes his first attack, presumably his first murder, as a monstrous act that was inappropriate based on how spontaneous and poorly planned it was. He was unmoved by the immorality of the crime. And although he indicated a sense of revulsion about the crime, likely untrue, his real revulsion appears to have been in terms of its planning and execution. It lacked the acumen that he would come to expect when committing kidnapping, rape, and murder. On the issue of revulsion about the crime, Bundy plainly stated, "I think we'd expect a person not to feel much remorse or regret for the actual crime—or guilt in the conventional sense for the harm done to another individual."[8] That is textbook psychopathy.

Consistent with the frustrating manipulation of psychopathic offenders, Bundy would openly deny involvement in cases where it is not only incontrovertible that he did it, but also that he had already been convicted and sentenced to death. In the next breath, however, he would effectively describe in third person the precise details of other murders for which he is suspected, but had not been prosecuted. He would vacillate between offering general information about what it takes to perpetrate sexual violence and then offering specific details about the events immediately preceding, during, and after the crimes.

Although noncompliance and deception are the norms when talking with serious offenders, I have also had the rare experience of talking with criminals who had perfect photographic recall of their official criminal record coupled with frank assessments of the extent of their true criminal acts. To illustrate, one offender had seventy-eight arrests mostly for property offenses such as burglary and theft, drug violations, and occasional violent crimes including armed robbery and assault. This defendant had significant psychopathology including mild intellectual disability, polysubstance dependence, ADHD, and antisocial personality disorder. He was moderately psychopathic especially in the antisocial and lifestyle dimensions. After release from one of his many jail incarcerations, this man sadly died from anorexia nervosa, a rare condition among males.

During a pretrial bond interview with me, this defendant recalled *all* of his arrest activity including the specific criminal charges, the month and year of the event, and the legal disposition. His recall was identical to the criminal records at my disposal. As we discussed his offending career, he asked if I wanted to know about all of his arrests or all of his crimes. To him, that was an important empirical distinction.

Upon follow-up, he informed me that he committed crimes, such as theft, burglary, drug use, and drug sales on a daily basis and engaged in violent disputes involving harassment, assault, or robbery on a weekly basis. He also informed that his criminal activity was much higher during periods of homelessness when his mental health problems centering on anxiety and depression were more problematic and disabling. It was clear that his actual criminal activity was orders of magnitude higher than the criminal record in his eidetic memory even though he never used the words dark figure of crime.

Similarly, it is obvious that Bundy's official criminal record and even the normally accepted roster of activity between 1974 and 1978 is at best a mere sampling of his true criminal activity. A quick heuristic about the dark figure of crime reveals how much antisocial behavior occurs that never sees the light of day in terms of justice system intervention. The most common form of antisocial behavior, underage drinking of alcohol, is so prevalent that it is normative to engage in this behavior, and statistically speaking, abnormal to abstain from it.[9]

As alluded to in an earlier chapter, most people will consume alcohol, and consume it with regularity during middle to late adolescence and early adulthood prior to its legal threshold, which in the United States is age 21 years. Moreover, it is normative to engage in ancillary criminal actions, such as producing or using a false identification card that inflates one's age, and purchasing alcohol under age.

Among active offenders, the magnitude of the dark figure of crime is more substantial because the criminal population engages in far more, and far more serious offenses than underage drinking, and criminological examples reveal how much sexual violence and homicides occur that never appear on official crime records. Studies of institutionalized youth, for instance, reveal that offenders report dozens to even hundreds of serious offenses for every time they are arrested. The most prolific offenders report hundreds of crimes for every arrest.[10]

In the federal criminal justice system, a common conviction offense is possession or receipt of child pornography that is usually punished by a sentence to the Bureau of Prisons followed by a term of supervised release in the community. Relative to other types of sexual offenders, such as rapists, child pornography offenders have generally higher socioeconomic status and limited criminal history. Many of these offenders have no official adult criminal record, similar to Bundy before his arrest in Utah in 1975.

A condition of their supervised release involves treatment and one of the modalities includes the use of polygraphed interviews to measure the offender's sexual history. These interviews indicate not only far more evidence of criminal activity, but also substantial evidence of prior contact sexual offending, such as rape, sodomy, and oral copulation. Approximately seventy percent of federal sexual offenders report prior contact victims, and the number of victims is occasionally as high as forty.

Importantly, these data indicate the number of previous contact victims, and do not capture the actual number of sexual crime events that were perpetrated against these victims, which sometimes number in the hundreds to thousands. For child pornography possession cases, nearly sixty percent have reported a prior contact sexual offense against a child when their official record indicates zero prior criminal acts.[11] Sexual offenders engage in exponentially more sexual aggression than their official records indicate, and the majority of sexual violence is never reported or detected.

The dark figure of crime also pertains to homicide offending. In prior research and practitioner roles, I have interacted with offenders who have multiple police contacts for murder, in some cases as many as five separate killings, but were never formally charged for these crimes because of limited evidence, poor cooperation from eyewitnesses, and the ambiguity of whether the homicide was effectively self-defense. In almost all of these cases, the offender had murdered another active offender during the midst of ongoing criminal activity.

In other cases, during a forensic interview, an offender reported to me his involvement in more than ten homicide offenses that occurred in prison settings, again, none of these crimes resulted in convictions. The actual occurrence of these homicides is documented, but again, offenders can avoid legal liability due to acquittals, lack of cooperation from eyewitnesses or sharply conflicting statements about details of the murder, and other sentencing factors, such as whether the inmate was already serving a life sentence. However, the discussion of his homicide offending also contained nebulous statements which intimated that he had killed frequently while also not explicitly stating so. Comments including "I've been around a lot of murders," "There were lots of killings in my facility," or "Several inmates were killed where I served time" are examples of this. He also told correctional staff that he was unwilling to discuss the numerous murders and orders to murder that he got away with during his life.[12]

All crimes, not just sexual and homicide offenses, illustrate the dark figure of crime where the true incidence of offending has a much earlier beginning, or onset, a much longer duration, or career span, and involves many more offenses, or frequency. Estimates vary across studies and depending on which type of criminal behavior is being studied, but the ratio of actual crimes to convictions can range from 10:1 to 50:1 or even higher.[13] In the case of underage drinking among professional audiences, the ratio is hundreds or thousands to zero.

Bundy admits to his interviewers that much of his normal life had to be rescheduled, postponed, changed, or simply skipped because he was spending so much time at night prowling for women to victimize. Although he does not ascribe specific dates or periods of his life to his antisocial development, Bundy describes a sort of psychic competition that existed between the normal parts of his personality and the antisocial features of his psychopathology. His earliest murders of a male contemporary or Ann Marie Burr derailed his social adjustment, but Bundy was at least able to maintain his educational progress enough to complete high school on time. Based on his lack of success in behavioral functioning after graduation from high school, it appears that Bundy was consistently losing his internal struggle against his antisocial drives as early as 1965.

Although his revelations to Michaud and Aynesworth were in third person to facilitate the juvenile pretense that he was not talking about himself, Bundy recurrently gave detailed accounts of the forensic awareness and fluid modus operandi that an offender like him would display. Bundy assiduously read the newspaper to monitor the status of police investigations of missing women whom he had murdered, and gauged the overall police and public reaction to the case. In the event the reaction to the case was moderate or high, Bundy would make alterations in his offense conduct, or simply move out of state, to portray that a different offender was at large.

The other critical issue was whether the body of the missing woman was found. According to Bundy, "one of the principal things in arousing the public and the police was the discovering of the body. And if you *had* no body, then essentially you didn't…you're eliminating a moving force behind the police investigation."[14] Bundy accomplished the no body scenario in multiple ways. Some of his victims were transported hundreds of miles after their initial abduction and sexual assault only to be sexually assaulted again, murdered, and dumped, such as at the Taylor Mountain site in Issaquah, Washington. Some of his victims were murdered and taken to dump site expressly because Bundy would return and engage in sexual activity with the corpse.

In his final conversations with Keppel just prior to his execution, Bundy offered several revelatory comments which indicated that the "no body, no crime" philosophy was far more prevalent in his offense history than law enforcement investigators knew. As the chapter opening quotation indicates, there are untold numbers of Bundy's victims who have never been, and likely will never be found because they were buried. When Keppel pressed Bundy about how many victims were buried, he replied that he was unsure, that he did not know their names, and that there were simply too many to remember. Bundy also admitted that he kept a hacksaw and a small military-style shovel in his car to use for the dismemberment and burials.

Later, during conversations with Keppel and Colorado police investigator Matt Lindvall who was there to question Bundy about outstanding murder cases in his state, Bundy suggested, "Because in every case where a woman was buried, there's no body to be found." When Lindvall responded by asking if there were other people buried in Colorado, Bundy responded with an emphatic, "Well, yeah."[15]

Lindvall queried Bundy about the Colorado cases where the victim's body was found and thus unburied, to which Bundy advised that when he was perpetrating murder, he was never an "automaton," and would mix up the ways that he killed and responded to the victim's body.

Although he was mostly evasive with Lindvall, Bundy later admitted there are additional buried remains in Colorado and also indicated there are undiscovered dump sites with other bodies."[16]

Still another approach, likely far more prevalent, involved Bundy targeting a woman on the open road, making contact and perpetrating a sexual homicide, and randomly disposing of the body. Both scenarios highlight the extraordinary mobility that he exhibited traveling across the United States. It is likely during the early and middle stages of his homicide career, far before the official 1974–1978 period, that Bundy was careful to not allow authorities to discover a body given its salience to a police investigation. During this phase of his murder career on the open roads, he was less confident, more careful, and more painstakingly ensured that no bodies would ever be found.

Complicating matters further was the dynamic modus operandi that Bundy would employ throughout his criminal career, a level of complexity and criminal sophistication that set him apart from other homicide offenders who transport bodies. For instance, a study of more than five-hundred murder cases some of which involved body transport and others that did not reveal numerous differences in terms of their offense behavior. Murderers who transport bodies usually engage in more preplanning, gag, blindfold, and strike the victim, are more likely to use a blunt instrument or strangulation, are less likely to use a sharp-bladed weapon, steal property, commit the murder in the vehicle, and destroy evidence.[17] Bundy mixed these actions during his murders, and, of additional importance, engaged in both body transportation and killing at the scene with no body removal.

In traversing the country and murdering young women whom he contacted along the way, Bundy was also displaying a certain amount of contempt for the societal unraveling of the 1960s and 1970s, a cultural breakdown that provided him so many opportunities for violence. According to Bundy, "as the culture declines, as people are cut loose and don't know what to do, they are floating around without the protection of the family, without protection of experience, tradition or anything. They become more vulnerable to people who want to exploit them."[18]

Bundy's contempt for the changes to American society emanates from multiple places. First, he was ideologically conservative and the vast changes to the social framework of the United States with their down-stream consequences on social institutions, including the family, likely annoyed him. In the aforementioned quotation, he refers to American culture as one that is in decline. Second, Bundy probably harbored resentment toward the women he picked up along the way who led a free, winsome, socially engaged, and adventurous life which stood in sharp contrast to his insecurity and ineptitude about his own functioning. Third and likely most importantly, Bundy seethed with homicidal thoughts and sexually sadistic fantasies that provided dysphoric and highly contemptuous fuel for the women he would murder.

Of the two media death row interviewers, Aynesworth is the more insistent about obtaining a total count of victims, to which Bundy consistently deflects, refuses, or offers a verbose but superficial explanation. Aynesworth presses Bundy about the likelihood that there are numerous homicide victims who have not been discovered, and potentially never will be. In turn, Bundy indicates there is a distinct possibility of numerous unknown victims and explicitly mentions hitchhiking as the means by which an offender could murder, virtually at will, without producing a body, and thus avoiding detection.[19]

During his death row conversations with Michaud and Aynesworth, Bundy employs a variety of vocabulary terms that have criminological and forensic importance, including accurate references to his own psychopathology as "psychopathology." In all of my conversations with criminal offenders of all kinds, none has ever used the word psychopathology, let alone refer to their own constellation of traits, symptoms, and conditions as such. And although Bundy did not spout off a list of conditions that he had, for instance, Bundy angrily disputed that he was a psychopath or that he met diagnostic criteria for antisocial personality disorder,[20] I have the deep sense that Bundy was well aware of how pathological his conditions were and that those conditions drove criminal conduct that was far more prevalent than anyone knew.

His knowledge about the depths of his homicidal and paraphilic drives and the full extent of his horrendous character gives me confidence that the information he provided to interviewers was his annoying and smug way to provide clues about his true murder count without actually doing so. Although Bundy usually would not answer Aynesworth directly, he did so indirectly particularly if one reads between the lines. Without using these precise words, Bundy was talking about the dark figure of his homicide offending.

Research on the dark figure of crime acknowledges that most crimes do not result in arrest because they are perpetrated in clandestine ways, are perpetrated in remote locations away from onlookers or potential witnesses, or are perpetrated in social contexts where the victim does not construe the event as a crime until it is too late. All of these conditions comport perfectly with Bundy's life history at least from 1965 onward as he traveled the country and as he meticulously found remote locations to perpetrate his crimes.

He was accustomed to taking women to the middle of nowhere where onlookers were nonexistent and the risk of detection was low. He grew increasingly comfortable and confident picking up young females who were hitchhiking toward greener pastures, many of whom likely were enjoying playful and flirty banter and were pleased to have found a ride from a nice, handsome, affable stranger—until they were rendered unconscious by a blow to the head. Throughout his interviews, he recurrently discussed hitchhikers, talked about the salience of a no body scenario to a missing person or homicide investigation, and speculated about bodies in ditches that will never be found. He was coyly giving it all away without saying so.

Regarding the various occasions where Bundy admitted that he killed more than one-hundred victims, skeptics would likely suggest this was hyperbole, another outrageous lie in the Bundy folder of deception. Indeed, that is true to his psychopathic nature. However, I view Bundy's one-hundred victim admissions as rare but truthful statements that reveal his psychopathic features in a different manner but one that cuts its sinister nature closer to the bone.

By telling his defense attorney Browne, law enforcement official in Florida, or journalists Michaud and Aynesworth that he killed "three digits," Bundy was able to thumb his nose at a society and the criminal justice systems that for many years were powerless to stop him. An honest admission of murdering that many people showed his grandiosity, his contempt, and his defiance toward the justice system, which he knew would never be able to locate all of the victims scattered across the United States.

He knew because so many of those girls and women were decomposing in bodies of water, were dismembered and could never be found, were already consumed by animals, or were lost to the degradation of weather and time. Moreover, Bundy knew that most of those victims, seventy percent or so according to my estimation, were killed on the open roads and are not even believed to be missing, let alone dead.

To Bundy: no body, no crime.

Something that he only told Robert Keppel before his execution was that burial also played a major role in his homicidal behavior. The world of homicide victims, whether confirmed or speculated, that we know about Ted Bundy are only those who have been found above ground. There is effectively another world of his murder victims underground whom Bundy is confident will never be located.

Ever so contemptuous and manipulative, Ted Bundy would play with journalists and law enforcement investigators for the rest of his life, which ended on January 24, 1989 with his electrocution while a carnival-like spectacle of retributive celebration raged outside of the Florida State Prison. In his cajoling and insincere matter, he would provide piecemeal information to potentially help to resolve cases, deny his involvement in many other cases, offer mealy mouthed confessions, but never fully accept responsibility for his crimes or take ownership of his reprehensible behavior. He did this not only because he was a despicable psychopath, but also because he knew that his tried and true no body, no crime modus operandi and his widespread use of burial would forever keep most of his murder cases in the unsolved ledger.

Notes

1. Keppel and Birnes (2005, pp. 381–382).
2. https://www.cbsnews.com/news/serial-killer-samuel-little-60-minutes-2020-09-06/, Accessed October 7, 2021.
3. Kendall (2020, p. 11).
4. *Bundy v. State*, 455 So. 2d 330 (1984).

5. Michaud and Aynesworth (2019, p. 51).
6. Schlesinger (2007).
7. Michaud and Aynesworth (2019, p. 74).
8. Michaud and Aynesworth (2019, p. 94).
9. Moffitt (1993).
10. Minkler et al. (2022).
11. DeLisi et al. (2016), Drury et al. (2020), and Scurich and John (2019).
12. DeLisi et al. (2021).
13. Farrington et al. (2014), Theobald et al. (2014), Bouchard and Lussier (2015), and Mathesius and Lussier (2014).
14. Michaud and Aynesworth (2019, p. 85, italics in original).
15. Keppel and Birnes (2005, p. 410).
16. Keppel and Birnes (2005, p. 412).
17. Lee and Park (2019).
18. Michaud and Aynesworth (2019, p. 124).
19. Michaud and Aynesworth (2019, p. 207).
20. Michaud and Aynesworth (2019, p. 227).

References

Bouchard, M., & Lussier, P. (2015). Estimating the size of the sexual aggressor population. In A. Blokland & P. Lussier (Eds.), *Sex offenders: A criminal career approach* (pp. 351–371). John Wiley & Sons.

Bundy v. State, 455 So.2d 330 (1984).

DeLisi, M., Caropreso, D. E., Drury, A. J., Elbert, M. J., Evans, J. L., Heinrichs, T., & Tahja, K. M. (2016). The dark figure of sexual offending: New evidence from federal sex offenders. *Journal of Criminal Psychology, 6*(1), 3–16.

DeLisi, M., Drury, A. J., & Elbert, M. J. (2021). Psychopathy and pathological violence in a criminal career: A forensic case report. *Aggression and Violent Behavior, 60,* 101521.

Drury, A. J., Elbert, M. J., & DeLisi, M. (2020). The dark figure of sexual offending: A replication and extension. *Behavioral Sciences & the Law, 38*(6), 559–570.

Farrington, D. P., Ttofi, M. M., Crago, R. V., & Coid, J. W. (2014). Prevalence, frequency, onset, desistance and criminal career duration in self-reports compared with official records. *Criminal Behaviour and Mental Health, 24*(4), 241–253.

Kendall, E., with a contribution from Molly Kendall. (2020). *The phantom prince: My life with Ted Bundy* (updated and expanded edition). Abrams Press.

Keppel, R. D., with Birnes, W. J. (2005). *The riverman: Ted Bundy and I hunt for the Green River killer*. Pocket Books.

Lee, S. J., & Park, J. (2019). Body transportation after homicides: Offender and offense characteristics. *Journal of Forensic Sciences, 64*(4), 1092–1095.

Mathesius, J., & Lussier, P. (2014). The successful onset of sex offending: Determining the correlates of actual and official onset of sex offending. *Journal of Criminal Justice, 42*(2), 134–144.

Michaud, S. G., & Aynesworth, H. (2019). *Ted Bundy: Conservations with a killer: The death row interviews*. Sterling.

Minkler, M., Bonner, T., DeLisi, M., Pechorro, P., & Vaughn, M. G. (2022). The dark figure of delinquency: New evidence and its underlying psychopathology. *Youth Violence and Juvenile Justice, 20*(4), 279–291.

Moffitt, T. E. (1993). Adolescence-limited and life-course-persistent antisocial behavior: A developmental taxonomy. *Psychological Review, 100*(4), 674–701.

Schlesinger, L. B. (2007). Sexual homicide: Differentiating catathymic and compulsive murders. *Aggression and Violent Behavior, 12*(2), 242–256.

Scurich, N., & John, R. S. (2019). The dark figure of sexual recidivism. *Behavioral Sciences & the Law, 37*(2), 158–175.

Theobald, D., Farrington, D. P., Loeber, R., Pardini, D. A., & Piquero, A. R. (2014). Scaling up from convictions to self-reported offending. *Criminal Behaviour and Mental Health, 24*(4), 265–276.

10

What Would Have to Be True?

And it advises me about women, women that I would see in the streets, in a very hateful manner, in a very angry, in a very malicious manner. 'Look at that bitch there. Do this and this and this, or whatever.'[1]
Ted Bundy

Although I have interviewed thousands of offenders during the course of my criminological career, I have interacted with several thousand more criminal histories, presentence investigation reports, legal affidavits, treatment reports, correctional files, and other criminal justice documents. Depending on the nature of my role with the offender, such as primary examiner on a criminal or civil case, researcher, or practitioner, and depending on the seriousness of their criminal career, some cases involve hundreds and even thousands of pages of legal and behavioral information. Some offenders have so much criminal history and associated legal documents that it takes an hour or two to print it. In my researcher experiences on large correctional projects with the federal criminal justice system, for instance, the data collection process can take one or two years to complete. One can really get to know another person by reading all of their paper.

© The Author(s), under exclusive license to Springer Nature
Switzerland AG 2023
M. DeLisi, *Ted Bundy and The Unsolved Murder Epidemic*,
https://doi.org/10.1007/978-3-031-21418-9_10

One of the strongest themes to emerge from reading extensive documentation of offenders' lives is the role that stability plays in their behavioral development. A profitable way to think about behavioral stability is to locate a person on a distribution of some variable, such as criminal propensity. At the left tail of the criminal propensity distribution are people who have very low criminal propensity and consequently very low likelihood of engaging in antisocial behavior. At the center of the distribution is the mean on criminal propensity where people usually engage in commensurately average amounts of antisocial behavior. At the right tail of the criminal propensity distribution, several standard deviations above the mean, are the most serious criminal offenders, people like Samuel Little, Rodney Alcala, Todd Kohlhepp, and Ted Bundy.

As a general rule, one tends to keep their general placement on a distribution, whether low, average, or high, such that, to continue with the example of criminal propensity, a person with very high criminal propensity will always be more criminally involved than a person with very low criminal propensity. In this example, although stability is consistently stable, or absolute, it is also true that criminal behavior develops along a meandering developmental course. It does not unfold in a perfectly linear fashion where one form of behavior precisely predates another which in turn precisely predates another. There is a considerable amount of randomness and intermittency to criminal careers. This was especially true of the offending careers profiled in this book.

Within the developmental pathways of a criminal career, there are also multiple types of continuity, one where the same behaviors or conditions are seen across time and thus are predictive of each other, known as homotypic continuity, and another where similar but different behaviors or conditions are seen across time and are related but not necessarily predictive, known as heterotypic continuity. For example, clinical depression during adolescence progressing to clinical depression during adulthood indicates homotypic continuity. Fussiness and the "blues" during childhood and the development of generalized anxiety disorder during adulthood indicate heterotypic continuity.

A critical point to recognize, however, is that regardless of whether a behavior or condition exhibits homotypic or heterotypic continuity across time, the behaviors or conditions often have a similar connotation, valence, or tone across developmental periods. In the above example, fussiness, suggesting emotional reactivity, having the blues, suggesting low-grade depressive feelings, and generalized anxiety disorder all are part of the anxiety/depression spectrum. Although distinct conditions, they are substantively similar and seem like cousins in terms of their emotional valence.

A similar kind of developmental commonality occurs for behavioral disorders where individuals exhibit difficult-to-manage temperaments, oppositional and defiant symptoms, and antisocial traits.[2] In many cases, the evidence for the continuity is seen in overt contacts by the juvenile and criminal justice systems, but at other times, absent police contacts and court interventions, behavioral disorders are inferred from ominous behavioral red flags that never activated police attention, were never reported, or were undiscovered. This is where the dark figure of crime begins in the lives of the worst offenders: numerous aggressive and frankly predatory acts where the damage to victims is all the more glaring because justice is never achieved.

Among most serious and violent offenders, the behavioral stability plays out along the lines of a very familiar life narrative, one I have read thousands of times on paper and seen directly during forensic interviews. The typical profile involves a boy who has conduct problems, is highly aggressive, and struggles with regulating his emotions and behavioral responses to the environment. Although this profile occurs among females, the conduct is not as extreme and it is overwhelmingly more common in males.

Already by early elementary school, the boy is discrepant from his peers in terms of his ability to regulate his conduct, runs afoul of school rules, and recurrently causes problems for teachers, other children, and staff. Because they grow tired of dealing with the young boy's unpredictable conduct and labile mood, other children tend to reject him in favor of appropriately behaved children. Everyone who has contact with this boy can readily identify his conduct problems, which are likely rising to the level of clinical impairment.

Due to limitations in his ability to appreciate how his conduct affects others, the peer rejection and frequent sanctioning from adults strike the boy as unfair, and he cultivates feelings of rejection, persecution, and fatalism which serve to make him feel better while also providing a rationalization for his continued behavior problems. As these behavioral problems persist, they also negatively impact school functioning, social functioning, and later, work functioning. Ineluctably, the boy's conduct results in justice system intervention, which further removes him from the confines of normal socialization and pushes him further down the road of chronic delinquency and justice system involvement. This is the modal background of a serious criminal offender. It is the profile of offenders like Samuel Little and Todd Kohlhepp, whose clinically remarkable conduct problems resulted in deep-end juvenile justice placements that were just the start of their life of crime.

A unique feature of Ted Bundy's life, one not commonly seen in an offender who perpetrates so many extraordinarily violent felonies, is that his childhood and adolescence were largely devoid of the overt conduct problems that engender police, court, and correctional reaction. That fact is highly unusual. Just like he compartmentalized his sexual homicides from the world for so long, the young Ted Bundy did not reveal his true self for the most part, but, because it was so pathological, it nevertheless occasionally broke through.

It broke through as early as age three years with the knife displays around his sleeping female relatives.

It broke through with the sudden spasms of violence where he would hit playmates with sticks as his blue eyes transitioned to a blackened hue.

It broke through with his lifelong compulsion to steal.

It broke through when he pulled mice apart in the woods, callously deciding which ones could live and which ones from his cruel and heartless perspective had to die.

The age three knife event is so important. At the time, his behavior appeared strange, unsettling, and bizarre, and to his family likely seemed out of character for a young boy who by all outward appearances was fairly normal in his conduct. He wasn't. The age three knife display was not an aberration, it was a totally transparent glimpse into what the young Bundy was thinking, what he wanted to be doing, and it is phenotypically consistent with the sexual violence he inflicted across the remainder of his life.

The imagination of a man's heart is evil from his youth.[3]

What also broke through during Bundy's childhood was his growing realization that he was very different from other people, and so he had to pretend all those years to hide from them who he truly was. He had friends and engaged in traditional leisure and academic activities for boys in 1950s America, but it was superficial, pretending, and fake. It was all a lie. The childhood Ted Bundy could go through the motions of who a young boy should be and what he should do because it was necessary to provide social cover for his nascent psychopathy and sexual sadism.

He came to realize that he really didn't have much connection to other people, something that upset his own sense of vanity and self-importance, but otherwise he did not care. When it came to other people, he did not care about much. But he was adept at talking and could manipulate people into doing what he wanted, and thus he related to others as if they were objects to be controlled, not people to get to know. He had far horizons about his value as a person and his potential for achievement, but he was shy, felt inferior, and seemed out of sorts, thus he was always in internal conflict.

Although he was generally well-behaved during childhood, at least in comparison to a chronic juvenile delinquent who is repeatedly placed into custody or one who is adjudicated for a serious felony, like Little and Kohlhepp, there was evidence of childhood misbehavior. Some of that misbehavior involved the consumption of pornography. Ted Bundy liked the naked bodies of young women in that pornography, but he liked other things too.

He liked women in bondage, he liked women in pain, he liked when the sex had a violent edge to it. When he was older and more resourceful, he particularly liked crime scene photographs of women who had been killed, who had been raped, who had been beaten, who had been strangled. As he told the investigative journalists while he was on death row, his sadistic fantasies and compulsion to kill were present very early and developed for years. He feasted on those fantasies for years.

Sooner than later, Bundy had to put his fantasies into behavioral motion, and by his own admission his first murder was of another young child, a boy, with whom Bundy was engaged in a sexual exploration game in the woods. Although he did not provide specific dates to his defense lawyer—and he *never* provided dates so he could hide all of the undiscovered homicides from investigators—this event occurred in approximately 1959 or 1960.

In 1961, Bundy very likely lured Ann Marie Burr from her home and killed her. If we trust Dr. Carlisle's correctional assessment of Bundy in 1976, and I do, the Burr murder was the signal event in his adolescence that distorted his social adjustment for the rest of his life. With that killing, he experienced an existential crisis about who he was and what his life's work would become.

Bundy's compartmentalization of his psychopathology and later sexual violence is a microcosm of the dark figure of crime as a whole and more specifically of the multitude of unsolved murders in the United States. For most of his life, he was hidden. He was hidden in what he refused to reveal about his innermost thoughts and desires. He was hidden about his travel and where he had been. And while he was hidden, Bundy never had an alibi and his location always seemed to correspond with the disappearance of young women, the majority of whom were never seen again, alive or dead.

A more overt criminal with greater arrest and prison history, much of Rodney Alcala's life was hidden too. Although it is known that he traversed the United States during the halcyon middle to late decades of the twentieth century, many segments of his life are also a mystery. Despite his multiple convictions for murder and other predatory crimes, we are left to imagine what he was doing for most of his criminal career. The cache of photographs he possessed is an important clue, and likely represents at least some of the other missing persons whom he killed. Alcala's creepy, malevolent conduct toward investigators just prior to his death is another clue.

After a lifetime of living in the shadows, Samuel Little finally provided investigators with graphic details of what a lifetime of murder looks like, and how unsolved murders accumulate over time. Preying on highly vulnerable women and thriving on remote locations in the middle of the night, his final confessions will hopefully provide final legal resolution to ninety-three unsolved murder cases. But there is at least a quarter of a million or more to go.

Of the notorious offenders repeatedly discussed in this book, Little, Alcala, and Bundy are deceased, and for the most part, they kept their homicidal secret to themselves to the very end. Todd Kohlhepp is still alive, wants to talk, and has suggested his victim count is also extensive. He too can likely reduce the total of unsolved murders.

Another strong theme in reading thousands of pages of criminal records and biographical accounts of the lives of serious criminal offenders is the frequency with which they engage in antisocial behavior. Disease and disability never take a day off, and an offender with multiple clinical disorders and incomparably high psychopathology engages in problematic behavior on a daily basis. As a result, their lives are a nihilistic campaign of violence, defiance, and self-destructiveness. As a former career criminal told me, "I was 100 mph all the time, and didn't give a fuck about you, me, anyone, or anything. You wouldn't believe all the shit I did, those records don't even tell the half of it."

Frequency of crime doesn't tell half of it about Ted Bundy either. He was compulsively driven by his sexual fantasies, and sexual motivation is something not often known for its temperance and delayed time horizon. Despite the pernicious antisocial nature of his personality functioning, Bundy was also paradoxically rather conscientious especially in terms of deliberation, competence, and achievement striving, unfortunately all of these usually positive personality features related to his pace of murder.

Once his appetite for sexual violence was whet around age twelve, thirteen, or fourteen, the preponderance of his time was spent peeping, stalking, observing, and later, driving. It was thousands of miles across the United States, hours upon hours at a time, across jurisdictional and state lines, and a stack of gas receipts an inch or two thick; so much frequency.

Referring back to the timeline chapter, beginning with assault and rape of Joni Lenz on January 4, 1974 and concluding with the abduction, sexual assault, and murder of Kimberly Leach on February 9, 1978, the following list is the number of elapsed days between Bundy murders and attempted murders during the "official" 1974 to 1978 offending period:

- 28 (Healy)
- 42 (Manson)

- 42 (Rancourt)
- 19 (Parks)
- 26 (Ball)
- 10 (Hawkins)
- 20 (Weaver)
- 13 (Ott)
- 0 (Naslund)
- 19 (Valenzuela)
- 0 (Unidentified woman)
- 60 (Wilcox)
- 16 (Smith)
- 13 (Aimee/Aime)
- 8 (DaRonch)
- 0 (Kent)
- 60 (Campbell)
- 60 (Cunningham)
- 22 (Oliverson)
- 9 (Cooley)
- 21 (Culver)
- 60 (Curtis)
- 3 (Robertson/Robinson)
- 3 (Baird)
- 14 (Levy)
- 0 (Bowman)
- 0 (Kleiner)
- 0 (Thomas)
- 0 (Chandler)
- 25 (Leach).

After years of carefully following his "no body, no crime" philosophy, which had begun with Ann Marie Burr or even earlier with the young male victim, and preying on young women along the nation's highways during a winsome and nostalgic period of American history, he had switched gears. For the most part, the thorough destruction or simple burial of his victims' bodies was no longer his modus operandi. These data show the frequency of a psychopathic sexual murderer at the pinnacle of his criminal career, a period when he had relinquished any pretense of living a normal life and where he was so confident in his ability to kidnap, rape, and murder with virtual impunity that he longer worried if the body of the victim was left at the scene or discovered later at a dump site.

Now consider the distances between these murders and attempted murders. Bundy traveled 107 miles from the Manson crimes to the Rancourt crimes, 303 miles from the Rancourt crimes to the Parks crimes, 250 miles from the Parks crimes to the Ball crimes, 10 miles from the Ball crimes to the Hawkins crimes, 830 miles from the Hawkins crimes to the Weaver crimes, 814 miles from the Weaver crimes to the Ott crimes, and 0 miles from the Ott crimes to the Naslund crimes.

He traveled 180 miles from the Naslund crimes to the Valenzuela crimes, 0 miles from the Valenzuela crimes to the unidentified woman's crimes, 761 miles from those crimes to the Wilcox crimes, 9 miles from the Wilcox crimes to the Smith crimes, 19 miles from the Smith crimes to the Aimee/Aime crimes, 21 miles from the Aimee/Aime crimes to the DaRonch crimes, and 18 miles from the DaRonch crimes to the Kent crimes.

Bundy drove 405 miles from the Kent crimes to the Campbell crimes, 87 miles from the Campbell crimes to the Cunningham crimes, 147 miles from the Cunningham crimes to the Oliverson crimes, 242 miles from the Oliverson crimes to the Cooley crimes, 581 miles from the Cooley crimes to the Culver crimes, 206 miles from the Culver crimes to the Curtis crimes, 473 miles from the Curtis crimes to the Robertson/Robinson crimes, 517 miles from the Robertson/Robinson crimes to the Baird crimes, and 1744 miles from the Baird crimes to the attacks of five women in Tallahassee. Finally, Bundy traveled 106 miles from the Florida State crimes to the Leach crimes.

These mileage estimates are the driving distance between the cities, they do not necessarily represent the actual driving distance which would be even greater when considering all of Bundy's reconnaissance for dump sites. In total, the conservative travel distance is 7770 miles during the 1974 to 1978 murder period. To put this into perspective, Interstate 80 is 3527 miles from the Atlantic Ocean to the Pacific Ocean. Thus, Bundy's conservative driving distance just during his official murder career is further than driving entirely across the United States, twice.

These distances are also gross underestimates when other facts are considered, many of which Bundy divulged. After his final escape from Colorado, Bundy traveled to Chicago, then Ann Arbor, then Atlanta before arriving in Tallahassee. Bundy told his attorney Browne that he selected a young woman to murder during his time in Ann Arbor, but decided against it. To take him at his word, he would have decided against it during a period of flight when Bundy described himself as bestial and highly energized to commit sexual violence. How many hitch-hiking females would he have seen while traveling across the Midwest and Southern United States in January 1978, and how many of them were contacted never to be seen again? How many women during this time disappeared?

There are documented eyewitness accounts from women who Bundy approached prior to the Rancourt crimes and on the day of the Ott and Naslund crimes suggesting that he was constantly approaching women during this era with a confidence and swagger that could only have been borne from years of murdering in a more cautious and discrete manner on the open roads. He wasn't just hunting on a daily basis, he was hunting on an hourly basis.

In the twenty-five days between the Chandler crimes and the Leach crimes, the driving distance between Tallahassee, Florida and Lake City, Florida is 106 miles. We know that Bundy filled his car with three tanks of gas just prior to the Leach crimes. To use the infamous 1968 Volk-swagen Beetle as an example, the car has a ten-gallon gas tank and gets about thirty-five miles per gallon. A tank of gas provides 350 miles of driving distance. Bundy used enough gas to drive about 1050 miles. We also know that he contacted Leslie Parmenter in Jacksonville, Florida but was foiled in his attempt to kidnap her on the day before the abduction of Leach. Jacksonville, Florida and Lake City, Florida are 61 miles apart. Where was he going and what was he doing to justify enough gas to travel more than one thousand miles?

Of the thirty victims on this list during his official offending career of 1974 to 1978, the most frequent number of elapsed days between crimes is zero. The mode is a measure of central tendency which tells the most frequently occurring amount or value of a variable. This means that based on these data, Ted Bundy was raping and murdering on a daily basis. That is not the crime pace of a novice, experimental offender, but someone who has been perpetrating these crimes for many years.

What factors would have to be true for Ted Bundy's criminal career to begin in January 1974, at age 27, with the assault of Lenz, conclude in February 1978 with the killing of Leach, and be limited to the crimes in between?

Despite the robust effects of clinical disorders on behavior and the powerful association between psychopathy and the most serious forms of crime, such as sexual homicide,[4] Bundy nevertheless would have had to abstain from criminal activity for nearly three decades. He would have abstained from criminal activity and perpetrated other murders despite being in the 97th to 100th percentile on the Psychopathy Checklist-Revised according to my assessment, and despite receiving psychopathy diagnoses or being described as significantly psychopathic by Drs. Cleckley, Carlisle, Tanay, and Otnow Lewis, clinicians who worked directly with him. The embodiment of the most virulent construct in psychiatry and criminology relating to antisocial behavior would have been on ice for nearly 30 years before its emergence. This is so forensically improbable that it borders on impossible.

Psychopathy was not Ted Bundy's only problem. There was also the sexual sadism disorder, necrophilia, biastophilia, pedohebophilia, and homicidal ideation all of which were as essential to Bundy's sexual interests, sexual motivation, and sexual tastes as normative sexual behavior is to a healthy adult who does not have paraphilic disorders. Most healthy, prosocial individuals with conventional sexual motivation do not abstain from sexual activity until age 27.

Why would Bundy?

Suggesting that he did would mean that Bundy would have had to completely mute and nullify the deviant sexual drives that, as the chapter opening quotation indicates, involve the targeting of women for criminal violence. The "do this and this and this, or whatever" in the quotation likely equates to kidnap, rape, murder, and necrophilia. How realistic is it that these behaviors were inert until January 1974? How plausible is it that a serial murderer would live as an ascetic for three decades?

Given his academic ability and socioeconomic motivation, both of which were more than adequate to facilitate the completion of a university degree, why did someone who graduated from high school in 1965 not graduate from university with his age contemporaries in 1969? Why did that graduation get delayed until 1972 when there is not any substantive reason for the delay? Aside from attending multiple universities in multiple states, what was Ted Bundy doing between 1965 and 1974? What incredibly time and travel intensive activity, one that was carefully hidden from others, was going on to explain Bundy's arrested development?

Several additional factors would have to be true for Bundy's crimes to be limited to the 1974 to 1978 period. Bundy's overwrought admission to John Henry Browne that his first murder was of another boy during late childhood or early adolescence would have to be a fabrication, as would his confession to Browne that he murdered at least one-hundred victims, and that he murdered multiple times in states where authorities at the time had no suspicion that he had even traveled to.

Bundy's acknowledgment to law enforcement officials in Florida that he murdered three digits of victims, something that he reiterated to journalists while on death row would have to be an exaggeration. All of his death row confessions to cases beyond this time period would have to be false even when they included details that were specific to the actual offense and only the killer would know. Bundy's comments to FBI Special Agent Hagmaier that his early murders were impulsive and poorly executed relative to his "prime predator" phase beginning in 1974 would also have to be untrue as would the implication that he was comparing his official murders to other murders from earlier in his life.

His apoplectic reaction to Ann Marie Burr's disappearance during his conversations with Carlisle, Keppel, Reichert, Michaud, and Aynesworth, and his strenuous denial that he had any involvement in her disappearance would have to be taken at face value even though Bundy offered numerous unconvincing lies about the case. Ann Rule's anecdotes regarding Burr's father seeing Bundy at the likely burial site on the day of her disappearance and the unsolicited contact from a schoolmate of Bundy's who claims that he asked her if she wanted to see where he had buried a body years ago would also have to be false.

Bundy's response to Elizabeth Kendall that the murder onset year of 1969 was years off from the truth—as in way too late—would have to be an inaccuracy. The various incidents that Kendall experienced between 1969 and 1974, including discovering Ted moving stealthily in the hallway to retrieve a crowbar that he hid underneath a radiator along with the unexplained surgical gloves in his pockets, the presence of meat cleavers, hatchets, crutches, and plaster of Paris in his apartment and vehicle, the strange and unexplained absences coinciding with a late night phone call from out of state that just happened to correspond with the disappearance and presumed killing of a young woman, his admissions that his "sickness" was taking up so much of his time that he could not focus on his undergraduate or law studies, and his malefic behaviors toward Elizabeth and Molly Kendall would all have to have been fabrications.

We would have to ignore Bundy's consultation on the Riverman case and his conversations with Keppel and Reichert where Bundy engaged in perhaps the most transparent discourse about his life. During those conversations, Bundy was emphatic that if a sexual murderer is not in custody and remains in the community, he is always "doing stuff."

A free killer is an active killer.

He consistently told the investigators that a killer has many other victims that authorities are not aware of and still many more victims who were buried and will never be found. He told the investigators about abduction sites, kill sites, and the most hallowed of the murderous geography, dump sites. Bundy implored investigators to surveil dump sites because the murderer would repeatedly come back to the site to engage in sexual acts with the body, to stay with the body, to dismember the body. Bundy was confident that the Riverman would be caught returning to one of his dump sites. Bundy told Keppel and Reichert that if there are periods of a murderer's life that are unaccounted for and involve constant travel, he is actively killing. We would have to ignore that Bundy's advisement to them describes precisely the decade of his life before the putative 1974 onset.

What would also have to be true is that Bundy's final confessions to Keppel in 1989, confessions that were nearly identical to his consulting opinions about the Riverman five years earlier would have to be incorrect.

In a country that currently has 250,000 to 330,000 unsolved murders and during an era in the middle to late twentieth century characterized by little to no surveillance, criminal justice systems with primitive information sharing capacity, and extensive hitchhiking norms to provide opportunities to abduct victims, a person who is among the most prolific serial sexual homicide offenders in the history of the United States would not have been responsible for any of those unsolved murders. How likely is that?

If Bundy was not responsible for scores of rapes and murders that remain unsolved, why did he urgently destroy the shoebox full of photographs of his victims after his release from jail pursuant to the DaRonch kidnapping? Why did he have a bag of women's underwear that Kendall had found? Whose were those? How many garments were there? How many women?

In addition to stability and frequency, the final theme that arises from the voluminous paper files and interviews with the most serious criminal offenders is the sheer declension, or moral depravity and deterioration, in their lives. As a chronic offender on federal supervision for cocaine base trafficking told me, "I can't remember a single positive thing that happened in my childhood or my life. Not a thing. It made me sad, and it made me mad. And I was like, fuck it, I'm going to do what I want and make everyone else feel how sad I was. I wrecked my life for forty years doing that." Still another federal offender who was almost continually in local, state, or federal custody from 1957 to 2012 stared at me with a most sobering look and stated, "I was the worst asshole that you've ever seen" in reference to his life of crime and multiple homicide offending. As a result, the life histories of the most severe offenders are a horribly depressing mix of violence, victimization, and vice.

More horrible and depressing is the dark figure of crime and the final moments for murder victims whose case will never result in arrest, prosecution, or conviction. We know from Little's confessions these final moments involved the intense violence of a cataclysmic struggle between a person trying to breath and fighting for life while her killer expertly, cruelly, and deliberatively prevailed. After his murderous sense of rapture, the body was strewn in the weeds, rolled down a ravine, left in the water, dismembered, or buried.

According to Aristotle, fear is pain arising from the anticipation of evil. This is so applicable to Bundy's victims. The assaults with the blunt objects created massive fractures to the skull and jaw areas. In some of the recovered victims, the jaw was missing from the skull. In the event that the women were conscious after the blow to the head, the terror they experienced as they realized what Bundy was doing is unimaginable especially given Bundy's predilection for having the women take off their own clothes to methodically build toward their own sexual victimization and imminent death.

In some of the cases, the strangulations were so violent, and the ligature cinched the neck to such a degree, that it appeared the victim had a fractured neck. So much force was used in some cases that the victim's neck appears distortedly small. I've seen some of these crime scene photographs. They cannot be unseen. Still other women were fatally stabbed or had their throat slit from ear to ear simultaneously to being sexually assaulted. Some of the victims were drowned in the bathtub in a lonely hotel room where they were kept after their abduction, others were drowned in a river and summarily dumped. Some of his victims were children, but he raped, strangled, and murdered them just the same. Amidst the blood spatter and the carnage, the crime scenes dripped with the full extent of Ted Bundy's psychopathy and paraphilic disorders.

The nefariousness of his crimes and the horrifying extent of his psychopathology should be Ted Bundy's legacy. He does not deserve lasting popularity because he was allegedly charming, somewhat handsome, or apparently ambitious and intelligent. He deserves no special designation because at least on the surface, he seemed normal. He also does not deserve a cultural legacy that strangely presents his crimes in a glamorous, almost meretricious way. He was a rapist, child molester, necrophile, sadist, psychopath, and murderer.

He is as reprehensible as any criminal offender in American history, and those who personally listened to Bundy describe his sexual homicides with such ebullient joy and complete disregard for the victims were forever affected by his evil. Those who survived his attacks lived the rest of their lives with psychological and physical injuries that never fully heal. Countless families whose young female relatives disappeared during the 1960s or 1970s never to be heard from again have also suffered heart wrenching grief. That pain likely would only worsen if they knew that their loved one's disappearance was at the hands of Ted Bundy.

Notes

1. Nelson (2018, p. 282).
2. Lahey et al. (2014), Copeland et al. (2013), and Putnam et al. (2008).
3. Genesis 8:21.
4. Fox & DeLisi (2019), and DeLisi (2016).

References

Copeland, W. E., Adair, C. E., Smetanin, P., Stiff, D., Briante, C., Colman, I., Fergusson, D., Horwood, J., Poulton, R., Jane Costello, E., & Angold, A. (2013). Diagnostic transitions from childhood to adolescence to early adulthood. *Journal of Child Psychology and Psychiatry, 54*(7), 791–799.

DeLisi, M. (2016). *Psychopathy as unified theory of crime*. Palgrave Macmillan.

Fox, B., & DeLisi, M. (2019). Psychopathic killers: A meta-analytic review of the psychopathy-homicide nexus. *Aggression and Violent Behavior, 44*, 67–79.

Genesis 8:21.

Lahey, B. B., Zald, D. H., Hakes, J. K., Krueger, R. F., & Rathouz, P. J. (2014). Patterns of heterotypic continuity associated with the cross-sectional correlational structure of prevalent mental disorders in adults. *JAMA Psychiatry, 71*(9), 989–996.

Nelson, P. (2018). *Defending the devil: My story as Ted Bundy's last lawyer*. Echo Point Books & Media.

Putnam, S. P., Rothbart, M. K., & Gartstein, M. A. (2008). Homotypic and heterotypic continuity of fine-grained temperament during infancy, toddlerhood, and early childhood. *Infant and Child Development: An International Journal of Research and Practice, 17*(4), 387–405.

11

Resolution

It's obvious you haven't found everyone. And there's a good chance that where you've found only one that there are probably more than one.[1]
Ted Bundy

Whether it was Samuel Little setting his spiderweb to catch disadvantaged and disempowered women in the ghettos, Rodney Alcala luring young men and women to remote locations for the photoshoot that he convinced them would launch their modeling career, or Ted Bundy trolling the nation's college and universities for young women or obliging hitchhikers on the nation's vast highways, the United States was once a loosely connected, frontier society where changing behavioral mores unwound the bonds that previously regulated behavior. It was a perfect milieu for obsessively motivated, psychopathic, sexually deranged career criminals whose wanderlust drove them across the United States many times over to the most remote and clandestine settings imaginable.

These structural factors facilitated homicide careers that seem too extreme to be true, but, unfortunately are true particularly when one considers the magnitude of unsolved murders and that about one percent of those were sexual homicides. There are upwards of 3500 unsolved

M. DeLisi, *Ted Bundy and The Unsolved Murder Epidemic*, https://doi.org/10.1007/978-3-031-21418-9_11

sexual homicides in the United States, perhaps more. From multiple scientific perspectives, we know for certain those offenses were primarily committed by the most aberrant, exceptional offenders in the population, a small but mighty group in terms of their responsibility for the most heinous forms of violence.

Many, perhaps even most, abnormal homicides will never be solved. The pathological offenders who perpetrated them were too skilled at their craft, benefited from a bygone historical era marked by technological limitations, were too effective at selecting which victims to kill—the missing missing—and were experts in knowing how to dispose of their bodies. As the chapter opening quotation makes clear, there are so many buried and destroyed bodies. Everyone will not be found.

That so many cases will forever remain unsolved is the worst offenders' final act of cruelty. Samuel Little's haunting confessions and detailed drawings of his victims and Todd Kohlhepp's impromptu confession to a quadruple murder are exceptional circumstances. More common is the insincere, cajoling, and incomplete admissions by Ted Bundy and the impudent and defiant display that Rodney Alcala gave the Wyoming investigators. Fortunately, there have been many technological innovations since the putatively halcyon days of late twentieth century America that not only reduce the likelihood that a single offender could murder dozens to even hundreds of victims, but also increase the likelihood that outstanding cases are solved.

One innovation is fingerprint technology. In early 1984, the Automated Fingerprint Identification System known as AFIS was unveiled. AFIS is an automated system for searching fingerprint files that can automatically extract and digitize ridge details and other identifying characteristics to match to computerized fingerprints in the system. In 1999, it was renamed the Integrated Automated Fingerprint Identification System or IAFIS, which is maintained by the Criminal Justice Information Services Division within the Federal Bureau of Investigation. In its first year of use, IAFIS processed over fourteen million fingerprint submissions, a volume that it now processes in about three months and provides data on criminal research requests usually within twenty minutes.[2]

In 2011, the IAFIS was discontinued. It was replaced by Next Generation Identification, which is the largest and most efficient electronic repository of criminal history information and biometric data in the world. The Next Generation Identification System uses Advanced Fingerprint Identification that replaced the prior IAFIS technology and improved the overall matching accuracy for fingerprints from ninety-two percent to 99.6%. It also is a more efficient and effective system for file maintenance. In 2013, the National Palm Print System was implemented to allow law enforcement searches of palm prints similar to the technology that is employed in the searching of fingerprints.[3]

There are other programs dedicated to fingerprints such as the National Fingerprint File, which contains fingerprints of federal offenders and offenders from each state where the individual had been arrested for a felony or reportable misdemeanor. Once a fingerprint card is electronically recorded, the FBI enters the individual's fingerprints, name, and other identifiers in the Interstate Identification Index. As of 2016, the National Fingerprint File has been implemented in twenty states including several states with large correctional populations, such as Florida, Georgia, New Jersey, New York, and Ohio.[4] The Repository for Individuals of Special Concern is a mobile identification device that allows law enforcement officers to search a limited but enhanced population of fingerprint records of wanted persons, known or suspected terrorists, subjects on the National Sexual Offender Registry, and other persons of public safety interest.[5] It specifically targets more serious offenders.

These fingerprint modalities would have been especially effective at slowing down the homicide careers of Samuel Little given how extensively he was arrested and Rodney Alcala, who had already been imprisoned for predatory sexual violence. They would have been less useful for Bundy because he avoided arrest until the end stages of his offending career. However, these improved fingerprint systems might be useful to link potential evidence in Bundy's crimes to his fingerprint record. During his conversations with Keppel and Reichert, Bundy advised that serial murderers often throw items used during their murder out of the car window as they drive away from the abduction site, murder site, or dump site. He indicated that they also throw the victims' possessions out of the car window, casting them to the wind presumably because they would never be located. But random items are often found in the middle of fields, near roads, or in other remote locations. In most cases, these items are viewed as junk that was either left behind by someone who used it, or the items are considered litter.

What if the discarded items are tire irons? Crowbars? Purses? Wallets? Make-up cases? Crutches? Arm slings? Ice picks? Handcuffs? Masks? Pantyhose? What if the discarded items are collectively the same objects found in Bundy's Volkswagen Beetle when he was arrested in Utah in 1975? How many murder kits currently sit in remote locations, unmoved from the moment that Ted Bundy or offenders of his ilk threw them out the car window? What fingerprint, blood, or semen evidence remains?

In a paradigm shift, other investigative developments focus on forensic evidence and justice system's dedication to resolving cold cases. A landmark legislation that ended the three-decade upsurge in crime and violence in the United States, the *Violent Crime Control and Law Enforcement Act of 1994* authorized the creation of a centralized database of DNA samples to be used for investigative purposes.[6] This became the Combined DNA Index System or CODIS. In recent years, the National Institute of Justice, which is the research arm of the United States Department of Justice, has appropriated considerable resources toward solving cold cases including unsolved homicides that probably involve serial murderers. Multiple initiatives including the National Missing and Unidentified Persons System or NamUs, Solving Cold Cases with DNA Program, and Prosecuting Cold Cases Using DNA and Other Forensic Technologies Program have dedicated more attention and resources to unsolved murders than ever before in American criminal justice history.

In 2003, the National Institute of Justice began allocating funding for research to use various DNA analyses for criminal justice system purposes including the identification of missing and unidentified persons, a substantial proportion of whom are unsolved homicide victims. For example, between 2005 and 2014, the National Institute of Justice awarded 213 grants totaling nearly $78 million to the Solving Cold Cases with DNA Program. Collectively, these awards resulted in the review of 141,371 cases including 34,289 cases where biological evidence remained. National Institute of Justice efforts has helped to confirm the responsibility of notorious sexual offenders like Albert DeSalvo to victims where his involvement was controversial, identify the remains of two victims of serial murderer John Wayne Gacy, and identify some of the remaining victims of Gary Ridgway, the prodigious murderer that Bundy referred to as the Riverman.[7] Moreover, the identification of probative DNA files to be submitted to CODIS is another positive outcome of the grants program in that the DNA file could later be linked to biological evidence taken from an unsolved homicide.

In 2005, the National Institute of Justice hosted a conference called the "Identifying the Missing Summit" that included criminal justice practitioners, scientists, and victim advocates that led to the creation of the National Missing Persons Task Force, an entity that culminated in the creation of the National Missing and Unidentified Persons System (NamUs). The NamUs consists of three databases: the Missing Persons Database, the Unidentified Persons Database, and the Unclaimed Persons Database. At this writing, there are 20,699 results in the missing persons search, 13,818 results in the unidentified persons search, and 11,939 results in the unclaimed persons search.[8] Several states with large correctional populations, including New York, New Jersey, and Michigan now require by law that law enforcement organizations enter missing persons data into NamUs. This is a sea change when considering the status of missing persons during the 1960s, 1970s, and 1980s.

In 2012, an analytical division that offered resources to criminal justice professionals to locate missing persons and family members for DNA sample collections and next of kin death notifications emerged. The NamUs AFIS/Fingerprint Unit was created to use the FBI's fingerprint databases to search the fingerprints of all unidentified deceased persons. It uses their friction ridge impression records for missing and unidentified persons to search through the FBI's Next Generation biometric database. As of September 30, 2019, 259 previously missing persons have been identified and twenty-eight of those who were identified were confirmed as homicide victims.[9]

The use of DNA to investigate cold cases is as technologically sophisticated as it is multifaceted. Short tandem repeat analysis allows for the testing of samples that in prior eras were too limited to test, but today can confirm that a DNA profile corresponds to a specific person. Mitochondrial DNA testing can be used to test compromised DNA samples because most human cells contain hundreds of copies of mitochondrial DNA genomes as opposed to the two copies of DNA that exist in a cell's nucleus.[10] DNA phenotyping is used to generate an image of an individual's face by combining information from multiple genetic loci. This can assist in showing what a potential homicide victim's face looked like prior to their injuries or other factors that degraded the body. DNA mixture interpretation is a form of analysis where multiple DNA profiles are separated to produce individual DNA profiles to produce a definitive match where prior analyses would have yielded inconclusive results.[11]

Public concern about the epidemic of unsolved murders increasingly informs federal legislation. The *DNA Analysis Backlog Elimination Act of 2000* provided grant money to states to increase their capacity for use of CODIS and provide DNA samples from pathological offenders specifically offenders involved in crimes, such as murder, kidnapping, and sexual assault.[12] The *Justice Served Act of 2018* offers funding to increase the capacity of local and state prosecutors to address the backlog of violent crime cases in which suspects have been identified through DNA evidence. The Act amends the *DNA Analysis Backlog Elimination Act of 2000* by providing additional resources.[13] The program was moved to the Bureau of Justice Assistance in 2020 and to date the Bureau has funded twelve grant awards of nearly $6 million. This is a start, but more investment is needed.

The Prosecuting Cold Cases Using DNA Program has three requirements including a local or state prosecutor must be a full partner in the project, suspects' DNA profiles have already been obtained, and forensic genetic genealogy must follow Department of Justice guidelines and policies. To date, multiple suspect profiles have been uploaded to CODIS or AFIS, cases with suspect DNA identified are pending prosecution, and three charged suspects currently await trial.[14]

The potential for resolution of unsolved murders is more possible today than ever before in terms of justice system resources dedicated to resolving these cases and the technological advances that make them possible. The precondition for a case achieving legal resolution is whether forensic evidence was collected, analyzed, or linked: cases where evidence was collected, analyzed, or linked fare much better than cases where it was not. A study of 4205 criminal cases from five jurisdictions is revealing. In cases where crime scene evidence was collected, cases are significantly more likely to result in arrest, referral for charges, formal filing of charges, guilty pleas, trial convictions, and any conviction compared to those where crime scene evidence was not collected. In cases where tangible physical evidence was collected, there was greater likelihood of arrest, referral and filing of charges, guilty plea, trial, and any convictions relative to those where tangible evidence was not collected.

The same trends were found in cases where forensic evidence was laboratory analyzed. In cases where it was, the likelihood of arrest, charging, and convictions via plea or trial were higher than in cases where it was not. In cases where the evidence linked the suspect to the victim or crime scene, there are significantly greater odds of arrest, referral, and filing of charges, guilty pleas, trial convictions, or any conviction. Across scenarios, the likelihood of criminal justice system arrest, charging, or conviction is two to three times greater in cases where forensic evidence is obtained than in cases where it is not. Laboratory-examined evidence was critical for a case progressing through the justice system. In cases where this occurred, there were 109% increased odds of referral, 313% increased odds of charging, 132% increased odds of trial conviction, and significantly greater sentence length.[15]

A disquieting factor in whether forensic information is analyzed or linked is that in many cases, law enforcement officials decline to upload DNA evidence because they do not have a suspect in mind. But there are two general types of upload to CODIS, one where there is a direct match to an individual offender, known as an offender or suspect hit, and one where there is forensic evidence but an unknown offender, known variously as a case hit or forensic hit. Forensic hits are essential for linking multiple cases involving the same unknown offender, but they require that the DNA evidence is uploaded.

Regrettably, a great deal of forensic evidence is collected, but goes unanalyzed. Forensic scientists examined nationally representative data and found that over a five-year period, fourteen percent of unsolved murders and eighteen percent of unsolved rapes, which corresponded to 3975 murders and 27,595 rapes in their study, contained forensic evidence that had not been submitted to laboratory for analysis.[16] In forty percent of these cases, there was DNA evidence and in approximately one in four cases there was trace evidence, which is evidence that is left during the physical contact between offender and victim, such as hair or fibers, latent fingerprints, which are finger or palm impressions left on a surface at the crime scene, or firearm or tool mark evidence.

In several ways, the failure to submit forensic evidence for analysis reflected a lack of understanding or appreciation about the potential of DNA to connect to a specific suspect or to connect disparate cases. Among forty-four percent of agencies, the reason that law enforcement did not submit forensic evidence for analysis was because there was not a clear suspect, even though the sample could have been linked to another sample in CODIS via a case or forensic hit. About twenty-four percent of law enforcement agencies declined to submit forensic evidence for analysis because the suspect was adjudicated in another case without forensic evidence, even though he could have been linked to other cases had forensic information been shared.

Nineteen percent of agencies declined to submit forensic evidence of crime laboratories because the case had been dismissed and twelve percent of agencies declined to submit forensic evidence because a suspect had been identified but not yet formally charged. These too are missed opportunities. In 2013, the United States Supreme Court held that the collection of DNA evidence via a buccal or cheek swab is consistent with other evidence gathering procedures during the booking process, such as fingerprinting, and thus is reasonable under the search and seizure clause of the Fourth Amendment.[17] Thirty states now allow for the collection of DNA evidence at the point of arrest thus it is immaterial whether the suspect is formally charged in the case.

There were many lost opportunities. Approximately seventeen percent of agencies were uncertain about the usefulness of forensic data and thus did not submit it for testing and fifteen percent declined to submit data because the prosecutor had not requested it. In fairness to law enforcement organizations, there are related criminal justice system processes that likely contribute to their reticence to upload forensic evidence. For example, several states including Colorado, Missouri, Nevada, New Mexico, Utah, and Wisconsin require a probable cause hearing for the collection of DNA evidence from a defendant and several other states including Illinois, Maryland, Minnesota, North Carolina, Tennessee, Vermont, and Virginia require a probable cause hearing prior to the analysis of DNA data. These are unnecessary judicial impediments.

Laboratory problems and the sheer size of the backlog of untested forensic evidence contributed even more to the reluctance of law enforcement to submit forensic evidence. Eleven percent of agencies did not submit forensic evidence for testing because of the inability of the crime laboratory to produce results in a timely manner and nine percent of agencies reported there was insufficient funding for laboratory analysis of evidence. Two percent of agencies were uncertain where to submit forensic evidence for analysis suggesting a historical departmental norm of never submitting forensic evidence for testing. Finally, six percent of law enforcement organizations reported that their local crime laboratory no longer accepted forensic evidence due to the backlog of untested evidence kits already in storage at the lab.[18]

The analysis of forensic evidence specifically DNA evidence is not a panacea that will resolve the unsolved murder problem in the United States and this is particularly true for older cases inflicted by Little, Alcala, and Bundy. Criminologists conducted a study of untested sexual assault kits in Texas where a 2011 statute required that all law enforcement agencies submit untested sexual assault kits collected between 1996 and 2011 for testing. Of the more than 6300 sexual assault kits that were analyzed, just fifteen percent of them produced an offender hit and only fifty-three offenders, representing less than one percent of all kits that were tested, were arrested and formally charged.[19] Similar studies of mandatory testing of sexual assault kits in other jurisdictions also found that the policy did not have significant impact on arrests for sexual assault.[20]

However, even if research produces findings that lack statistical punch, there remains a substantive value to testing forensic data in unsolved murders. For instance, archival medical examiner specimens might contain perpetrator DNA that can be used to solve cold homicide cases. One study examined 376 homicides from 1990 to 1999 of which thirteen slides from the medical examiner archives had testable sperm, and of these, six murders were still unsolved. These forensic data had been in storage between twenty-three to thirty years in murders where the cause of death included gunshot wound, traumatic asphyxia, strangulation, blunt force trauma, and multiple stab wounds. Of the six cases, four had enough data to upload to CODIS and two of these submissions matched to a convicted offender resulting in one arrest. In two other cases, three suspects were eliminated and the data remain in CODIS to potentially be connected to other cases.[21]

The open road that was the environmental context of so many murders decades ago has also been revisited. A federal justice initiative to redress the unsolved murders problem across the nation's interstates is the Highway Serial Killings Initiative, which began in 2004 when a crime data analyst within the Oklahoma Bureau of Investigation noticed a pattern of murder victims who were dumped along Interstate 40 across Oklahoma, Texas, Arkansas, and Mississippi. These and other cases were entered into the Violent Criminal Apprehension Program, or VICAP, a database that contains information on homicides, sexual assaults, missing persons, and unidentified human remains that is available to law enforcement organizations. At present, analysts within the Violent Criminal Apprehension Program produced a roster of 750 murder victims whose bodies were found along interstates and highways and developed a list of 450 potential suspects. According to the Federal Bureau of Investigation, the Highway Serial Killings Initiative has resulted in ten arrests of offenders who are responsible for nearly three dozen murders.[22] One of those cases involves John Robert Williams, who is serving a life sentence for murder and other crimes in Mississippi, but confessed his responsibility in more than one dozen additional murders, confessions he has since recanted.[23]

All of these developments are encouraging in that they disseminate forensic evidence on rare, violent crimes that are disproportionately committed by the rarest offenders. Although widespread testing of previously unanalyzed sexual assault kits does not always produce the desired arrest results, greater testing has consistently shown the undue burden of serial offenders, some of whom have been arrested and prosecuted. A paradigm shift has already occurred when we compare the modern age to a half century ago when linkage blindness was so prevalent and surveillance data so scarce that sexual homicides clustered in proximal geographic areas with no law enforcement sense they were related.

There is an emerging frontier in forensic science that has also benefited from technological innovation and holds considerable promise with unearthing the unknown victims of the worst offenders. These technologies show promise at identifying clandestine graves or homicide burial sites. For example, ground penetrating radar involves the transmission of electromagnetic energy into the ground that is transmitted back to an antenna and thus provides imaging information on items that exist below ground.[24] Ground penetrating radar is commonly used in archaeology, but has obvious import for forensic investigations especially since murder victims are usually buried not very deeply below the surface.

In his various conversations with Robert Keppel, Ted Bundy offered several matter-of-fact statements about the direct association between a murder victim being found and their burial status. Here, his statements about serial murderers throwing evidence out of their car window as they left a burial site are valuable. Those discarded items including tire irons, crowbars, purses, wallets, identification cards, cosmetic accessories, crutches, arm slings, ice picks, handcuffs, masks, and pantyhose are worth a closer look because they likely are close to those buried bodies.

These are the breadcrumbs that Ted Bundy left proximal to the numerous dump sites that he created throughout the western states, and likely, across the entire United States. He knew where those sites were, and he knew he would likely get away with it. And that is the darkest figure of crime of all: the unfortunate souls contacted by the worst criminal predators, who forever disappeared.

Notes

1. Keppel and Birnes (2005, p. 255).
2. Moses et al. (2010).
3. https://www.fbi.gov/services/cjis/fingerprints-and-other-biometrics/ngi, Accessed September 29, 2021.
4. Goggins and DeBacco (2018).

5. https://www.fbi.gov/file-repository/repository-for-individuals-of-special-concern-brochure.pdf/view, Accessed September 29, 2021.
6. *Violent Crime Control and Law Enforcement Act of 1994*, 42 U. S. C. § 14132.
7. Martin et al. (2020).
8. https://namus.nij.ojp.gov/, Accessed September 24, 2021.
9. Martin et al. (2020).
10. Heurich (2008).
11. Martin et al. (2020).
12. *DNA Analysis Backlog Elimination Act of 2000*, 42 U.S.C. § 13701.
13. *Justice Served Act of 2018*, 34 U. S. C. § 10101.
14. https://bja.ojp.gov/sites/g/files/xyckuh186/files/media/document/fact-sheet-prosecuting-cold-cases-using-dna.pdf, Accessed September 24, 2021.
15. Peterson et al. (2013).
16. Strom and Hickman (2010).
17. *Maryland v. King* (2013).
18. Strom and Hickman (2010).
19. Davis et al. (2021).
20. Mourtgos et al. (2021).
21. Clark et al. (2019).
22. https://archives.fbi.gov/archives/news/stories/2009/april/highwayserial_040609; https://www.fbi.gov/news/stories/violent-criminal-apprehension-program-part-2, Accessed September 29, 2021.
23. Glover (2009).
24. Berezowski et al. (2021).

References

Berezowski, V., Mallett, X., Ellis, J., & Moffat, I. (2021). Using ground penetrating radar and resistivity methods to locate unmarked graves: A review. *Remote Sensing, 13*(15), 2880.

Clark, M., Gill, J., Sasinouski, K., & McGuire, A. (2019). Cold case homicides: DNA testing of retained autopsy sexual assault smears. *Journal of Forensic Sciences, 64*(4), 1100–1104.

Davis, R. C., Jurek, A., Wells, W., & Shadwick, J. (2021). Investigative outcomes of CODIS matches in previously untested sexual assault kits. *Criminal Justice Policy Review, 32*(8), 841–864.

Glover, S. (2009). FBI makes a connection between long-haul truckers, serial killings. https://www.latimes.com/archives/la-xpm-2009-apr-05-me-serialkillers5-story.html, Accessed September 29, 2021

Goggins, B. R., & DeBacco, D. A. (2018). *Survey of state criminal history information systems, 2016: A criminal justice information policy report.* U.S. Department of Justice, Office of Justice Programs, Bureau of Justice Statistics.

Heurich, C. (2008). Cold cases: Resources for agencies, resolution for families. *National Institute of Justice (NIJ) Journal, 260*, 20–23.

Keppel, R. D., with Birnes, W. J. (2005). *The riverman: Ted Bundy and I hunt for the Green River killer.* Pocket Books.

Martin, E., Schwarting, D. E., & Chase, R. J. (2020). Serial killer connections through cold cases. *National Institute of Justice (NIJ) Journal, 282*, 29–44.

Maryland v. King, 569 U. S. 435 (2013).

Moses, K. R., Higgins, P., McCabe, M., Probhakar, S., & Swann, S. (2010). Fingerprint Sourcebook-Chapter 6: Automated fingerprint identification system (AFIS). https://www.ojp.gov/pdffiles1/nij/225326.pdf. Accessed September 27, 2021.

Mourtgos, S. M., Adams, I. T., Nix, J., & Richards, T. (2021). Mandatory sexual assault kit testing policies and arrest trends: A natural experiment. *Justice Evaluation Journal, 4*(1), 145–162.

Peterson, J. L., Hickman, M. J., Strom, K. J., & Johnson, D. J. (2013). Effect of forensic evidence on criminal justice case processing. *Journal of Forensic Sciences, 58*, S78–S90.

Strom, K. J., & Hickman, M. J. (2010). Unanalyzed evidence in law-enforcement agencies: A national examination of forensic processing in police departments. *Criminology & Public Policy, 9*(2), 381–404.

References

Abel, G. G., Becker, J. V., Mittelman, M., Cunningham-Rathner, J., Rouleau, J. L., & Murphy, W. D. (1987). Self-reported sex crimes of nonincarcerated paraphiliacs. *Journal of Interpersonal Violence, 2*(1), 3–25.

Alcala, Rodney James v. The Superior Court of Orange County and the People of the State of California, G036911, S. Ct. C42861, 2007.

Alexander, J. (2013). *Best Aristotle quotes.* Crombie Jardine Publishing.

American Psychiatric Association. (2013). *Diagnostic and statistical manual of mental disorders (DSM-5®).* American Psychiatric Publishing.

Bachman, R. (1998). The factors related to rape reporting behavior and arrest: New evidence from the National Crime Victimization Survey. *Criminal Justice and Behavior, 25*(1), 8–29.

Balemba, S., Beauregard, E., & Martineau, M. (2014). Getting away with murder: A thematic approach to solved and unsolved sexual homicides using crime scene factors. *Police Practice and Research, 15*(3), 221–233.

Baur, E., Forsman, M., Santtila, P., Johansson, A., Sandnabba, K., & Långström, N. (2016). Paraphilic sexual interests and sexually coercive behavior: A population-based twin study. *Archives of Sexual Behavior, 45*(5), 1163–1172.

© The Editor(s) (if applicable) and The Author(s), under exclusive
license to Springer Nature Switzerland AG 2023
M. DeLisi, *Ted Bundy and The Unsolved Murder Epidemic,*
https://doi.org/10.1007/978-3-031-21418-9

Beauregard, E., & DeLisi, M. (2018). Stepping stones to sexual murder: The role of developmental factors in the etiology of sexual homicide. *Journal of Criminal Psychology, 8*(3), 199–214.

Beauregard, E., & DeLisi, M. (2021). Unraveling the personality profile of the sexual murderer. *Journal of Interpersonal Violence, 36*(7–8), 3536–3556.

Beauregard, E., & Martineau, M. (2014). No body, no crime? The role of forensic awareness in avoiding police detection in cases of sexual homicide. *Journal of Criminal Justice, 42*(2), 213–220.

Berezowski, V., Mallett, X., Ellis, J., & Moffat, I. (2021). Using ground penetrating radar and resistivity methods to locate unmarked graves: A review. *Remote Sensing, 13*(15), 2880.

Biderman, A. D., & Reiss, A. J., Jr. (1967). On exploring the "dark figure" of crime. *The Annals of the American Academy of Political and Social Science, 374*(1), 1–15.

Bouchard, M., & Lussier, P. (2015). Estimating the size of the sexual aggressor population. In A. Blokland & P. Lussier (Eds.), *Sex offenders: A criminal career approach* (pp. 351–371). John Wiley & Sons.

Briken, P., Habermann, N., Kafka, M. P., Berner, W., & Hill, A. (2006). The paraphilia-related disorders: An investigation of the relevance of the concept in sexual murderers. *Journal of Forensic Sciences, 51*(3), 683–688.

Brouillette-Alarie, S., & Lussier, P. (2018). The risk assessment of offenders with a history of sexual crime: Past, present and new perspectives. In P. Lussier & E. Beauregard (Eds.), *Sexual offending: A criminological perspective* (pp. 349–375). Routledge.

Browne, J. H. (2016). *The devil's defender: My Odyssey through American criminal justice from Ted Bundy to the Kandahar massacre*. Chicago Review Press.

Bundy v. State, 455 So.2d 330 (1984).

Campedelli, G. M., & Yaksic, E. (2021). Survival of the recidivistic? Revealing factors associated with the criminal career length of multiple homicide offenders. *Homicide Studies.* https://doi.org/10.1177/10887679211010882

Carbone, J. T., Holzer, K. J., Vaughn, M. G., & DeLisi, M. (2020). Homicidal ideation and forensic psychopathology: Evidence from the 2016 Nationwide Emergency Department Sample (NEDS). *Journal of Forensic Sciences, 65*(1), 154–159.

Carlisle, A. (2020). *The 1976 psychological assessment of Ted Bundy*. Carlisle Legacy Books.

Caspi, A., Houts, R. M., Belsky, D. W., Goldman-Mellor, S. J., Harrington, H., Israel, S., Meier, M. H., Ramrakha, S., Shalev, I., Poulton, R., &

Moffitt, T. E. (2014). The p factor: One general psychopathology factor in the structure of psychiatric disorders? *Clinical Psychological Science, 2*(2), 119–137.

Caspi, A., Houts, R. M., Belsky, D. W., Harrington, H., Hogan, S., Ramrakha, S., Poulton, R., & Moffitt, T. E. (2016). Childhood forecasting of a small segment of the population with large economic burden. *Nature Human Behaviour, 1*(1), 1–10.

Chai, A. M. M., Beauregard, E., & Chopin, J. (2021). "Drop the body": Body disposal patterns in sexual homicide. *International Journal of Offender Therapy and Comparative Criminology, 65*(6–7), 692–714.

Chan, H. C. O. (2017). Sexual homicide: A review of recent empirical evidence (2008 to 2015). In F. Brookman, E. R. Maguire, & M. Maguire (Eds.), *The handbook of homicide* (pp. 105–130). John Wiley & Sons.

Chan, H. C., & Beauregard, E. (2016). Choice of weapon or weapon of choice? Examining the interactions between victim characteristics in single-victim male sexual homicide offenders. *Journal of Investigative Psychology and Offender Profiling, 13*(1), 70–88.

Chopin, J., & Beauregard, E. (2021). Body dismemberment in sexual homicide cases: Lust murder or rational decision? *Psychology, Crime & Law, 27*(9), 869–889.

Chopin, J., & Beauregard, E. (2021). Patterns of necrophilic behaviors in sexual homicide: A criminological perspective. *International Journal of Offender Therapy and Comparative Criminology, 65*(15), 1676–1699.

Chopin, J., Beauregard, E., & DeLisi, M. (2021). Homicidal child sexual abuse: Identifying the combinations of factors predicting a lethal outcome. *Child Abuse & Neglect, 111*, 104799.

Chopin, J., Beauregard, E., Bitzer, S., & Reale, K. (2019). Rapists' behaviors to avoid police detection. *Journal of Criminal Justice, 61*, 81–89.

Clark, M., Gill, J., Sasinouski, K., & McGuire, A. (2019). Cold case homicides: DNA testing of retained autopsy sexual assault smears. *Journal of Forensic Sciences, 64*(4), 1100–1104.

Cleckley, H. M. (1941). *The mask of sanity: An attempt to clarify some issues about the so-called psychopathic personality.* The C. V. Mosby Company.

Coid, J., Yang, M., Ullrich, S., Roberts, A., & Hare, R. D. (2009). Prevalence and correlates of psychopathic traits in the household population of Great Britain. *International Journal of Law and Psychiatry, 32*(2), 65–73.

Collishaw, S., Gardner, F., Maughan, B., Scott, J., & Pickles, A. (2012). Do historical changes in parent–child relationships explain increases in youth conduct problems? *Journal of Abnormal Child Psychology, 40*(1), 119–132.

Copeland, W. E., Adair, C. E., Smetanin, P., Stiff, D., Briante, C., Colman, I., Fergusson, D., Horwood, J., Poulton, R., Jane Costello, E., & Angold, A. (2013). Diagnostic transitions from childhood to adolescence to early adulthood. *Journal of Child Psychology and Psychiatry, 54*(7), 791–799.

Darjee, R. (2019). Sexual sadism and psychopathy in sexual homicide offenders: An exploration of their associates in a clinical sample. *International Journal of Offender Therapy and Comparative Criminology, 63*(9), 1738–1765.

Davis, R. C., Jurek, A., Wells, W., & Shadwick, J. (2021). Investigative outcomes of CODIS matches in previously untested sexual assault kits. *Criminal Justice Policy Review, 32*(8), 841–864.

DeLisi, M. (2005). *Career criminals in society*. Sage.

DeLisi, M. (2016). *Psychopathy as unified theory of crime*. Palgrave Macmillan.

DeLisi, M., Angton, A., Vaughn, M. G., Trulson, C. R., Caudill, J. W., & Beaver, K. M. (2014). Not my fault: Blame externalization is the psychopathic feature most associated with pathological delinquency among confined delinquents. *International Journal of Offender Therapy and Comparative Criminology, 58*(12), 1415–1430.

DeLisi, M., & Piquero, A. R. (2011). New frontiers in criminal careers research, 2000–2011: A state-of-the-art review. *Journal of Criminal Justice, 39*(4), 289–301.

DeLisi, M., Bunga, R., Heirigs, M. H., Erickson, J. H., & Hochstetler, A. (2019). The past is prologue: Criminal specialization continuity in the delinquent career. *Youth Violence and Juvenile Justice, 17*(4), 335–353.

DeLisi, M., Caropreso, D. E., Drury, A. J., Elbert, M. J., Evans, J. L., Heinrichs, T., & Tahja, K. M. (2016). The dark figure of sexual offending: New evidence from federal sex offenders. *Journal of Criminal Psychology, 6*(1), 3–16.

DeLisi, M., Drury, A. J., & Elbert, M. J. (2021). Psychopathy and pathological violence in a criminal career: A forensic case report. *Aggression and Violent Behavior, 60*, 101521.

DeLisi, M., Drury, A., Elbert, M., Tahja, K., Caropreso, D., & Heinrichs, T. (2017). Sexual sadism and criminal versatility: Does sexual sadism spillover into nonsexual crimes? *Journal of Aggression, Conflict and Peace Research, 9*(1), 2–12.

DeLisi, M., Tahja, K., Drury, A. J., Caropreso, D., Elbert, M., & Heinrichs, T. (2017). The criminology of homicidal ideation: Associations with criminal careers and psychopathology among federal correctional clients. *American Journal of Criminal Justice, 42*(3), 554–573.

DeLisi, M., Vaughn, M. G., Beaver, K. M., & Wright, J. P. (2010). The Hannibal Lecter myth: Psychopathy and verbal intelligence in the MacArthur violence risk assessment study. *Journal of Psychopathology and Behavioral Assessment, 32*(2), 169–177.

DeLisi, M., Vaughn, M. G., Salas-Wright, C. P., & Jennings, W. G. (2015). Drugged and dangerous: Prevalence and variants of substance use comorbidity among seriously violent offenders in the United States. *Journal of Drug Issues, 45*(3), 232–248.

Dietz, P. E., Hazelwood, R. R., & Warren, J. (1990). The sexually sadistic criminal and his offenses. *Bulletin of the American Academy of Psychiatry and the Law, 18*(2), 163–178.

Drury, A. J., Elbert, M. J., & DeLisi, M. (2020). The dark figure of sexual offending: A replication and extension. *Behavioral Sciences & the Law, 38*(6), 559–570.

Durose, M. R., & Antenangeli, L. (2021). *Recidivism of prisoners released in 34 states in 2012: A 5-year follow-up period (2012–2017).* U.S. Department of Justice, Office of Justice Programs, Bureau of Justice Statistics.

Egger, S. A. (2002). *The killers among us: An examination of serial murder and its investigation* (2nd ed.). Prentice Hall.

Eher, R., Rettenberger, M., & Turner, D. (2019). The prevalence of mental disorders in incarcerated contact sexual offenders. *Acta Psychiatrica Scandinavica, 139*(6), 572–581.

Fallik, S., & Wells, W. (2015). Testing previously unsubmitted sexual assault kits: What are the investigative results? *Criminal Justice Policy Review, 26*(6), 598–619.

Farrington, D. P. (1986). Age and crime. *Crime and Justice, 7*, 189–250.

Farrington, D. P., Ttofi, M. M., Crago, R. V., & Coid, J. W. (2014). Prevalence, frequency, onset, desistance and criminal career duration in self-reports compared with official records. *Criminal Behaviour and Mental Health, 24*(4), 241–253.

Fedora, O., Reddon, J. R., Morrison, J. W., Fedora, S. K., Pascoe, H., & Yeudall, L. T. (1992). Sadism and other paraphilias in normal controls and aggressive and nonaggressive sex offenders. *Archives of Sexual Behavior, 21*(1), 1–15.

Firestone, P., Bradford, J. M., Greenberg, D. M., Larose, M. R., & Curry, S. (1998). Homicidal and nonhomicidal child molesters: Psychological, phallometric, and criminal features. *Sexual Abuse: A Journal of Research and Treatment, 10*(4), 305–323.

Fox, B., & DeLisi, M. (2018). From criminological heterogeneity to coherent classes: Developing a typology of juvenile sex offenders. *Youth Violence and Juvenile Justice, 16*(3), 299–318.

Fox, B., & DeLisi, M. (2019). Psychopathic killers: A meta-analytic review of the psychopathy-homicide nexus. *Aggression and Violent Behavior, 44,* 67–79.

Fox, J. A. (2004). Missing data problems in the SHR: Imputing offender and relationship characteristics. *Homicide Studies, 8*(3), 214–254.

Genesis 8:21.

Glover, S. (2009). *FBI makes a connection between long-haul truckers, serial killings.* https://www.latimes.com/archives/la-xpm-2009-apr-05-me-serialkillers5-story.html. Accessed September 29, 2021.

Goggins, B. R., & DeBacco, D. A. (2018). *Survey of state criminal history information systems, 2016: A criminal justice information policy report.* U.S. Department of Justice, Office of Justice Programs, Bureau of Justice Statistics.

Hare, R. D. (1991). *Manual for the psychopathy checklist-revised.* Multi-Health Systems.

Healey, J., Lussier, P., & Beauregard, E. (2013). Sexual sadism in the context of rape and sexual homicide: An examination of crime scene indicators. *International Journal of Offender Therapy and Comparative Criminology, 57*(4), 402–424.

Heurich, C. (2008). Cold cases: Resources for agencies, resolution for families. *National Institute of Justice (NIJ) Journal, 260,* 20–23.

Hirschi, T., & Gottfredson, M. (1983). Age and the explanation of crime. *American Journal of Sociology, 89*(3), 552–584.

Holt, S. E., Meloy, J. R., & Strack, S. (1999). Sadism and psychopathy in violent and sexually violent offenders. *Journal of the American Academy of Psychiatry and the Law, 27*(1), 23–32.

James, J., & Beauregard, E. (2018). How sexual murderers thwart investigations. In J. Proulx, E. Beauregard, A. J. Carter, A. Mokros, R. Darjee, & J. James (Eds.), *Routledge international handbook of sexual homicide studies* (pp. 574–593). Routledge.

Justice Served Act of 2018, 34 U.S.C. 10101.

Keller, L. (1989). *Confessed mass murderer Ted Bundy…South Florida Sun Sentinel.* Retrieved May 27, 2021 from https://www.sun-sentinel.com/news/fl-xpm-1989-01-24-8901040963-story.html

Kendall, E., with a contribution from Molly Kendall. (2020). *The phantom prince: My life with Ted Bundy* (updated and expanded edition). Abrams Press.

Keppel, R. D., with Birnes, W. J. (2005). *The riverman: Ted Bundy and I hunt for the Green River killer*. Pocket Books.

Koeppel, S., Schlesinger, L. B., Craun, S. W., Keel, T. G., Rubin, D., & Kum, J. (2019). Foreign object insertions in sexual homicide. *International Journal of Offender Therapy and Comparative Criminology, 63*(9), 1726–1737.

Kruh, I. P., Whittemore, K., Arnaut, G. L., Manley, J., Gage, B., & Gagliardi, G. J. (2005). The concurrent validity of the Psychopathic Personality Inventory and its relative association with past violence in a sample of insanity acquittees. *International Journal of Forensic Mental Health, 4*(2), 135–145.

Lahey, B. B., Zald, D. H., Hakes, J. K., Krueger, R. F., & Rathouz, P. J. (2014). Patterns of heterotypic continuity associated with the cross-sectional correlational structure of prevalent mental disorders in adults. *JAMA Psychiatry, 71*(9), 989–996.

Larsson, H., Andershed, H., & Lichtenstein, P. (2006). A genetic factor explains most of the variation in the psychopathic personality. *Journal of Abnormal Psychology, 115*(2), 221–230.

Lee, S. J., & Park, J. (2019). Body transportation after homicides: Offender and offense characteristics. *Journal of Forensic Sciences, 64*(4), 1092–1095.

Li, W., & Lartey, J. (2022). *As murders spiked, police solved about half in 2020.* Retrieved August 26, 2022 from https://www.themarshallproject.org/2022/01/12/as-murders-spiked-police-solved-about-half-in-2020

Lilienfeld, S. O., & Andrews, B. P. (1996). Development and preliminary validation of a self-report measure of psychopathic personality traits in noncriminal population. *Journal of Personality Assessment, 66*(3), 488–524.

Lovell, R., Huang, W., Overman, L., Flannery, D., & Klingenstein, J. (2020). Offending histories and typologies of suspected sexual offenders identified via untested sexual assault. *Criminal Justice and Behavior, 47*(4), 470–486.

Lovell, R., Luminais, M., Flannery, D. J., Bell, R., & Kyker, B. (2018). Describing the process and quantifying the outcomes of the Cuyahoga County sexual assault kit initiative. *Journal of Criminal Justice, 57*, 106–115.

Lovell, R., Luminais, M., Flannery, D. J., Overman, L., Huang, D., Walker, T., & Clark, D. R. (2017). Offending patterns for serial sex offenders identified via the DNA testing of previously unsubmitted sexual assault kits. *Journal of Criminal Justice, 52*, 68–78.

Magee, L. A., Fortenberry, J. D., Tu, W., & Wiehe, S. E. (2020). Neighborhood variation in unsolved homicides: A retrospective cohort study in Indianapolis, Indiana, 2007–2017. *Injury Epidemiology, 7*(1), 1–10.

Martin, E., Schwarting, D. E., & Chase, R. J. (2020). Serial killer connections through cold cases. *National Institute of Justice (NIJ) Journal, 282*, 29–44.

Martineau, M., & Beauregard, E. (2016). Journey to murder: Examining the correlates of criminal mobility in sexual homicide. *Police Practice and Research, 17*(1), 68–83.

Martinez, N. N., Lee, Y., Eck, J. E., & SooHyun, O. (2017). Ravenous wolves revisited: A systematic review of offending concentration. *Crime Science, 6*(1), 1–16.

Maryland v. King, 569 U. S. 435 (2013).

Mathesius, J., & Lussier, P. (2014). The successful onset of sex offending: Determining the correlates of actual and official onset of sex offending. *Journal of Criminal Justice, 42*(2), 134–144.

McClellan, J. (2007). Unsolved homicides: What we do and do not know. *Journal of Security Education, 2*(3), 53–69.

Michaud, S. G., & Aynesworth, H. (1983). *The only living witness*. Signet.

Michaud, S. G., & Aynesworth, H. (1999). *The only living witness: The true story of serial sex killer Ted Bundy*. Authorlink Press.

Michaud, S. G., & Aynesworth, H. (2019). *Ted Bundy: Conservations with a killer: The death row interviews*. Sterling.

Minkler, M., Bonner, T., DeLisi, M., Pechorro, P., & Vaughn, M. G. (2022). The dark figure of delinquency: New evidence and its underlying psychopathology. *Youth Violence and Juvenile Justice, 20*(4), 279–291.

Moffitt, T. E. (1993). Adolescence-limited and life-course-persistent antisocial behavior: A developmental taxonomy. *Psychological Review, 100*(4), 674–701.

Mokros, A., Osterheider, M., Hucker, S. J., & Nitschke, J. (2011). Psychopathy and sexual sadism. *Law and Human Behavior, 35*(3), 188–199.

Moses, K. R., Higgins, P., McCabe, M., Probhakar, S., & Swann, S. (2010). Fingerprint Sourcebook-Chapter 6: Automated fingerprint identification system (AFIS). https://www.ojp.gov/pdffiles1/nij/225326.pdf. Accessed September 27, 2021.

Mourtgos, S. M., Adams, I. T., Nix, J., & Richards, T. (2021). Mandatory sexual assault kit testing policies and arrest trends: A natural experiment. *Justice Evaluation Journal, 4*(1), 145–162.

Myers, W. C., Chan, H. C., & Mariano, T. Y. (2016). Sexual homicide in the USA committed by juveniles and adults, 1976–2007: Age of arrest and incidence trends over 32 years. *Criminal Behaviour and Mental Health, 26*(1), 38–49.

Nelson, P. (2018). *Defending the devil: My story as Ted Bundy's last lawyer.* Echo Point Books & Media.

Newiss, G. (2004). Estimating the risk faced by missing persons: A study of homicide victims as an example of an outcome-based approach. *International Journal of Police Science & Management, 6*(1), 27–36.

Newiss, G. (2006). Understanding the risk of going missing: Estimating the risk of fatal outcomes in cancelled cases. *Policing: An International Journal of Police Strategies & Management, 29*(2), 246–260.

Patrick, C. J. (2010). Conceptualizing the psychopathic personality: Disinhibited, bold, … or just plain mean? In R. T. Salekin & D. R. Lynam (Eds.), *Handbook of child & adolescent psychopathy* (pp. 15–48). The Guilford Press.

Patrick, C., Fowles, D., & Krueger, R. (2009). Triarchic conceptualization of psychopathy: Developmental origins of disinhibition, boldness, and meanness. *Development and Psychopathology, 21*, 913–938.

Peterson, J. L., Hickman, M. J., Strom, K. J., & Johnson, D. J. (2013). Effect of forensic evidence on criminal justice case processing. *Journal of Forensic Sciences, 58*, S78–S90.

Proulx, J., Blais, E., & Beauregard, E. (2006). Sadistic sexual offenders. In J. Proulx, E. Beauregard, M. Cusson, & A. Nicole (Eds.), *Sexual murderers: A comparative analysis and new perspectives* (pp. 107–122). John Wiley & Sons.

Putnam, S. P., Rothbart, M. K., & Gartstein, M. A. (2008). Homotypic and heterotypic continuity of fine-grained temperament during infancy, toddlerhood, and early childhood. *Infant and Child Development: An International Journal of Research and Practice, 17*(4), 387–405.

Quinet, K. (2007). The missing missing: Toward a quantification of serial murder victimization in the United States. *Homicide Studies, 11*(4), 319–339.

Ramsland, K. (2013, Fall). The many sides of Ted Bundy. *The Forensic Examiner, 2013*, 18–25.

Reale, K., Beauregard, E., & Martineau, M. (2020). Is investigative awareness a distinctive feature of sexual sadism? *Journal of Interpersonal Violence, 35*(7–8), 1761–1778.

Regoeczi, W. C., Jarvis, J., & Riedel, M. (2008). Clearing murders: Is it about time? *Journal of Research in Crime and Delinquency, 45*(2), 142–162.

Ressler, R. K., Burgess, A. W., & Douglas, J. E. (1988). *Sexual homicide: Patterns and motives.* The Free Press.

Riedel, M. (1998). Counting stranger homicides: A case study of statistical prestidigitation. *Homicide Studies, 2*(2), 206–219.

Rule, A. (1980). *The stranger beside me.* W. W. Norton.

Rule, A. (2018). *The stranger beside me: The shocking inside story of serial killer Ted Bundy.* Gallery Books.

Samuel, D. B., & Widiger, T. A. (2007). Describing Ted Bundy's personality and working towards DSM-V. *Independent Practitioner, 27*(1), 20–22.

Schlesinger, L. B. (2004). *Sexual murder: Catathymic and compulsive subtypes.* CRC Press.

Schlesinger, L. B. (2007). Sexual homicide: Differentiating catathymic and compulsive murders. *Aggression and Violent Behavior, 12*(2), 242–256.

Schlesinger, L. B., Kassen, M., Mesa, V. B., & Pinizzotto, A. J. (2010). Ritual and signature in serial sexual homicide. *Journal of the American Academy of Psychiatry and the Law, 38*(2), 239–246.

Scurich, N., & John, R. S. (2019). The dark figure of sexual recidivism. *Behavioral Sciences & the Law, 37*(2), 158–175.

Seto, M. C., Hanson, R. K., & Babchishin, K. M. (2011). Contact sexual offending by men with online sexual offenses. *Sexual Abuse, 23*(1), 124–145.

Sleep, C. E., Weiss, B., Lynam, D. R., & Miller, J. D. (2019). An examination of the Triarchic Model of psychopathy's nomological network: A meta-analytic review. *Clinical Psychology Review, 71*, 1–26.

Statista. (2021). Retrieved May 27, 2021 from: https://www.statista.com/statistics/187592/death-rate-from-homicide-in-the-us-since-1950/

Stein, M. L., Schlesinger, L. B., & Pinizzotto, A. J. (2010). Necrophilia and sexual homicide. *Journal of Forensic Sciences, 55*(2), 443–446.

Strom, K. J., & Hickman, M. J. (2010). Unanalyzed evidence in law-enforcement agencies: A national examination of forensic processing in police departments. *Criminology & Public Policy, 9*(2), 381–404.

Strom, K., Scott, T., Feeney, H., Young, A., Couzens, L., & Berzofsky, M. (2021). How much justice is denied? An estimate of unsubmitted sexual assault kits in the United States. *Journal of Criminal Justice, 73*, 101746.

Sullivan, K. (2017). *The Bundy secrets: Hidden files on America's worst serial killer.* Wildblue Press.

Sullivan, K. M. (2009). *The Bundy murders: A comprehensive history.* McFarland and Company.

Theobald, D., Farrington, D. P., Loeber, R., Pardini, D. A., & Piquero, A. R. (2014). Scaling up from convictions to self-reported offending. *Criminal Behaviour and Mental Health, 24*(4), 265–276.

Tracy, P. E., Wolfgang, M. E., & Figlio, R. M. (1990). *Delinquency careers in two birth cohorts*. Plenum Press.

Trulson, C. R., Haerle, D. R., Caudill, J. W., & DeLisi, M. (2016). *Lost causes: Blended sentencing, second chances, and the Texas youth commission*. University of Texas Press.

United States Sentencing Commission. (2017). *The past predicts the future: Criminal history and recidivism of federal offenders*. Government Printing Office.

United States Sentencing Commission. (2021). *Federal Armed career criminals: Prevalence, patterns, and pathways*. Government Printing Office.

University of Chicago Crime Lab. (2017). *Gun violence in Chicago, 2016*. University of Chicago.

Vaughn, M. G., & DeLisi, M. (2008). Were Wolfgang's chronic offenders psychopaths? On the convergent validity between psychopathy and career criminality. *Journal of Criminal Justice, 36*(1), 33–42.

Vaughn, M. G., & DeLisi, M. (2018). Criminal energetics: A theory of antisocial enhancement and criminal attenuation. *Aggression and Violent Behavior, 38*, 1–12.

Vaughn, M. G., Carbone, J., DeLisi, M., & Holzer, K. J. (2020). Homicidal ideation among children and adolescents: Evidence from the 2012–2016 Nationwide Emergency Department Sample. *The Journal of Pediatrics, 219*, 216–222.

Vaughn, M. G., DeLisi, M., Gunter, T., Fu, Q., Beaver, K. M., Perron, B. E., & Howard, M. O. (2011). The severe 5%: A latent class analysis of the externalizing behavior spectrum in the United States. *Journal of Criminal Justice, 39*(1), 75–80.

Vaughn, M. G., Howard, M. O., & DeLisi, M. (2008). Psychopathic personality traits and delinquent careers: An empirical examination. *International Journal of Law and Psychiatry, 31*(5), 407–416.

Vaughn, M. G., Salas-Wright, C. P., DeLisi, M., & Maynard, B. R. (2014). Violence and externalizing behavior among youth in the United States: Is there a severe 5%? *Youth Violence and Juvenile Justice, 12*(1), 3–21.

Vaughn, M. G., Salas-Wright, C. P., DeLisi, M., Maynard, B. R., & Boutwell, B. (2015). Prevalence and correlates of psychiatric disorders among former juvenile detainees in the United States. *Comprehensive Psychiatry, 59*, 107–116.

Viding, E., Blair, R. J. R., Moffitt, T. E., & Plomin, R. (2005). Evidence for substantial genetic risk for psychopathy in 7-year-olds. *Journal of Child Psychology and Psychiatry, 46*(6), 592–597.

Viding, E., Jones, A. P., Frick, P., Moffitt, T. E., & Plomin, R. (2008). Heritability of antisocial behaviour at 9: Do callous-unemotional traits matter? *Developmental Science, 11*(1), 17–22.

Weiss, D., Schwarting, D., Heurich, C., & Waltke, H. (1998). Lot but not forgotten: Findings the nation's missing. *National Institute of Justice (NIJ) Journal, 279*, 58–69.

Wells, W., Fansher, A. K., & Campbell, B. A. (2019). The results of CODIS-hit investigations in a sample of cases with unsubmitted sexual assault kits. *Crime & Delinquency, 65*(1), 122–148.

Welner, M., DeLisi, M., Baglivio, M. T., Guilmette, T. J., & Knous-Westfall, H. M. (2021). Incorrigibility and the juvenile homicide offender: An ecologically valid integrative review. *Youth Violence and Juvenile Justice*. https://doi.org/10.1177/15412040211030980

Wolfgang, M. E., Figlio, R. M., & Sellin, T. (1987). *Delinquency in a birth cohort*. University of Chicago Press.

Wright, N., Pickles, A., Sharp, H., & Hill, J. (2021). A psychometric and validity study of callous-unemotional traits in 2.5-year-old children. *Scientific Reports, 11*(1), 1–10.

Yaksic, E. (2015). Addressing the challenges and limitations of utilizing data to study serial homicide. *Crime Psychology Review, 1*(1), 108–134.

Index

© The Editor(s) (if applicable) and The Author(s), under exclusive
license to Springer Nature Switzerland AG 2023
M. DeLisi, *Ted Bundy and The Unsolved Murder Epidemic*,
https://doi.org/10.1007/978-3-031-21418-9

Printed by Printforce, the Netherlands